Oxford School *Shakespeare*

HAMLET

edited by
Roma Gill, OBE
M.A. *Cantab.*, B. Litt. *Oxon*

OXFORD
UNIVERSITY PRESS

OXFORD

UNIVERSITY PRESS

Great Clarendon Street, Oxford OX2 6DP

Oxford University Press is a department of the University of Oxford.
It furthers the University's objective of excellence in research, scholarship,
and education by publishing worldwide in

Oxford New York

Auckland Cape Town Dar es Salaam Hong Kong Karachi Kuala Lumpur
Madrid Melbourne Mexico City Nairobi New Delhi Taipei Toronto Shanghai

With offices in

Argentina Austria Brazil Chile Czech Republic France Greece Guatemala
Hungary Italy Japan South Korea Poland Portugal Singapore Switzerland
Thailand Turkey Ukraine Vietnam

Oxford is a registered trade mark of Oxford University Press
in the UK and in certain other countries

© Oxford University Press 1992
First published 1992
Trade edition first published 1994
This revised edition first published 2002
British Library Cataloguing in Publication Data available
ISBN 0–19–832049–3

7 9 10 8

Illustrations by Alexy Pendle

Photographs by Donald Cooper (Photostage), except for p.174. Cover
shows Stephen Dillane as Hamlet in the Gielgud Theatre, London, 1994
production.

For Matthew

Oxford School Shakespeare
edited by Roma Gill

Typeset in Minion and Trade Gothic
by Herb Bowes Graphics, Oxford
Printed and bound by Creative Print and Design Wales, Ebbw Vale

Contents

Introduction

About the Play

REVENGE! OR GETTING YOUR OWN BACK

It's only natural—you hit me, I hit you back! It doesn't matter whether we are children quarrelling in the playground, or mighty nations fighting global warfare. The impulse to retaliate, to give tit for tat, is strong, and primitive, and human.

Most societies make rules to control this natural urge. In the Bible, we can read how the Jews of the Old Testament were instructed under the law of Moses to exact strict penalties for injuries: an eye for an eye, a tooth for a tooth, and a life for a life (Exodus, chapter 21). In the New Testament, however, Jesus taught Christians to love their enemies, and to 'turn the other cheek' to their assailants (St Luke, chapter 6).

For the well-being of any community, hidden injuries must be revealed, and wrongs must be punished. And there is in all of us, surely, a desire to see that justice is done, and that everyone gets what they deserve? In real life, of course, this does not always happen; but sometimes in the imaginary world of fiction we can have the satisfaction of seeing the crime disclosed, the criminal unmasked, and the forces of good triumphing over evil. Even if the victims cannot always be recompensed—the murdered cannot be restored to life—at least their suffering is avenged.

Such fiction, sometimes based on fact, has always been popular: today there is no shortage of 'whodunnit' detective novels and television plays. In times past, the theatre was the place to find this kind of entertainment.

Revenge drama has a very long history, going back at least as far as the time of Aeschylus (*c.* 500 BC) and his great Oresteian trilogy. About five centuries later, the Greek plays were adapted for Roman audiences by the dramatist Seneca—and in the sixteenth century Seneca's plays, translated from Latin into English, became the model for the English playwrights.

The most famous of early English revenge plays is *The Spanish Tragedy* (*c.* 1588), written by Thomas Kyd. Other notable plays are Shakespeare's own *Titus Andronicus* (*c.* 1590), *Antonio's Revenge* (*c.* 1599), by John Marston, *The Revenger's Tragedy* (*c.* 1607), attributed to Cyril Tourneur, and John Webster's *Duchess of Malfi* (*c.* 1614).

Hamlet is the finest of all the plays in the English revenge tradition. It is the most serious, because it asks so many questions; and it is also the most understandable. Shakespeare's characters are like real people—people of today—even though the action of the play belongs to a remote past. Later writers tried to follow Shakespeare's example, copying his ideas and theatrical devices just as he had copied those of his predecessors. But no one—even today—could imitate the character of Shakespeare's Prince. Hamlet is unique.

Leading Characters in the Play

Hamlet   The Prince of Denmark, son of Gertrude and nephew of Claudius. He is presented with a terrible problem when the Ghost of his dead father accuses Claudius of murder and demands revenge. Doubt makes him indecisive, and for a time he pretends to be mad. But when he knows the truth he is resolute and fearless.

TWO BROTHERS

King Hamlet   Father of the prince. He is now dead, and we see only his Ghost. But other characters, and especially Prince Hamlet, speak of his courage and virtues.

Claudius   Brother to the dead king, and now King of Denmark. He is newly married to Gertrude, his dead brother's wife. At first he seems to be courteous and efficient, but the play reveals him as a 'smiling, damned villain'.

VICTIMS OF THE DISASTER

Gertrude   Hamlet's mother, and the queen of Denmark. She married Claudius as soon as her first husband was dead, and now acquiesces in all his plans.

Ophelia   The daughter of Polonius and sister of Laertes. She loves Hamlet, and is distressed by his treatment of her.

Polonius   The king's trusted counsellor, whose interference triggers off the action of the play. He is the father of Laertes and Ophelia, and takes himself very seriously.

Laertes   Son to Polonius, and brother of Ophelia. He is passionate in defence of the family honour, and (unlike Hamlet) does not scruple to avenge his injuries.

Rosencrantz and Guildenstern   Said to be schoolfriends of Hamlet. They are summoned to court by the King (Claudius), and used as his instruments.

THE SURVIVORS

Fortinbras
Prince of Norway. Headstrong and (as his name—French *fort* = strong—suggests) physically active. He is the complete opposite of Hamlet, although their situations are alike: Fortinbras's uncle has also succeeded to his brother's throne.

Horatio
Hamlet's friend. He is a model of friendship and can always be trusted to give sensible advice and an honest opinion. Sometimes he is not so much a *character* as a choric figure, giving necessary information to the audience.

Synopsis

ACT 3

Scene 1   Claudius and Polonius try unsuccessfully to trick Hamlet into declaring love for Ophelia. Polonius volunteers to conceal himself in order to hear an interview between the queen and her son.

Scene 2   Hamlet lectures the actors on their art, but the performance of their play is interrupted by the king's guilty alarm. Hamlet is called to his mother's presence.

Scene 3   Claudius tries to pray—and offers Hamlet an unexpected opportunity to take his revenge.

Scene 4   Startled by a sudden noise in his mother's chamber, Hamlet stabs through the arras and kills the hidden Polonius. He confronts his mother with accusations of guilty lust, but his wrath is subdued when the Ghost appears and rebukes him.

ACT 4

Scene 1   The queen tells Claudius about the murder of Polonius.

Scene 2   Rosencrantz and Guildenstern encounter Hamlet.

Scene 3   Claudius reveals that he has sent Hamlet to England to be murdered.

Scene 4   The Norwegian prince makes a brief appearance on his way to defend his territory, and Hamlet compares his own inactivity with this energy.

Scene 5   Ophelia has gone mad with distress at Hamlet's treatment of her, and her brother—who has returned to investigate the suspicious circumstances of his father's death—is outraged. Claudius blames Hamlet for everything.

Scene 6   Horatio has news from Hamlet, who has returned to Denmark.

Scene 7   Claudius arranges a fencing match between Laertes and Hamlet which should be fatal for the prince. The queen describes the death of Ophelia.

Act 5

Scene 1 Hamlet and Horatio come into the graveyard, and Hamlet learns of Ophelia's suicide.

Scene 2 Hamlet describes his adventures at sea and his treatment of Rosencrantz and Guildenstern. The entire court assembles for the fencing match, in which Laertes is wounded. Claudius drops poison into a goblet, but it is the queen who drinks and dies. Laertes denounces Claudius, and Hamlet strikes at the king with the poisoned rapier and forces him to drink from the poisoned goblet. But Hamlet is also fatally wounded, and with his dying voice gives the kingdom over to Young Fortinbras.

Hamlet: commentary

ACT 1

Scene 1 'Who's there?'—The play opens with a challenge. The scene is set on the gun-platform outside the castle of Elsinore, and the soldiers on guard-duty must be professionally suspicious. Tonight they are more than usually tense, because they have been frightened by something which they dare not even name—a 'thing', 'a dreaded sight', an 'apparition'.

They are joined by a civilian, Horatio, who makes light of their fears, just as a father might comfort a nervous child: 'Tush, tush, 'twill not appear'. Sitting in a huddle on the ground, they listen as Barnardo begins his ghost story. And we, the play's audience, listen too, sharing in the suspense.

The Ghost startles us all when it suddenly appears, and then vanishes in an instant. It makes no sound, although (as we learn in Scene 2) it is clad in full armour. The frightened soldiers discuss what we have *all* witnessed, turning to Horatio to confirm the Ghost's identity: 'Is it not like the king?' Horatio was once sceptical, and dismissed the soldiers' fears as 'fantasy'. But now he has seen the Ghost himself, and he must believe 'the sensible and true avouch' of his own eyes.

Because Horatio is convinced of the Ghost's reality, we—Shakespeare's audience—are also persuaded to believe in it, no matter what we may think of ghosts. Like Horatio, though, we may question its nature and the reason for its appearance at this time.

There was a very old superstition that ghosts would return from the dead in order to give some kind of warning to the living. This is Horatio's first thought, especially now that the whole country of Denmark is getting ready for war and expecting trouble from Young Fortinbras of Norway. All this is explained (like a lesson in modern history) to the soldiers—but really for the benefit of the audience! And Horatio recalls a historic precedent for such supernatural manifestations: he describes the ghosts that were seen in ancient Rome when Julius Caesar was murdered.

At the climax of his speech the Ghost returns, and Horatio challenges it boldly. But he gets no response. The cock crows, and the Ghost disappears. Dawn breaks, life returns to normal, and Horatio takes Barnardo and Marcellus in search of Young Hamlet. Perhaps the Ghost will speak to *him*.

Scene 2   After the eerie silence of the guards' midnight watch and its mysterious happenings, we are taken into the daytime activity of the royal court. The sound of trumpets heralds the entry of Claudius, the new king of Denmark, with his queen and all the members of his Council. Prince Hamlet follows, at the end of the royal procession.

From the tone of his address, it sounds as though Claudius is making his first public appearance as the king; he delivers a well-prepared speech, calculated to make a good impression. He speaks of grief for his brother's death, and pleasure at his own marriage—sorrow has been mixed with joy, there has been 'mirth in funeral' and 'dirge in marriage'. He thanks the counsellors, who have guided him with their 'better wisdoms'. And then he moves on to talk of less embarrassing matters, demonstrating his efficiency in handling the Norwegian threat, and dispatching ambassadors with his official letter to the king of Norway.

He turns now to Laertes, speaking more naturally and showing some affection to the young man, the son of his most valued counsellor: 'What wouldst thou have, Laertes?' Laertes asks permission to leave Denmark and go back to Paris. His wish is granted. But no such graciousness is extended to Hamlet, whose request to go back to his university is flatly refused: 'It is most retrograde to our desires'.

The prince is marked off from the rest of the courtiers by the 'nighted colour' of his clothes—his 'inky cloak' and 'suits of solemn black'. Hamlet is still in mourning for his father, and he refuses to accept the trite words of consolation offered by Claudius and the queen. In public, Hamlet's grief and bitterness are controlled, hidden behind the sardonic wit when he tells Claudius that he is 'A little more than kin, and less than kind'. In private, however, his anger bursts out in passionate reproaches—and we now learn that his mother's hasty remarriage has almost broken Hamlet's heart.

Sorrow has a moment's respite when Hamlet recognizes Horatio, and finds a much-needed friend. Horatio comes, with Marcellus and Barnardo, to recount the experience of the previous night; Hamlet is convinced that they have indeed seen his father's spirit—and he too suspects the worst. He is impatient—'Would night were come'.

Scene 3   But we must allow for a little time to pass. The suspense is slackened as the mood and pace of the play change once again. The scene is now domestic, showing an intimate glimpse of a loving and close-knit family. The brother, Laertes, is going away to Paris, but he does not want to lose touch with his sister—'let me hear from you'. He worries about her boyfriend—perhaps Prince Hamlet *says* he loves her—and perhaps he does love her *now*—but she must remember that a prince is not like ordinary men, who are free to choose wives for themselves. Ophelia must be careful to protect her good name—and her virginity.

Their father adds some of his store of worldly wisdom, first counselling Laertes about his behaviour in Paris—the sort of friends he should make, how he should dress, and how to handle his money. When his son has left, Polonius turns his attention to his daughter, lecturing Ophelia about her friendship with Prince Hamlet. He scoffs at the idea of love, because he is afraid that Hamlet will seduce his daughter, and he orders Ophelia to end their friendship.

Scene 4   Midnight has come at last, and Hamlet waits with the guards on the gun-platform outside the palace. From the banqueting hall within, they can hear the sound of revelry. Guns are fired in celebration when the king drinks a toast. With some disgust, Hamlet describes how the heavy drinking of the Danes lowers their reputation in the eyes of other nations.

His moralizing breaks off when the Ghost appears, startling Hamlet so that he invokes divine protection: 'Angels and ministers of grace defend us'. He is determined to speak to this apparition, regardless of whether it is a good spirit or an evil one, because he recognizes its likeness to his father. The tone of his demands becomes almost hysterical, but the Ghost speaks no word—only indicating that Hamlet should follow where it leads. His companions try to restrain Hamlet, fearing that an evil spirit might be trying to lead him into suicidal madness. But Hamlet's grim wit threatens to 'make a ghost' of anyone who holds him back.

Scene 5   Alone with Hamlet, the Ghost speaks. It has come from some terrifying purgatory, where it is being punished for the sins of a lifetime. But the Ghost does not ask pity—it demands revenge! Hamlet's father claims to have been betrayed by his 'most seeming-virtuous queen' and murdered by 'that adulterate beast', his brother Claudius. The Ghost's language is violent with hatred, and Hamlet is faint with disgust and horror. The signs of dawn appear, which means that the Ghost must depart. Hamlet has sworn to avenge his father, and will keep his word.

Now Horatio and Marcellus come on the scene, searching for Hamlet. They find him in a very odd mood, and his words do not make sense: they are 'wild and whirling'. He makes them swear never to reveal what they have seen, and they take their oath on the cross-piece of

Hamlet's sword. A ghostly voice speaks from under the ground each time Hamlet—with a strange joke—repeats the oath. He speaks of a madness—an 'antic disposition'—that he means to pretend, and which they are sworn not to disclose. His final words are cryptic: 'The time is out of joint. O cursed spite, That ever I was born to set it right'. Hamlet seems to have found a vocation, a purpose for his life.

His friends must be bewildered. They have all seen the Ghost, *but only Hamlet*—and the audience—*knows what the Ghost has said.*

ACT 2

Scene 1   Some time has passed. Laertes is now in Paris, and his father—always suspicious—is sending Reynaldo to spy on him. Although Reynaldo accepts the job, he does not like what he has to do. Ophelia comes to find her father. She has been badly frightened by Prince Hamlet, and she describes how he came into her private room, only half-dressed— his doublet was not buttoned, and his stockings hung loose around his ankles. He did not say anything, but he was obviously upset.

Polonius decides at once that Hamlet is mad with love for Ophelia, and he is even more sure of his diagnosis when he hears that Ophelia (as he had ordered in *Act 1*, Scene 3) has been refusing either to see the prince, or to receive his letters. Full of his own importance, Polonius hurries his daughter off to see the king.

Scene 2   We find Claudius interviewing Rosencrantz and Guildenstern. He had commanded the two young men to come to the court, and now he tells them of the distressing change in Hamlet's behaviour; perhaps these two boys, being of Hamlet's own age ('so neighbour'd to his youth'), will be able to find out what is wrong with him. In fact, Rosencrantz and Guildenstern are being set to spy on Hamlet, just as Reynaldo was told to spy on Laertes.

Dismissing them, the king listens to the report of the ambassadors who have returned from their successful mission to Norway. They tell Claudius how 'old Norway' has rebuked his nephew, sending him to fight against the Poles (which means, incidentally, that he will need to pass, peaceably, through Denmark). Then at last it is Polonius's turn to speak.

At first, his pompous formality irritates the queen, but Polonius carries on to tell everything he knows about Hamlet's love for Ophelia. He has found one of the prince's love-letters, which he reads aloud. He is quick to point out that he has not encouraged this affair, and that he has told his daughter that 'Lord Hamlet is a prince out of thy star'. But, he concludes, Ophelia's rejection of his love must have driven Hamlet out of his mind. The king seems unconvinced, and asks for some proof of what Polonius says. The two men decide that they will hide where they can listen to a meeting (which will be arranged by Polonius) between Hamlet and Ophelia.

The prince comes in just as they are making their plans. When Polonius tries to talk to him, Hamlet replies with answers that make no sense to Polonius, who seems to accept that it is only another fit of madness. But the audience may suspect that Hamlet is assuming his 'antic disposition' (as he promised in *Act 1*, Scene 5) in order to insult Polonius. This suspicion is confirmed by Hamlet himself after Polonius has left the stage; he drops his disguise with an exasperated comment, 'These tedious old fools'.

Hamlet's manner changes when he meets his old friends Rosencrantz and Guildenstern. He laughs with them—but it is no joke when he tells them 'Denmark's a prison'! He soon becomes suspicious of them, and starts to ask questions. They have to admit that they have come to Elsinore because they were 'sent for'. Hamlet tells them only what he wants them to know—that he is depressed and nothing seems to satisfy him. But news of some travelling players diverts him for a while.

He recognizes the actors, and recalls a particular production that he has seen. The leading actor (flattered, no doubt, by the royal attention) declaims the whole of the speech that Hamlet remembers. And this gives Hamlet an idea! He chooses the programme for the evening's entertainment, asking for a performance of *The Murder of Gonzago*—with an additional speech which he will write himself. The players go off to get ready, Rosencrantz and Guildenstern are dismissed, and Hamlet is left alone to ponder on what he has seen.

The audience is taken into his confidence as he thinks aloud. The pretended grief of the actor has sharpened Hamlet's sense of his own grief, and spurred him to take some action. He wonders *why* he cannot get anything done—after all, he has never been frightened of defending himself, and he has a very good cause to fight for now . . . Only at the end of the speech do we find out what is really worrying Hamlet: can he trust the Ghost? It could be an *evil* spirit, which will lead him to damnation. But if the actors could perform 'something like the murder of my father', perhaps Claudius will show his guilt by his reaction. And that would be better proof than the word of a ghost!

ACT 3

Scene 1   Rosencrantz and Guildenstern report to Claudius. They have nothing much to tell him, since Hamlet, 'with a crafty madness', refuses to confide in them. They are dismissed, and Claudius explains his next stratagem to Gertrude—whose concern for Hamlet seems to be genuine. Ophelia is set in position by her father, then Polonius takes the king aside—but not before Claudius has mumbled a few words (overheard only by the audience) about his 'heavy burden' of guilt.

Hamlet, meditating on the problems of living and dying, is surprised when he comes upon Ophelia—especially when she hands back to him the little presents ('remembrances') that he had given to her in the past. Angered by this, he lets loose on Ophelia all the bitterness he has been feeling since his mother's marriage to Claudius. He begins to suspect Ophelia too, and seems conscious that there are unseen listeners to this conversation. In his apparent madness, he drops a veiled threat (which Claudius *must* hear): 'I say we will have no mo marriage. Those that are married already—*all but one*—shall live'.

His departure—with a final insult—leaves Ophelia terribly upset and quite convinced of his madness. Claudius is not so sure about this—he is certain, however, that the cause of Hamlet's strange behaviour is not love. He says he will send his nephew to England, to collect an unpaid debt; perhaps the change of air will do him good!

Polonius prefers his love-sickness theory, and suggests that the queen should have a word with her son—and he, Polonius, will be there to listen; he will hide behind the 'arras'—the great tapestry that hangs in Gertrude's room.

Scene 2   Hamlet is lecturing to the actors on the theory of drama ('to hold as 'twere the mirror up to nature') and the art of acting. The professional actors listen meekly to the royal amateur until they are sent away to get ready for their performance. After a speech in praise of Horatio's friendship, Hamlet explains what he is planning. Apparently Horatio has already been told about the Ghost's accusation, and now he too is to watch the king 'the whilst this play is playing', and look for any tell-tale signs of guilt. Afterwards, they can compare notes.

The idle chatter of an assembling audience (on stage) becomes heavy with insult and irony—from Hamlet—which is only interrupted by the dumb-show. The mime prepares *us*—Shakespeare's audience—for what is to come in the play's main action. Then, like Horatio, we shall probably be watching Claudius.

The Murder of Gonzago is written in an obviously 'old-fashioned' style; its heavily regular verse sounds artificial, and contrasts with the language spoken by the 'real' people of Shakespeare's play. Its plot, however, is very relevant to the situation in Elsinore. A king, feeling that death is near, recalls his happy marriage and wonders whether his wife will ever marry again. She insists that she will never think of a second husband. At the end of the first little scene, Hamlet asks his mother for her opinion. Gertrude is evidently uneasy, and Claudius is beginning to feel uncomfortable.

The second scene has hardly started—the murderer has just poisoned his victim—when Claudius brings it to a sudden end. He leaves the hall, and his courtiers follow. The actors disappear. Only Hamlet and Horatio are left behind. Hamlet is triumphant—his plot has worked, and Claudius has convicted himself.

Rosencrantz and Guildenstern come to summon Hamlet: the queen wishes to speak to her son. But Hamlet must first show his former friends that he understands what they are doing; and he warns them that they will fail: 'though you fret me, you cannot play upon me'. Polonius comes to call Hamlet: the queen is waiting. Hamlet will come—but before he leaves the stage, he lets the audience see something of his new-found resolution.

Scene 3   Claudius is now sure that his secret is known, and he proceeds with his plan to send Hamlet to England, guarded by Rosencrantz and Guildenstern. Hamlet's former friends appreciate the importance of their job to the national security. They go to pack for the journey. Polonius drops in for a moment—he is on his way to hide behind the arras in the queen's room.

For the very first time, we see Claudius alone and hear what *he* thinks about the whole business. He is a very unhappy man, trapped in a horrible dilemma—of his own making. He admits his guilt (to himself), but feels that he cannot pray, or repent, or ask for God's forgiveness, since he is still in possession of the rewards of his crime—his queen and his throne. But he tries to pray, forcing himself to kneel. In this position he is discovered by Hamlet, who draws his sword—but fails to act. Hamlet argues with himself that this would not be true revenge for his father's murder: the Ghost had told him of its sufferings in Purgatory, but Claudius would avoid these if he were to die just now, when he is in a state of grace. So Hamlet will wait, until he can find a more suitable occasion.

Ignorant of the danger he has just missed, Claudius gets to his feet. He has not been able to pray, after all.

Scene 4   Another trap is being set. Gertrude is prepared for the part that she is to play, and Polonius conceals himself behind the arras. The interview starts well enough—a mother scolding her son: 'Hamlet, thou hast thy father much offended'. But her son immediately takes control of the situation: 'Mother, you have my father much offended'. His passion alarms Gertrude, and her call for help is echoed by the unseen listener hidden behind the arras. Hamlet runs his sword through the tapestry, thinking that this must be the king. But he has killed Polonius.

His passion undiminished, Hamlet forces his mother to look at two portraits, 'the counterfeit presentment of two brothers'. He describes them to her—though his description tells us more about Hamlet himself than about the brothers. One is idealized, and given all the attributes of the Greek gods: 'Hyperion's curls, the front of Jove himself, An eye like Mars . . . ' The other receives nothing but contempt: he is 'a mildew'd ear'—Hamlet's scorn lacks words!

His disgust speaks out, however, when he talks of his mother's relationship with Claudius. He loathes the very idea of her lust, and dwells on its physical aspects with horrified fascination as he contemplates Gertrude and Claudius 'honeying and making love Over the nasty sty'. The queen pleads with him to stop, but Hamlet has got carried away by his own emotion, and he will not hear her. He stops only when he sees the Ghost which seems to have come (as Hamlet understands it) to urge Hamlet on to some action. Gertrude sees and hears nothing but her son's strange behaviour, and she worries even more about his sanity. After the Ghost has left them, Hamlet speaks once more to his mother. He is calmer now, but he continues to exhort her to repent of her marriage to Claudius, and to put an end to their sexual relationship.

Hamlet turns to the body of Polonius, which has been lying on stage throughout this scene. His death was regrettable, and Hamlet repents of the murder. But by this deed, Hamlet himself has become a murderer—and will now become the object of another revenge plot.

Before he parts from his mother, Hamlet refers to the king's decision to send him to England. All preparations have been made, and Hamlet is ready to go.

ACT 4

Scene 1 The king comes to Gertrude's room to find out about her interview with Hamlet. He is accompanied by Rosencrantz and Guildenstern, but these are quickly dismissed by the queen. She confirms that her son is completely mad, and tells of the murder of Polonius. Claudius is quick to realize that *he* was the intended victim: 'It had been so with us had we been there'. He says that Hamlet's madness is a threat to *everyone*, and it must be dealt with immediately: Hamlet must be sent to England, and Claudius himself must devise some kind of cover-up story. Rosencrantz and Guildenstern are sent off to find the prince, and to get the body of Polonius.

From this point the action of the play moves quickly; the conventional—and useful—division into 'scenes' can seem an interruption.

Scene 2 Rosencrantz and Guildenstern encounter Hamlet. He evades their questions—but he lets them know that he understands their roles as the king's informers.

Scene 3 Claudius is now very frightened. Hamlet answers his questions with a grim playfulness—but Claudius knows that there is a deadly seriousness behind all that Hamlet says. The letters for England are 'seal'd and done', ready for Rosencrantz and Guildenstern to carry them. When everyone has gone, Claudius reveals that his letter 'imports . . . The present death of Hamlet'—he has told the king of England to have Hamlet murdered.

Scene 4 Young Fortinbras leads his army across the stage. He is going to fight in Poland and needs to cross Denmark. A captain is dispatched to the Danish court to remind the king—*and the audience*—that this has all been pre-arranged (in *Act 2*, Scene 2).

The captain meets Hamlet and his escort, who are on their way to the port, to take ship for England. Questions are asked, and Hamlet learns that Young Fortinbras and his army will be fighting only 'to gain a little patch of ground That hath in it no profit but the name'. The captain is not enthusiastic, but Hamlet is filled with admiration for the enterprise. The example of Young Fortinbras, engaging in such a battle over a matter of honour, serves as a reproach to Hamlet for his own inactivity, and strengthens his resolve to act.

Scene 5   Hamlet has left Elsinore to go to England, and Horatio is attending on the queen. A gentleman brings news of Ophelia, and almost immediately, the girl herself comes in. She is literally mad with grief. Her father is dead, murdered by the man she loves! Everyone understands her anguish—even Claudius, who also witnesses the scene.

     When Ophelia has left the room, Claudius tells Gertrude of a new danger—Laertes has returned from France and, hearing rumours of the suspicious circumstances of his father's death, is threatening rebellion. The threat becomes real when Laertes bursts into the room. The king takes control of the situation, calming Laertes's anger for a moment. But then the appearance of Ophelia, crazily singing of love and death, gives her brother more cause for passion. Claudius seizes his opportunity, and takes Laertes aside to explain his plot.

Scene 6   There is news from sea. Horatio learns that pirates have captured Hamlet—and rescued him from Rosencrantz and Guildenstern. He is now back in Denmark.

Scene 7   Claudius has given *his* account of the events which have taken place while Laertes has been away from Denmark, and is now explaining why he has not been able to do anything about the situation. He seems to have a plan, however, and he is just about to divulge it when Hamlet's letters are brought in.

     Claudius thinks quickly. He flatters Laertes with talk of fencing and of Hamlet's jealousy; then he returns to the subject of Polonius's death. A fencing match is arranged—Laertes will fight Hamlet—but one of the foils will be 'unbated': there will be nothing to protect its sharp point. Laertes has bought some poison, and he will put this on the point of the sword, so that the least scratch will prove fatal. In case this fails, the king will have prepared a cup of wine—and this too will be poisoned. Hamlet will not escape!

     The queen interrupts their scheming with news of fresh disaster. Ophelia is drowned. There is a lyrical beauty in Gertrude's description of Ophelia's death which forbids us to ask how the queen knew all these details. Laertes weeps—but promises action.

ACT 5

Scene 1   The pace of the play slows down, and there is even time for a kind of humour as we watch a gravedigger going about his work, and we listen as he talks to another character (who is not identified). Gradually, we realize that it is Ophelia whose grave is being dug. Was her death accidental, or did she commit suicide? The two characters debate the issues until one goes off to fetch the beer and the other sings to himself as he digs.

Hamlet and Horatio come to the graveyard and watch the man at work. Hamlet speaks his thoughts on death, and starts up a conversation with the gravedigger. A funeral procession interrupts them, and Hamlet recognizes the mourners. But the funeral is conducted with very little ceremony. A young man questions the priest about this—and Hamlet identifies Laertes, 'a very noble youth'. The priest will allow no further rites of burial, because there is some doubt about the cause of death.

In his agonized grief, Laertes refers to his 'sister' and this, together with Gertrude's tender farewell, reminds Hamlet that he had once loved Ophelia. He reveals himself to Laertes, who is so enraged that he attacks Hamlet. They start to fight by Ophelia's open grave. The other mourners separate them. With a strange threat, Hamlet leaves the scene.

Scene 2   Hamlet tells Horatio the full story of his adventures at sea. It is a story full of accidents, and Hamlet is now convinced that there is a divine power in control of everything that happens: 'There's a divinity that shapes our ends'.

Hamlet describes how, unable to sleep one night when he was on the ship sailing to England, he had discovered the letter that Rosencrantz and Guildenstern were carrying. From it, he learned that Claudius was plotting to have him killed. Hamlet substituted *another* letter, which he had just written, ordering the deaths of the two messengers. But Hamlet's own life was saved when the ship was attacked by pirates (as Horatio had learned from Hamlet's letter in *Act 4*, Scene 6). They took the prince as their only prisoner, leaving Rosencrantz and Guildenstern behind—who have sailed to meet their deaths. Hamlet feels no remorse for this, although he regrets his behaviour to Laertes. He now has no doubt of the king's guilt, and Horatio too is convinced. But time is short.

A courtier, Osric, interrupts; he has come to inform Hamlet of the planned fencing bout with Laertes, and the king's wager on Hamlet's skill. Osric's affectation amuses and irritates Hamlet, but he replies in a similar style. He accepts the challenge, but Horatio warns him—'You will lose this wager, my lord'. We in the audience must share his fatalism, because we have heard the talk about the 'shuffling' planned in *Act 4*,

Scene 7: we know about the 'unbated' rapier with the poisoned tip, and the poison in the cup of wine.

The thought of death does not worry Hamlet: 'If it be now, 'tis not to come; if it be not to come, it will be now'.

The entire court assembles to watch the duel. Hamlet begs pardon of Laertes, blaming his 'madness' for some of the things he has done. Laertes accepts the apology, but says that his 'terms of honour' demand the satisfaction of a duel. They choose their rapiers. Hamlet is easily pleased, but Laertes needs to make sure that he has got the deadly weapon. The wine is set on the table, and the king orders trumpets and guns to mark his toast—just as his drinking was celebrated in *Act 1, Scene 4*.

Hamlet and Laertes fight, and Hamlet makes the first hit. The king drinks to Hamlet—and drops the poison in the cup. Hamlet refuses to drink, and they fight again. Again Hamlet hits Laertes. The queen drinks to Hamlet—and Claudius (in an 'aside') reveals that she has drunk from the poisoned cup.

In a further bout of fighting, Laertes wounds Hamlet; the rapiers are dropped and picked up—but this time Hamlet gets the poisoned one. There is a further bout of fighting, and Hamlet wounds Laertes. The queen falls, and dies. Laertes confesses the poisoning of the weapon and the wine. He denounces Claudius: 'The king—the king's to blame'.

Hamlet, incensed, wounds the king with the poisoned rapier, and forces him to drink from the poisoned cup. Claudius dies. Laertes, having asked Hamlet's forgiveness, also dies—and Hamlet himself feels the approach of death. He orders Horatio (who is willing, himself, to drink from the poisoned cup) to 'Report me and my cause aright' to the world.

Before he dies, he hears the noise of marching soldiers. Fortinbras has returned from the war in Poland (to which he was going in *Act 4, Scene 4*), and now Hamlet elects him to the throne of Denmark. The Prince dies.

Fortinbras is accompanied by the English ambassadors, who have come to report the deaths of Rosencrantz and Guildenstern. Horatio shows them what has happened, and Fortinbras takes command.

Shakespeare's Verse

Easily the best way to understand and appreciate Shakespeare's verse is to read it aloud—and don't worry if you don't understand everything! Try not to be captivated by the dominant rhythm, but decide which are the most important words in each line and use the regular metre to drive them forward to the listeners.

Shakespeare's plays are mainly written in 'blank verse', the form preferred by most dramatists in the sixteenth and early seventeenth centuries. It is a very flexible medium, which is capable—like the human speaking voice—of a wide range of tones. Basically the lines, which are unrhymed, are ten syllables long. The syllables have alternating stresses, just like normal English speech; and they divide into five 'feet'. The technical name for this is 'iambic pentameter'.

> **Horatio**
> Befóre my Gód, I míght not thís beliéve
> Withoút the sénsible and trúe avoúch 60
> Of míne own eyés.
> **Marcellus**
>   Is ít not líke the kíng?
> **Horatio**
> As thóu art tó thysélf.
> Such wás the véry ármour hé had ón
> When hé th'ambítious Nórway cómbattéd.
> So frówn'd he ónce, when ín an ángry párle 65
> He smóte the slédded Pólacks ón the íce.
> 'Tis strange.
> **Marcellus**
> Thus twíce befóre, and júmp at thís dead hóur,
> With mártial stálk hath hé gone bý our wátch. _1_, 1, 59–69

In this quotation, most of the lines are regular in length and normal in iambic stress pattern. But sometimes Shakespeare deviates from the norm, writing lines that are longer or shorter than ten syllables, and varying the stress patterns for unusual emphasis. In lines 62 and 67, for instance, Horatio speaks only part of a pentameter; it is as though his bewilderment can only be expressed in silence. When two speakers share a pentameter (as in line 61), Shakespeare can show the closeness of their thoughts, and the quickness of their reactions to each other.

The verse line sometimes contains the grammatical unit of meaning—'When he th'ambitious Norway combatted'—thus allowing for a pause at the end of the line, before a new idea is started; at other times, the sense runs on from one line to the next—'the sensible and true avouch Of mine own eyes'. This makes for the natural fluidity of speech, avoiding monotony but still maintaining the iambic rhythm. Occasionally, for the sake of rhythm, words are elided or otherwise abbreviated ('th'ambitious Norway')—but this is also a feature of normal spoken English.

Source, Date, and Text

Once upon a time there was a real Prince Amleth whose father, the king of Jutland, was murdered by King Fengo, his brother . . . The story was told in the thirteenth century by a Danish historian, Saxo Grammaticus. It was retold in the sixteenth century, with additions, by Belleforest, a Frenchman. His version, translated into English, was probably the source for Shakespeare's tragedy.

There was an earlier play, perhaps written by Thomas Kyd, which might have linked Shakespeare's *Hamlet* with Belleforest's *Histoire Tragique* of Hamblet. But this link is now missing—the play was never published.

Shakespeare's play was known in England at the end of the sixteenth century, but the version we have today cannot have been written before 1601. This date is fixed by two topical references in the play itself. The boy actors described in *Act* 2, Scene 2 had a very successful season at the Blackfriars playhouse in 1601; and the 'innovation' spoken of in 2, 2, 326 could have been the rebellion which was led by the Earl of Essex in February of that year.

Hamlet was first published in a quarto volume (Q1) in 1603. A second edition (Q2) appeared the following year, giving a rather different version of the play. Yet another text, different from both the others, was published in 1623 in the collection of all Shakespeare's plays, which is known as the First Folio (F).

Throughout the twentieth century there was much scholarly argument about the respective merits of these editions, but towards the end of the century a masterly study, which has not been surpassed, was published by Professor Harold Jenkins in his Arden edition of the play (1982), and this is the text now followed in this *Oxford School Shakespeare* edition. Professor Jenkins believed that Q2 is the most reliable of the three texts, and probably based directly on Shakespeare's own manuscript. But even Q2 is obscure in some places, and a modern edition must seek help from Q1 and F to clarify the difficulties.

Characters in the Play

Ghost	*of* Hamlet King of Denmark, *recently deceased*
Gertrude	*his wife, now married to* Claudius
Claudius	*his brother, now King of Denmark*
Hamlet	*Prince of Denmark, son to the late* King Hamlet *and his wife,* Gertrude
Horatio	*friend to* Prince Hamlet
Rosencrantz **Guildenstern** }	*former schoolfriends of* Prince Hamlet
Polonius	*the* King's *counsellor*
Laertes	*his son*
Ophelia	*his daughter*
Reynaldo	*his servant*
Fortinbras	*Prince of Norway*
A Norwegian Captain	

At the King's Court in Elsinore

Voltemand **Cornelius** }	*Danish ambassadors sent to Norway*
Osric	*a foppish courtier*
A Lord	
A Gentleman	
Francisco **Barnardo** **Marcellus** }	*soldiers of the* King's *guard*
A Gravedigger	
Another	*the* Gravedigger's *companion*
A Priest	

Players Visiting the Court in Elsinore

First Player	*acting the part of the king*
Second Player	*acting the part of the queen*
Third Player	*acting the part of the king's nephew*
Fourth Player	*speaking the Prologue*

English Ambassadors, Messengers, Lords, Attendants, Guards, Players, Soldiers, Sailors

Scene: *Elsinor—in the royal castle and its environs*

'What, has this thing appear'd again tonight?' (*1*, 1, 24). Tom Wilkinson as Horatio, Royal Shakespeare Company, 1980.

ACT 1

Act 1 Scene 1

It is cold; and it is midnight. In a country preparing for war the sentries who guard the castle are nervous. They have been frightened by something extraordinary, and tonight they have asked Horatio, whose opinion they value, to accompany their watch. The Ghost appears, then vanishes; and the awe-struck men discuss what they have witnessed. The Ghost returns, and Horatio tries to make contact—but it will not hear him, and disappears again. They must tell Hamlet.

2 *answer me*: It is the sentry on duty who has the right to challenge.
unfold: reveal.
3 Barnardo's response—perhaps an accepted password—shows him to be a friend.
6 *carefully*: promptly.

9 *I am . . . heart*: I've had enough.

14 *rivals*: partners.

Scene 1

Enter Barnardo *and* Francisco, *two Sentinels*

Barnardo
Who's there?
Francisco
Nay, answer me. Stand and unfold yourself.
Barnardo
Long live the king!
Francisco
Barnardo?
Barnardo
5 He.
Francisco
You come most carefully upon your hour.
Barnardo
'Tis now struck twelve. Get thee to bed, Francisco.
Francisco
For this relief much thanks. 'Tis bitter cold,
And I am sick at heart.
Barnardo
10 Have you had quiet guard?
Francisco
Not a mouse stirring.
Barnardo
Well, good night.
If you do meet Horatio and Marcellus,
The rivals of my watch, bid them make haste.
Francisco
15 I think I hear them.

Enter Horatio *and* Marcellus

Stand, ho! Who is there?

16 *this ground*: this country.
the Dane: the Danish king.

17 *Give you*: may God give you.

19 *hath*: has taken.

22 *a piece of him*: Horatio perhaps
extends a hand as a mock proof of his
identity.

24 *this thing*: Shakespeare begins to
build up suspense.

26 *but our fantasy*: just our imagination.

28 *dreaded*: dreadful.
29 *Therefore*: that is why. *The audience*
needs to be told this—Barnardo
already knows.
along: to come along.
32 *approve our eyes*: believe what we
have seen.

34 *assail your ears*: get you to listen.
35 *fortified*: i.e. by reason. The imagery is
appropriate for a soldier.

Horatio
Friends to this ground.
   Marcellus
                     And liegemen to the Dane.
   Francisco
Give you good night.
   Marcellus
O, farewell honest soldier, who hath reliev'd you?
   Francisco
Barnardo hath my place. Give you good night.   [*Exit*
   Marcellus
20 Holla, Barnardo!
   Barnardo
Say, what, is Horatio there?
   Horatio
A piece of him.
   Barnardo
Welcome, Horatio. Welcome, good Marcellus.
   Horatio
What, has this thing appear'd again tonight?
   Barnardo
25 I have seen nothing.
   Marcellus
Horatio says 'tis but our fantasy,
And will not let belief take hold of him,
Touching this dreaded sight twice seen of us.
Therefore I have entreated him along
30 With us to watch the minutes of this night,
That if again this apparition come,
He may approve our eyes and speak to it.
   Horatio
Tush, tush, 'twill not appear.
   Barnardo
                     Sit down awhile,
And let us once again assail your ears,
35 That are so fortified against our story,
What we have two nights seen.
   Horatio
                       Well, sit we down.
And let us hear Barnardo speak of this.

Barnardo
Last night of all,
When yond same star that's westward from the pole,
40 Had made his course t'illume that part of heaven
Where now it burns, Marcellus and myself,
The bell then beating one—

Enter Ghost

Marcellus
Peace, break thee off. Look where it comes again.
Barnardo
In the same figure like the king that's dead.
Marcellus
45 Thou art a scholar, speak to it, Horatio.
Barnardo
Looks 'a not like the king? Mark it, Horatio.
Horatio
Most like. It harrows me with fear and wonder.
Barnardo
It would be spoke to.
Marcello
                              Question it, Horatio.
Horatio
What art thou that usurp'st this time of night,
50 Together with that fair and warlike form
In which the majesty of buried Denmark
Did sometimes march? By heaven, I charge thee speak.
Marcellus
It is offended.
Barnardo
                    See, it stalks away.
Horatio
Stay, speak, speak, I charge thee speak.   [*Exit* Ghost
Marcellus
55 'Tis gone and will not answer.
Barnardo
How now, Horatio? You tremble and look pale.
Is not this something more than fantasy?
What think you on't?

39 *pole*: pole star.
40 *illume*: light up.

42 *beating*: striking.

44 *figure*: shape.

45 *a scholar*: Horatio would know Latin, the proper language in which to address any supernatural being (although theatrical convention permits English here).
46 *'a*: he.
47 *harrows me*: breaks me up.

48 *would*: wants to be. A ghost could not start a conversation.

49 *usurp'st*: Horatio challenges the Ghost's right to appear at that time and in that particular shape.
50 *warlike*: martial.
51 *majesty of buried Denmark*: dead king of Denmark.

53 *offended*: The Ghost turns away because the questioner is not the man it seeks.

60-1 *without . . . eyes*: if I had not seen for myself: his eyes give the evidence ('avouch') of his senses. Horatio's conversion helps the audience to accept the Ghost's reality.

64 *Norway*: the king of Norway (father of Fortinbras). The conflict between the two kings is described in lines 85–9.
65 *parle*: argument (not merely verbal).
66 *smote*: struck.
sledded Polacks: Polish soldiers on sledges. Horatio perhaps knew of a famous battle fought on the frozen Baltic Sea.
68 *jump*: exactly.

70 'I don't really know what to think of it.'
71 *in the gross and scope*: in general.
72 *bodes*: threatens. Horatio tries to find a meaning in the apparition.
strange eruption: violent disturbance.
73 *Good now*: please.
he that: if anyone.
74-81 Marcellus describes the activity of a nation preparing for war—the forging of armaments by night as well as by day, seven days a week; and the international trade in weapons.
74 *watch*: wakefulness.
75 *the subject of the land*: all the king's subjects.
77 *mart*: trading.
78 *impress*: conscription.
80 *What . . . toward*: what is going on.

83 *whisper*: rumour.
84 *even but*: only just.
86 *prick'd*: urged.
emulate: competitive.
87 *Dar'd*: challenged.
Hamlet: the family name, to which Prince Hamlet is heir.
88 *this side of our known world*: our western world.
89 *seal'd compact*: certified (bearing official seals) agreement. The stress is on the second syllable of 'compact'.
90 *heraldry*: the code of chivalry.

Horatio
Before my God, I might not this believe
60 Without the sensible and true avouch
Of mine own eyes.
    Marcellus
                Is it not like the king?
    Horatio
As thou art to thyself.
Such was the very armour he had on
When he th'ambitious Norway combated.
65 So frown'd he once, when in an angry parle
He smote the sledded Polacks on the ice.
'Tis strange.
    Marcellus
Thus twice before, and jump at this dead hour,
With martial stalk hath he gone by our watch.
    Horatio
70 In what particular thought to work I know not,
But in the gross and scope of my opinion,
This bodes some strange eruption to our state.
    Marcellus
Good now, sit down, and tell me, he that knows,
Why this same strict and most observant watch
75 So nightly toils the subject of the land,
And why such daily cast of brazen cannon
And foreign mart for implements of war,
Why such impress of shipwrights, whose sore task
Does not divide the Sunday from the week.
80 What might be toward that this sweaty haste
Doth make the night joint-labourer with the day,
Who is't that can inform me?
    Horatio
                  That can I.
At least the whisper goes so: our last king,
Whose image even but now appear'd to us,
85 Was as you know by Fortinbras of Norway,
Thereto prick'd on by a most emulate pride,
Dar'd to the combat; in which our valiant Hamlet
(For so this side of our known world esteem'd him)
Did slay this Fortinbras, who by a seal'd compact
90 Well ratified by law and heraldry

92 *seiz'd of*: in possession of; the rival
monarchs had wagered lands which
they *personally* possessed, *not* their
kingdoms.

93 *moiety competent*: sufficient portion.
Hamlet did not need to wager all his
possessions to equal those of
Fortinbras.

94 *gaged*: gagèd; wagered.
had return'd: would have gone to.

96 *same cov'nant*: the 'compact' of
line 89.

97 'In accordance with the clause
referred to.'

98 *His*: i.e. the land of Fortinbras;
Horatio in these lines has been
speaking the language of lawyers.

99 *unimproved mettle*: unimprovèd;
undisciplined energy.
full: vigorous.

100 *skirts*: remote parts.

101 *Shark'd up*: got together.
list of lawless resolutes: band of
determined outlaws.

102–3 *For . . . in't*: to supply the power
and energy for some demanding
adventure that needs them (as a
hungry stomach needs food).

104 *doth well appear*: looks very much like
it.
state: government.

105 *of*: from.
strong hand: force.

106 *terms compulsatory*: compulsion.

109 *chief head*: fountain-head.

110 *post-haste*: furious activity.
rummage: turmoil.

111 *but e'en so*: just as it is.

112 *Well may it sort*: it is appropriate.
portentous: ominous.

113 *armed*: armèd.

114 *question*: cause.

115 *mote*: speck of dust.

116–23 *In . . . eclipse*: Horatio describes
the phenomena that also feature in
Shakespeare's *Julius Caesar* (*1*, 3,
and *2*, 2).

116 *palmy*: flourishing.

117 *the mightiest Julius*: Julius was the
first and most powerful of all the
Caesars.

118 *sheeted dead*: bodies in their shrouds.

119 *squeak and gibber*: wail in high-
pitched voices.

Did forfeit, with his life, all those his lands
Which he stood seiz'd of to the conqueror;
Against the which a moiety competent
Was gaged by our king, which had return'd
95 To the inheritance of Fortinbras,
Had he been vanquisher; as, by the same cov'nant
And carriage of the article design'd,
His fell to Hamlet. Now, sir, young Fortinbras,
Of unimproved mettle, hot and full,
100 Hath in the skirts of Norway here and there
Shark'd up a list of lawless resolutes
For food and diet to some enterprise
That hath a stomach in't, which is no other,
As it doth well appear unto our state,
105 But to recover of us by strong hand
And terms compulsatory those foresaid lands
So by his father lost. And this, I take it,
Is the main motive of our preparations,
The source of this our watch, and the chief head
110 Of this post-haste and rummage in the land.

  Barnardo
I think it be no other but e'en so.
Well may it sort that this portentous figure
Comes armed through our watch so like the king
That was and is the question of these wars.

  Horatio
115 A mote it is to trouble the mind's eye.
In the most high and palmy state of Rome,
A little ere the mightiest Julius fell,
The graves stood tenantless and the sheeted dead
Did squeak and gibber in the Roman streets;

120 *As*: The awkwardness of the syntax here suggests that something has been lost from the text.
stars . . . fire: comets with fiery tails.
dews of blood: red dews (which are actually caused by insects, not by comets).

121 *Disasters*: portents (Shakespeare uses an astrological term).

121–3 *moist . . . eclipse*: the moon was almost totally eclipsed; the moon, 'moist' because it was thought to draw up water from the sea, was known to influence the movement of the tides ('Neptune's empire').

124–8 'The same sort of thing has happened in our country, and always been a warning of some coming crisis.'

124 *precurse*: forerunner.

125 *harbingers*: heralds.
still: always.
fates: calamities; *and* the powers that ordain them.

126 *omen*: disaster.

128 *climatures*: regions of the earth.

129 *soft*: hush.

130 *cross it*: i.e. cross its path (and so expose himself to a dangerous influence).
blast: damn.

131–42 *Stay . . . speak*: Horatio's incantatory questioning suggests some of the common superstitions about the appearance of ghosts.

134 *to thee . . . to me*: Perhaps the body has not been properly laid to rest; and to bury it would be accounted as a credit to Horatio.

136 *privy to*: secretly aware of.

137 *happily*: perhaps (also 'fortunately').

120 As stars with trains of fire and dews of blood,
Disasters in the sun; and the moist star,
Upon whose influence Neptune's empire stands,
Was sick almost to doomsday with eclipse.
And even the like precurse of fear'd events,
125 As harbingers preceding still the fates
And prologue to the omen coming on,
Have heaven and earth together demonstrated
Unto our climatures and countrymen.

Enter Ghost

But soft, behold. Lo, where it comes again.
130 I'll cross it though it blast me.

Ghost spreads its arms

                   Stay, illusion:
If thou hast any sound or use of voice,
Speak to me.
If there be any good thing to be done
That may to thee do ease, and grace to me,
135 Speak to me;
If thou art privy to thy country's fate,
Which, happily, foreknowing may avoid,

O speak;
Or if thou hast uphoarded in thy life
140 Extorted treasure in the womb of earth,
For which they say your spirits oft walk in death,
Speak of it, stay and speak.

The cock crows

                                    Stop it, Marcellus.
Marcellus
Shall I strike at it with my partisan?

Horatio
Do if it will not stand.
Barnardo
145 'Tis here.
Horatio
'Tis here.   [*Exit* Ghost
Marcellus
'Tis gone.
We do it wrong, being so majestical,
To offer it the show of violence,
150 For it is as the air, invulnerable,
And our vain blows malicious mockery.
Barnardo
It was about to speak when the cock crew.
Horatio
And then it started like a guilty thing
Upon a fearful summons. I have heard
155 The cock, that is the trumpet to the morn,

139–40 *uphoarded . . . earth*: buried a hoard of ill-gotten treasure in your lifetime.
140 *Extorted*: ill-gotten.
141 *your*: these.

143 *partisan*: pike.

148 *being*: since it is.
149 *show*: The violence can be only in appearance.
150 'Because the Ghost is incorporeal, and therefore cannot be harmed.'
151 *vain*: useless.
malicious mockery: only the pretence of hurting.
154 *I have heard*: Horatio's early scepticism is waning.

155 *trumpet*: trumpeter. The farmyard cock crows just before daybreak.

156 *lofty*: outstretched.

157 *god of day*: Phoebus Apollo, the classical sun-god. In the Christian tradition the cock, as herald of light, is also the harbinger of Christ.

158–60 *Whether . . . confine*: any spirit who is straying beyond its limits ('extravagant and erring') returns quickly ('hies') to its prison ('his confine') in one of the four elements.

160 *herein*: in this matter.

161 *made probation*: proved.

163–9 This Christmas story seems to have no other authority; but now the mood of the scene switches to one of hope and comfort with the coming of light.

163 *'gainst*: in preparation for.

164 *our Saviour*: Christ.

166 *stir abroad*: wander from its confines.

167 *strike*: exert an evil influence.

168 *takes*: casts a spell.

169 *hallow'd*: sanctified.
gracious: filled with heavenly grace.

170 *in part*: Horatio's scepticism has not entirely disappeared.

171–2 A literary description of the reddish ('russet') sky at daybreak.

173 *watch*: guard.

175 *young Hamlet*: This is the play's first reference to the Prince of Denmark.

178 *needful in our loves*: necessary because we all love him.

Doth with his lofty and shrill-sounding throat
Awake the god of day, and at his warning,
Whether in sea or fire, in earth or air,
Th'extravagant and erring spirit hies
160 To his confine; and of the truth herein
This present object made probation.
    Marcellus
It faded on the crowing of the cock.
Some say that ever 'gainst that season comes
Wherein our Saviour's birth is celebrated,
165 This bird of dawning singeth all night long;
And then, they say, no spirit dare stir abroad,
The nights are wholesome, then no planets strike,
No fairy takes, nor witch hath power to charm,
So hallow'd and so gracious is that time.
    Horatio
170 So have I heard and do in part believe it.
But look, the morn in russet mantle clad
Walks o'er the dew of yon high eastward hill.
Break we our watch up, and by my advice
Let us impart what we have seen tonight
175 Unto young Hamlet; for upon my life
This spirit, dumb to us, will speak to him.
Do you consent we shall acquaint him with it
As needful in our loves, fitting our duty?
    Marcellus
Let's do't, I pray, and I this morning know
180 Where we shall find him most convenient.   [*Exeunt*

Act 1 Scene 2
King Claudius addresses the Danish court, speaking of his recent marriage to the wife of their former, deceased, king. Ambassadors are sent to Norway, and Laertes asks permission to return to France. This is granted, but Prince Hamlet cannot be allowed to return to his university studies. Horatio tells Hamlet of the appearance of his father's Ghost.

Os.d. *Flourish*: fanfare, heralding the approach of the royal party.

1–16 *Hamlet . . . thanks*: Denmark was an elective monarchy in which Claudius might have come legitimately to his dead brother's throne, but the unctuousness of his address to the court suggests that he is uneasy in his position.

2 *green*: fresh.
that . . . befitted: although it would have been more suitable for us (i.e. Claudius himself—using the royal plural—and the whole kingdom).

4 *contracted*: knit together.

5–7 *so far . . . ourselves*: practical considerations have fought against emotions so that now we can grieve for him and also remember our own position.

8 *sometime sister*: former sister-in-law.

9 *jointress*: woman sharing property with her husband.

10 *defeated*: subdued (by sorrow).

11 *an auspicious . . . eye*: one eye smiling and the other weeping.

12 *dirge*: lamentation.

13 *In . . . weighing*: measuring out equally.
dole: sorrow.

14 *Taken to wife*: In English law at this time, such a marriage would have been considered incestuous.
barr'd: rejected.

15 *better*: more mature.

15–16 *freely . . . along*: generously agreed to this marriage.

18 *weak supposal*: poor opinion.

20 *disjoint*: broken up, disturbed.
frame: order.

21 *Colleagued . . . advantage*: allied with imagination of personal gain.

23 *Importing*: concerning.

SCENE 2

Flourish. Enter Claudius, King of Denmark, Gertrude the Queen, Council, *including* Voltemand, Cornelius, Polonius *and his son* Laertes, Hamlet *dressed in black, with* Others

King
Though yet of Hamlet our dear brother's death
The memory be green, and that it us befitted
To bear our hearts in grief, and our whole kingdom
To be contracted in one brow of woe,
5   Yet so far hath discretion fought with nature
That we with wisest sorrow think on him
Together with remembrance of ourselves.
Therefore our sometime sister, now our queen,
Th'imperial jointress to this warlike state,
10 Have we, as 'twere with a defeated joy,
With an auspicious and a dropping eye,
With mirth in funeral and with dirge in marriage,
In equal scale weighing delight and dole,
Taken to wife. Nor have we herein barr'd
15 Your better wisdoms, which have freely gone
With this affair along. For all, our thanks.
Now follows that you know young Fortinbras,
Holding a weak supposal of our worth,
Or thinking by our late dear brother's death
20 Our state to be disjoint and out of frame,
Colleagued with this dream of his advantage,
He hath not fail'd to pester us with message
Importing the surrender of those lands

26 *this . . . meeting*: this present
meeting.

28 *Norway*: the King of Norway—who,
like Claudius, has taken the throne
from his brother, the elder Fortinbras.

29 *impotent*: powerless.

30–1 *suppress . . . herein*: stop him going
any further in this business.

31 *in that*: because.

32 *lists*: enrolments.
full proportions: supporting force.

33 *subject*: subjects.

37 *business*: negotiate, do business.

38 *dilated*: detailed.

39 *let . . . duty*: show your duty in your
speed.

42 *Laertes*: The caressing repetitions of
the name emphasize Claudius's
affection—and introduce the contrast
with Hamlet.

43 *suit*: request.

45 *lose*: waste.
thou: Claudius uses the intimate form
of address.

46 *my . . . asking*: my gift, not your
request.

47 *native*: closely related.

49 *the throne*: the entire monarchy (not
merely Claudius himself).

53 *duty*: allegiance.

55 *bend*: turn.

56 *pardon*: indulgence.

Lost by his father, with all bonds of law,
25 To our most valiant brother. So much for him.
Now for ourself, and for this time of meeting,
Thus much the business is: we have here writ
To Norway, uncle of young Fortinbras—
Who, impotent and bedrid, scarcely hears
30 Of this his nephew's purpose—to suppress
His further gait herein, in that the levies,
The lists, and full proportions are all made
Out of his subject; and we here dispatch
You, good Cornelius, and you, Voltemand,
35 For bearers of this greeting to old Norway,
Giving to you no further personal power
To business with the king more than the scope
Of these dilated articles allow.
Farewell, and let your haste commend your duty.
    Cornelius and **Voltemand**
40 In that, and all things, will we show our duty.
    King
We doubt it nothing. Heartily farewell.
        [*Exeunt* Voltemand *and* Cornelius
And now, Laertes, what's the news with you?
You told us of some suit: what is't, Laertes?
You cannot speak of reason to the Dane
45 And lose your voice. What wouldst thou beg, Laertes,
That shall not be my offer, not thy asking?
The head is not more native to the heart,
The hand more instrumental to the mouth,
Than is the throne of Denmark to thy father.
50 What wouldst thou have, Laertes?
    Laertes
                  My dread lord,
Your leave and favour to return to France,
From whence though willingly I came to Denmark
To show my duty in your coronation,
Yet now I must confess, that duty done,
55 My thoughts and wishes bend again toward France
And bow them to your gracious leave and pardon.
    King
Have you your father's leave? What says Polonius?

58 *wrung . . . leave*: slowly forced me to grant permission.

60 *Upon . . . consent*: I stamped my hard-won seal of approval on his desire.

62 *Take . . . thine*: enjoy your youth, Laertes, as long as you like.

63 *thy . . . will*: use your finest accomplishments as you wish.

64 *cousin*: kinsman.

65 *more . . . kind*: more than kindred and less than natural; Hamlet puns on different senses of 'kind'.

67 *sun*: Hamlet resents being called 'son' by Claudius.

68 *nighted*: black.

69 *Denmark*: a) the country; b) the King of Denmark, Claudius.

70 *vailed lids*: vailèd; downcast eyes.

72 *common*: usual, normal.

75 *particular*: different, personal.

76 *Seems*: Hamlet snatches Gertrude's word to contrast his genuine grief with the general display of hypocrisy.

78 *customary*: conventional.

79 *windy . . . breath*: uncontrollable sighing.

81 *haviour*: expression.

82 *shapes*: appearances.

83 *denote me*: express my feelings.

84 *play*: act out.

85 *passes show*: goes beyond outward appearance.

Polonius
He hath, my lord, wrung from me my slow leave
By laboursome petition, and at last
60 Upon his will I seal'd my hard consent.
I do beseech you give him leave to go.
       King
Take thy fair hour, Laertes, time be thine,
And thy best graces spend it at thy will.
But now, my cousin Hamlet, and my son—
       Hamlet
65 A little more than kin, and less than kind.
       King
How is it that the clouds still hang on you?
       Hamlet
Not so, my lord, I am too much in the sun.
       Queen
Good Hamlet, cast thy nighted colour off,
And let thine eye look like a friend on Denmark.
70 Do not for ever with thy vailed lids
Seek for thy noble father in the dust.
Thou know'st 'tis common: all that lives must die,
Passing through nature to eternity.
       Hamlet
Ay, madam, it is common.
       Queen
                              If it be,
75 Why seems it so particular with thee?
       Hamlet
Seems, madam? Nay, it is. I know not 'seems'.
'Tis not alone my inky cloak, good mother,
Nor customary suits of solemn black,
Nor windy suspiration of forc'd breath,
80 No, nor the fruitful river in the eye,
Nor the dejected haviour of the visage,
Together with all forms, moods, shapes of grief,
That can denote me truly. These indeed seem,
For they are actions that a man might play;
85 But I have that within which passes show,
These but the trappings and the suits of woe.

'Good Hamlet, cast thy nighted colour off' (*1, 2, 68*). John Stride as Claudius, Virginia McKenna as Gertrude, and Roger Rees as Hamlet, Royal Shakespeare Company, 1985.

King
'Tis sweet and commendable in your nature, Hamlet,
To give these mourning duties to your father,
But you must know your father lost a father,

90 That father lost, lost his—and the survivor bound
In filial obligation for some term
To do obsequious sorrow. But to persever
In obstinate condolement is a course
Of impious stubbornness, 'tis unmanly grief,

95 It shows a will most incorrect to heaven,
A heart unfortified, a mind impatient,
An understanding simple and unschool'd;
For what we know must be, and is as common
As any the most vulgar thing to sense—

100 Why should we in our peevish opposition
Take it to heart? Fie, 'tis a fault to heaven,
A fault against the dead, a fault to nature,
To reason most absurd, whose common theme
Is death of fathers, and who still hath cried

105 From the first corse till he that died today,
'This must be so'. We pray you throw to earth
This unprevailing woe, and think of us
As of a father; for let the world take note
You are the most immediate to our throne,

110 And with no less nobility of love
Than that which dearest father bears his son
Do I impart toward you. For your intent
In going back to school in Wittenberg,
It is most retrograde to our desire,

115 And we beseech you bend you to remain
Here in the cheer and comfort of our eye,
Our chiefest courtier, cousin, and our son.

Queen
Let not thy mother lose her prayers, Hamlet.
I pray thee stay with us, go not to Wittenberg.

Hamlet

120 I shall in all my best obey you, madam.

King
Why, 'tis a loving and a fair reply.
Be as ourself in Denmark. Madam, come.
This gentle and unforc'd accord of Hamlet

---

90 *bound*: was bound.

92 *do . . . sorrow*: perform the rites of grieving.
persever: persèver; persist.
93 *condolement*: mourning.
95 *incorrect*: disobedient.
96 *unfortified*: unsupported by religious belief.
impatient: lacking the virtue of patience.
97 *simple*: ignorant.
98–101 *For . . . heart*: why should we be so perverse ('peevish') and obstinate as to be distressed by what we know to be inevitable and that we can see to be most common.
101 *fault*: sin.
104 *still*: always.
105 *the first corse*: the first man to die (i.e. Abel, killed by his brother Cain—Genesis 4:8).
106 *throw to earth*: overcome (like a wrestler).
109 *most immediate*: next in succession.
110–12 *with . . . you*: I feel the most honourable love towards you that the most loving father can have for his son.
112 *For*: as for.
113 *Wittenberg*: The university of Martin Luther—and the famous eponymous hero of Marlowe's *Doctor Faustus*.
114 *retrograde*: contrary.
115 *bend you*: incline yourself.
116 *eye*: sight, presence.

120 *all my best*: to the best of my ability.
madam: Hamlet responds only to his mother—but she has aligned herself with Claudius.

123 *unforc'd accord*: willing agreement.

124 *grace whereof*: thanksgiving for which.

125 *jocund health*: cheerful toast; Claudius seems to omit no occasion for a drink.

126 *great cannon . . . tell*: See *1, 4, 6*s.d. note.

127 *rouse*: carousal.
bruit again: re-echo the noise of the cannon.

Sits smiling to my heart; in grace whereof
125 No jocund health that Denmark drinks today
But the great cannon to the clouds shall tell,
And the king's rouse the heaven shall bruit again,
Re-speaking earthly thunder. Come away.

[*Flourish. Exeunt all but* Hamlet

Hamlet
O that this too too sullied flesh would melt,
130 Thaw and resolve itself into a dew,
Or that the Everlasting had not fix'd
His canon 'gainst self-slaughter. O God! God!
How weary, stale, flat, and unprofitable
Seem to me all the uses of this world!
135 Fie on't, ah fie, 'tis an unweeded garden
That grows to seed; things rank and gross in nature
Possess it merely. That it should come to this!
But two months dead—nay, not so much, not two—
So excellent a king, that was to this
140 Hyperion to a satyr, so loving to my mother
That he might not beteem the winds of heaven
Visit her face too roughly. Heaven and earth,
Must I remember? Why, she would hang on him
As if increase of appetite had grown
145 By what it fed on; and yet within a month—
Let me not think on't—Frailty, thy name is woman—
A little month, or ere those shoes were old
With which she follow'd my poor father's body,
Like Niobe, all tears—why, she—
150 O God, a beast that wants discourse of reason
Would have mourn'd longer—married with my uncle,

129 *sullied*: contaminated, impure (because human and liable to sin, and because it has been soiled by his mother's incestuous marriage). Variant readings in the other texts are 'sallied' (Q1, 2) and 'solid' (F).

130 *resolve*: dissolve.

132 *canon . . . slaughter*: religious law against suicide; the sixth commandment, 'Thou shalt not kill' (Exodus 20:13) was generally thought to include self-murder.

134 *all the uses*: the whole business.

136 *things . . . nature*: i.e. weeds, which smell foul and spread wildly.

137 *merely*: entirely.

138 *But*: only.
to this: compared to this man.

140 *Hyperion*: the glorious sun-god of classical mythology.
a satyr: a lustful mythological creature, half-man and half-goat.

141 *beteem*: permit.

144 *appetite*: affection.

147 *or ere*: before.

149 *Niobe*: The type of sorrowing womanhood in classical mythology; she wept for the deaths of all her children until she was turned into a stone fountain.

150 *wants . . . reason*: is incapable of rational thought processes.

153 *Hercules*: the superman of classical
mythology; Hamlet is already
conscious of his own inadequacy,
although he is ignorant of the task
that will be required from him.
154 *unrighteous*: insincere.
155 *left . . . eyes*: ceased to make her eyes
red and sore with rubbing.
galled: gallèd.
157 *dexterity*: skill.
incestuous: See note to line 8.

163 *change . . . you*: Hamlet echoes the
words spoken by Jesus: 'Henceforth I
call you not servants, for the servant
knoweth not what his lord doeth: but I
have called you friends' (John 15:15).
164 *what make you*: what are you doing.
from: away from.
166 *Good even*: The greeting was used at
any time after noon.

170 *say so*: say that of you.

175 *deep*: heartily; Hamlet speaks
ironically of the Danish drinking
habits.

My father's brother—but no more like my father
Than I to Hercules. Within a month,
Ere yet the salt of most unrighteous tears
155 Had left the flushing in her gallèd eyes,
She married—O most wicked speed! To post
With such dexterity to incestuous sheets!
It is not, nor it cannot come to good.
But break, my heart, for I must hold my tongue.

Enter Horatio, Marcellus, *and* Barnardo

Horatio
160 Hail to your lordship.
Hamlet
                                          I am glad to see you well.
Horatio, or I do forget myself.
Horatio
The same, my lord, and your poor servant ever.
Hamlet
Sir, my good friend, I'll change that name with you.
And what make you from Wittenberg, Horatio?—
165 Marcellus.
Marcellus
My good lord.
Hamlet
I am very glad to see you.—[*To* Barnardo] Good even,
    sir.—
But what in faith make you from Wittenberg?
Horatio
A truant disposition, good my lord.
Hamlet
170 I would not hear your enemy say so,
Nor shall you do my ear that violence
To make it truster of your own report
Against yourself. I know you are no truant.
But what is your affair with Elsinore?
175 We'll teach you to drink deep ere you depart.
Horatio
My lord, I came to see your father's funeral.

Hamlet

I prithee do not mock me, fellow-student.

I think it was to see my mother's wedding.

Horatio

Indeed, my lord, it follow'd hard upon.

Hamlet

180 Thrift, thrift, Horatio. The funeral bak'd meats

Did coldly furnish forth the marriage tables.

Would I had met my dearest foe in heaven

Or ever I had seen that day, Horatio.

My father—methinks I see my father—

Horatio

185 Where, my lord?

Hamlet

In my mind's eye, Horatio.

Horatio

I saw him once; 'a was a goodly king.

Hamlet

'A was a man, take him for all in all:

I shall not look upon his like again.

Horatio

My lord, I think I saw him yesternight.

Hamlet

190 Saw? Who?

Horatio

My lord, the king your father.

Hamlet

The king my father?

Horatio

Season your admiration for a while

With an attent ear till I may deliver

Upon the witness of these gentlemen

195 This marvel to you.

Hamlet

For God's love let me hear!

Horatio

Two nights together had these gentlemen,

Marcellus and Barnardo, on their watch

In the dead waste and middle of the night

Been thus encounter'd: a figure like your father

200 Armed at point exactly, cap-à-pie,

180–1 *The . . . tables*: the food cooked for the funeral was served up cold for the wedding feast.
182 *Would*: I wish.
 dearest foe: worst enemy.
183 *Or ever*: before.

185 *mind's eye*: imagination.

186 *once*: some time ago.

187 *'A was . . . in all*: he was the ideal of manhood, perfect in every way.

192 *Season your admiration*: control your wonderment.
193 *attent*: attentive.
 deliver: report. Horatio's speech has been called (by S. T. Coleridge) 'a perfect model of dramatic narration and dramatic style, the purest poetry and the most natural style'.
194 *Upon the witness of*: witnessed by.

198 *dead waste*: most desolate part.
200 *Armed*: armèd.
 at point: correctly in every detail.
 cap-à-pie: from head to foot (the phrase is French).

203 *oppress'd*: troubled.
fear-surprised: surprisèd.
204 *truncheon*: military baton.
distill'd: dissolved, melted.
205 *act*: action, effect.

207 *dreadful*: Marcellus and Barnardo
were full of fear.
209–10 *in time, Form*: in time and form.

211 *knew*: was acquainted with.

212 *These . . . like*: The Ghost was as like
Hamlet's father as Horatio's hands are
like each other.

213 *platform*: terrace of a fort, where the
guns are mounted.
watch: keep guard.

216 *it*: its.
216–17 *address . . . speak*: begin to move
as though it were going to speak.
218 *even then*: at that very moment.

224–43 The lines here have the rhythm of
verse, although they are not always
strict pentameter lines.

Appears before them, and with solemn march
Goes slow and stately by them; thrice he walk'd
By their oppress'd and fear-surprised eyes
Within his truncheon's length, whilst they, distill'd
205 Almost to jelly with the act of fear,
Stand dumb and speak not to him. This to me
In dreadful secrecy impart they did,
And I with them the third night kept the watch,
Where, as they had deliver'd, both in time,
210 Form of the thing, each word made true and good,
The apparition comes. I knew your father;
These hands are not more like.

Hamlet
But where was this?

Marcellus
My lord, upon the platform where we watch.

Hamlet
Did you not speak to it?

Horatio
My lord, I did,
215 But answer made it none. Yet once methought
It lifted up it head and did address
Itself to motion like as it would speak.
But even then the morning cock crew loud,
And at the sound it shrunk in haste away
220 And vanish'd from our sight.

Hamlet
'Tis very strange.

Horatio
As I do live, my honour'd lord, 'tis true;
And we did think it writ down in our duty
To let you know of it.

Hamlet
Indeed, sirs; but this troubles me.
225 Hold you the watch tonight?

All
We do, my lord.

Hamlet
Arm'd, say you?

All
Arm'd my lord.

Hamlet
From top to toe?
All
                      My lord, from head to foot.
Hamlet
Then saw you not his face?
Horatio

229 *beaver*: face-guard of a helmet.

O yes, my lord, he wore his beaver up.
Hamlet

230 *What*: how.
frowningly: i.e. as a warrior ought to look.

230 What look'd he, frowningly?
Horatio
A countenance more in sorrow than in anger.
Hamlet
Pale, or red?
Horatio
Nay, very pale.
Hamlet
            And fix'd his eyes upon you?
Horatio
Most constantly.
Hamlet

234 *I would*: I wish.

            I would I had been there.
Horatio

235 *amaz'd*: bewildered.

235 It would have much amaz'd you.
Hamlet
                    Very like.
Stay'd it long?
Horatio

237 *tell*: count.

While one with moderate haste might tell a hundred.
Marcellus and **Barnardo**
Longer, longer.
Horatio
Not when I saw't.
Hamlet

240 *grizzled*: grey.

240 His beard was grizzled, no?
Horatio
It was as I have seen it in his life,

242 *sable silver'd*: black with silver hairs.

A sable silver'd.
Hamlet

243 *Perchance*: perhaps.
war'nt: warrant.

           I will watch tonight.
Perchance 'twill walk again.

Horatio

I war'nt it will.

Hamlet

If it assume my noble father's person,

245 I'll speak to it though hell itself should gape

And bid me hold my peace. I pray you all,

If you have hitherto conceal'd this sight,

Let it be tenable in your silence still;

And whatsomever else shall hap tonight,

250 Give it an understanding but no tongue.

I will requite your loves. So fare you well.

Upon the platform 'twixt eleven and twelve

I'll visit you.

All

Our duty to your honour.

Hamlet

Your loves, as mine to you. Farewell.

[*Exeunt* Horatio, Marcellus, *and* Barnardo

255 My father's spirit—in arms! All is not well.

I doubt some foul play. Would the night were come.

Till then sit still, my soul. Foul deeds will rise,

Though all the earth o'erwhelm them, to men's eyes.

[*Exit*

---

244 *assume . . . person*: has the appearance of my father (spirits, both good and bad, could manifest themselves in the likeness of human beings).

245 *hell . . . gape*: The gaping hell-mouth (open to receive those who communicated with evil spirits) was a common property on the Elizabethan stage.

249 *whatsomever*: whatever.
hap: happen.

251 *requite*: reward.
loves: friendship. Hamlet emends the formal respect of the guards' 'duty'.

255 *My father's spirit*: The belief that ghosts were spirits of the dead dates back to classical times, and was reinforced for Christians by the Roman Catholic doctrine of purgatory.

256 *doubt*: suspect. Hamlet is quick to suggest another reason (not mentioned by Horatio in the first scene) for a ghost's appearance: it wishes to reveal a crime that has been committed.

Scene 3

Enter Laertes *and* Ophelia, *his sister*

Laertes

My necessaries are embark'd. Farewell.

And sister, as the winds give benefit

And convoy is assistant, do not sleep,

But let me hear from you.

Ophelia

Do you doubt that?

Laertes

5 For Hamlet, and the trifling of his favour,

Hold it a fashion and a toy in blood,

A violet in the youth of primy nature,

Forward, not permanent, sweet, not lasting,

Act 1 Scene 3
Laertes warns Ophelia not to put too much trust in Prince Hamlet, and his warnings are echoed by their father, Polonius, who comes to say goodbye to his son—and to give Laertes some words of worldly wisdom.

1 *necessaries*: luggage.

2 *as . . . benefit*: when the winds are favourable.

3 *convey is assistant*: there is a ship available.

5 *trifling . . . favour*: the feeling he's pretending.

6 *Hold it a fashion*: think it just a passing fancy.
toy in blood: youthful sport.

7 *primy nature*: springtime of youth. Later in the play (*5, 1, 131–49*) Hamlet is said to be much older.

8 *Forward*: early-flowering.

9 *suppliance*: pastime.
10 *No more but so*: nothing else. Ophelia questions her brother's judgement of Hamlet's love.
11 *crescent*: as it grows.
12 *thews and bulk*: muscles and size.
     this temple: i.e. the body, which in Christian teaching is called the temple of the Holy Ghost (see Corinthians, 3:16).
14 *Grows wide withal*: increases too. Laertes suggests that Hamlet will have more to think about than his love for Ophelia.
15 *soil*: stain.
     cautel: deceit.
16 *the virtue of his will*: the honourableness of his intentions. 'Will' is capable of a wide range of meanings, and in this line the sexual overtones are strong.
17 *greatness*: high position.
     weigh'd: taken into consideration.
18 *birth*: rank (just as the citizens are subject to their king).
19 *unvalu'd persons*: ordinary people.
20 *Carve for himself*: choose for himself.
21 *sanity*: well-being.
23 *voice*: approval.
     yielding: consent.
     that body: i.e. the body politic, the state. Laertes assumes that Hamlet will inherit his father's throne.
26 *in . . . place*: in his position.
27 *give . . . deed*: do what he says.
28 *main voice*: general approval.
     goes withal: agrees to.
29 *weigh*: consider.
     honour: reputation.
30 *credent*: credulous.
     list his songs: listen to his charms.
31 *chaste treasure*: virginity.
32 *unmaster'd importunity*: uncontrolled demands.
34 *keep . . . affection*: hold back in your desires.
36 *The . . . moon*: the most modest girl shows herself quite enough if she reveals her beauty to the moonlight.
38 *scapes*: escapes. Laertes is uttering Elizabethan commonplaces.
39 *canker*: canker-worm.
     galls: injures.
     infants of the spring: young spring flowers.
40 *buttons be disclos'd*: buds have opened.

The perfume and suppliance of a minute,
10 No more.
    Ophelia
          No more but so?
    Laertes
                    Think it no more.
For nature crescent does not grow alone
In thews and bulk, but as this temple waxes,
The inward service of the mind and soul
Grows wide withal. Perhaps he loves you now,
15 And now no soil nor cautel doth besmirch
The virtue of his will; but you must fear,
His greatness weigh'd, his will is not his own.
For he himself is subject to his birth:
He may not, as unvalu'd persons do,
20 Carve for himself, for on his choice depends
The sanity and health of this whole state;
And therefore must his choice be circumscrib'd
Unto the voice and yielding of that body
Whereof he is the head. Then if he says he loves you,
25 It fits your wisdom so far to believe it
As he in his particular act and place
May give his saying deed; which is no further
Than the main voice of Denmark goes withal.
Then weigh what loss your honour may sustain
30 If with too credent ear you list his songs,
Or lose your heart, or your chaste treasure open
To his unmaster'd importunity.
Fear it, Ophelia, fear it, my dear sister,
And keep you in the rear of your affection
35 Out of the shot and danger of desire.
The chariest maid is prodigal enough
If she unmask her beauty to the moon.
Virtue itself scapes not calumnious strokes.
The canker galls the infants of the spring
40 Too oft before their buttons be disclos'd,

41 *liquid*: bright.
42 *Contagious blastments*: infections.
  The dawn—of day and of youth—is a
  time of brightest promise and greatest
  danger.
43 *fear*: i.e. of danger.
44 *to itself*: by itself.
  none: no other temptation.
45 *effect*: substance.
47 *pastors*: a) shepherds; b) preachers.

49 *puff'd*: proud.
50 *primrose path*: easy way.
  dalliance: wanton amusement.
51 *recks . . . rede*: ignores his own
  advice.

And in the morn and liquid dew of youth
Contagious blastments are most imminent.
Be wary then: best safety lies in fear.
Youth to itself rebels, though none else near.
   Ophelia
45 I shall th'effect of this good lesson keep
As watchman to my heart. But good my brother,
Do not as some ungracious pastors do,
Show me the steep and thorny way to heaven,
Whiles like a puff'd and reckless libertine
50 Himself the primrose path of dalliance treads,
And recks not his own rede.
   Laertes
                 O fear me not.
I stay too long.

Enter Polonius

          But here my father comes.
A double blessing is a double grace:
Occasion smiles upon a second leave.

54 *Occasion smiles*: it is a happy
  opportunity.
  leave: leave-taking.
56 *sits . . . sail*: i.e. is favourable.
57 *you are stay'd for*: they are waiting for
  you.
  There: Polonius lays his hand on the
  head of the kneeling Laertes.
58 *precepts*: The matters on which
  Polonius advises Laertes were
  common topics for a father's parting
  words to his son.
59 *character*: engrave.
60 *unproportion'd*: reckless.
  his act: its deed.
61 'Be friendly enough, but don't make
  yourself cheap.'
62 *their adoption tried*: when you have
  tested their friendship.
63 *hoops*: bonds.
64–5 'Don't shake hands (in friendship)
  with every fresh young man.'
66 *entrance to*: beginning.
67 *Bear't*: conduct yourself in such a way.
  opposed: opposèd.
69 *censure*: opinion.
70 *habit*: dress.
71 *express'd in fancy*: with fancy
  trimmings.

   Polonius
55 Yet here, Laertes? Aboard, aboard for shame.
The wind sits in the shoulder of your sail,
And you are stay'd for. There, my blessing with thee.
And these few precepts in thy memory
Look thou character. Give thy thoughts no tongue,
60 Nor any unproportion'd thought his act.
Be thou familiar, but by no means vulgar;
Those friends thou hast, and their adoption tried,
Grapple them unto thy soul with hoops of steel,
But do not dull thy palm with entertainment
65 Of each new-hatch'd, unfledg'd courage. Beware
Of entrance to a quarrel, but being in,
Bear't that th'opposed may beware of thee.
Give every man thy ear, but few thy voice;
Take each man's censure, but reserve thy judgement.
70 Costly thy habit as thy purse can buy,
But not express'd in fancy; rich, not gaudy;
For the apparel oft proclaims the man,

73–4 'French noblemen are particularly renowned for having the height of good taste in clothes.'

77 *husbandry*: thrift.

81 *season*: ripen. His father's blessing will enrich these 'few precepts'.

83 *invests*: urges.
tend: attend.

86 *keep the key*: i.e. no one else can open the lock.

89 *touching*: relating to.

90 *Marry*: by the Virgin Mary (a mild oath).
bethought: remembered.

93 'Have willingly paid a lot of attention to him.'
94 *'tis put on me*: I am given to understand.
95 *in way of caution*: as a warning.
97 *it behoves*: it is fitting for.
98 *Give me up*: tell me.

99 *tenders*: declarations, offers. Polonius picks up the word's commercial usages.

101 *green*: inexperienced.
102 *Unsifted*: untried.

And they in France of the best rank and station
Are of a most select and generous chief in that.
75 Neither a borrower nor a lender be,
For loan oft loses both itself and friend,
And borrowing dulls the edge of husbandry.
This above all: to thine own self be true,
And it must follow as the night the day
80 Thou canst not then be false to any man.
Farewell, my blessing season this in thee.
  Laertes
Most humbly do I take my leave, my lord.
  Polonius
The time invests you; go, your servants tend.
  Laertes
Farewell, Ophelia, and remember well
85 What I have said to you.
  Ophelia
      'Tis in my memory lock'd,
And you yourself shall keep the key of it.
  Laertes
Farewell.   [*Exit*
  Polonius
What is't, Ophelia, he hath said to you?
  Ophelia
So please you, something touching the Lord Hamlet.
  Polonius
90 Marry, well bethought.
'Tis told me he hath very oft of late
Given private time to you, and you yourself
Have of your audience been most free and bounteous.
If it be so—as so 'tis put on me,
95 And that in way of caution—I must tell you
You do not understand yourself so clearly
As it behoves my daughter and your honour.
What is between you? Give me up the truth.
  Ophelia
He hath, my lord, of late made many tenders
100 Of his affection to me.
  Polonius
Affection? Pooh, you speak like a green girl,
Unsifted in such perilous circumstance.

Do you believe his tenders, as you call them?
> **Ophelia**
I do not know, my lord, what I should think.
> **Polonius**
105 Marry, I will teach you. Think yourself a baby
That you have ta'en these tenders for true pay
Which are not sterling. Tender yourself more dearly
Or—not to crack the wind of the poor phrase,
Running it thus—you'll tender me a fool.
> **Ophelia**
110 My lord, he hath importun'd me with love
In honourable fashion.
> **Polonius**
Ay, fashion you may call it. Go to, go to.
> **Ophelia**
And hath given countenance to his speech, my lord,
With almost all the holy vows of heaven.
> **Polonius**
115 Ay, springes to catch woodcocks. I do know,
When the blood burns, how prodigal the soul
Lends the tongue vows. These blazes, daughter,
Giving more light than heat, extinct in both
Even in their promise as it is a-making,
120 You must not take for fire. From this time
Be something scanter of your maiden presence,
Set your entreatments at a higher rate
Than a command to parley. For Lord Hamlet,
Believe so much in him that he is young,
125 And with a larger tether may he walk
Than may be given you. In few, Ophelia,
Do not believe his vows; for they are brokers
Not of that dye which their investments show,
But mere implorators of unholy suits,
130 Breathing like sanctified and pious bawds
The better to beguile. This is for all.
I would not, in plain terms, from this time forth
Have you so slander any moment leisure
As to give words or talk with the Lord Hamlet.
135 Look to't, I charge you. Come your ways.
> **Ophelia**
I shall obey, my lord.   [*Exeunt*

107 *sterling*: real money.
Tender . . . dearly: take more care of yourself.
108–9 'Not to overwork the metaphor (as excessive work breaks a horse's wind).'
109 *you'll . . . fool*: give me a fool for a daughter.
111 *fashion*: manner. Polonius again twists the sense of the word.
112 *Go to*: An exclamation of impatience.
113 *countenance to*: confirmation of.
115 *springes . . . woodcocks*: woodcocks were (proverbially) said to be foolish birds, easily caught in snares ('springes').
116 *blood*: sexual passion.
prodigal: with careless generosity.
117 *blazes*: flaring passions.
118 *extinct in both*: both light and heat are extinguished.
119 *it*: the promise.
121 *somewhat scanter of*: rather less generous with.
122–3 'Don't enter into negotiations with him just because he asks you to.' The presentation of courtship in terms of military strategy is traditional.
125 *larger tether*: longer rope—i.e. less restriction.
126 *few*: short.
127 *brokers*: traders, go-betweens.
128 *Not of that dye*: of a different colour.
investments: clothing. This word leads to the pun on 'suits' in the next line.
129 *implorators . . . suits*: solicitors making sinful entreaties.
130 *Breathing*: persuading.
sanctified and pious: apparently genuine and sincere.
131 *beguile*: deceive.
for all: all I have to say.
132 *slander . . . leisure*: misuse any of your free time.
135 *Come your ways*: come along now.

Act 1 Scene 4
Hamlet and Horatio join Marcellus on the
midnight watch, whilst the King and
courtiers enjoy a drunken revel within the
castle. The Ghost walks again; and Hamlet,
recognizing the likeness of his father, obeys
the beckoning command.

  1 *shrewdly*: sharply.

  3 *lacks of*: not quite.

  6 *held . . . walk*: usually walked.

6s.d. *pieces*: i.e. the cannon
      commanded at *1, 2, 126*.

  8 *wake*: stay up late.
      takes his rouse: carouses.
  9 *Keeps . . . reels*: drinks off toasts and
      sways about in a riotous dance.
  10 *Rhenish*: Rhine wine.

Scene 4

Enter Hamlet, Horatio, *and* Marcellus

Hamlet
The air bites shrewdly, it is very cold.
   Horatio
It is a nipping and an eager air.
   Hamlet
What hour now?
   Horatio
                  I think it lacks of twelve.
   Marcellus
No, it is struck.
   Horatio
             Indeed? I heard it not.
5 It then draws near the season
Wherein the spirit held his wont to walk.

*A flourish of trumpets, and two pieces of ordnance
go off*

What does this mean, my lord?
   Hamlet
The king doth wake tonight and takes his rouse;
Keeps wassail, and the swagg'ring upspring reels;
10 And as he drains his draughts of Rhenish down,

11 *kettle-drum and trumpet*: These give signals to the cannon.
12 *triumph*: celebration.
pledge: toast.
Is it a custom: Horatio asks for the benefit of the audience.
15 *to the manner born*: inheriting this tradition. Hamlet's disapproval of this custom emphasizes his alienation.
16 *in the breach*: by breaking it.
observance: performance.
17–38 The whole of this passage is omitted in both the Q1 and F texts.
17–18 'These drunken orgies give us a bad reputation in other countries both to the east and to the west.'
18 *traduc'd*: censured.
tax'd of: criticized by.
19 *clepe*: call.
19–20 *with . . . addition*: blacken our distinguished name by calling us pigs.
20–2 *takes . . . attribute*: takes the heart out of our reputation however noble our achievements.
23 *particular men*: certain individuals.
24 *for*: on account of.
mole: defect.
25 *As*: for instance.
26 *his*: its.
27 *o'ergrowth . . . complexion*: being temperamentally unbalanced (with an excess of one of the four 'humours'— blood, choler, phlegm, melancholy— determining human personality).
28 *pales*: fences.
29 *habit*: habitual practice.
o'erleavens: influences excessively.
30 *form . . . manners*: decent behaviour.
32 *Nature's . . . star*: innate quality or the chance of fate.
33 *else*: otherwise.
34 *undergo*: support.
35 *general censure*: opinion of everybody.
35–6 *take . . . fault*: be contaminated by a single character flaw.
36 *dram*: very small amount.
37 *dout*: subdue.
38 *his . . . scandal*: its own shame.

39 *ministers of grace*: guardian angels; Hamlet calls for divine protection.
40 *a spirit . . . damn'd*: an angel or a devil; Hamlet articulates what should be the feelings of the audience.
42 *Be thy intents*: whether your intentions are.

The kettle-drum and trumpet thus bray out
The triumph of his pledge.

Horatio
                               Is it a custom?

Hamlet
Ay marry is't,
But to my mind, though I am native here
15 And to the manner born, it is a custom
More honour'd in the breach than the observance.
This heavy-headed revel east and west
Makes us traduc'd and tax'd of other nations—
They clepe us drunkards, and with swinish phrase
20 Soil our addition; and indeed it takes
From our achievements, though perform'd at height,
The pith and marrow of our attribute.
So, oft it chances in particular men
That for some vicious mole of nature in them,
25 As in their birth, wherein they are not guilty
(Since nature cannot choose his origin),
By their o'ergrowth of some complexion,
Oft breaking down the pales and forts of reason,
Or by some habit, that too much o'erleavens
30 The form of plausive manners—that these men,
Carrying, I say, the stamp of one defect,
Being Nature's livery or Fortune's star,
His virtues else, be they as pure as grace,
As infinite as man may undergo,
35 Shall in the general censure take corruption
From that particular fault. The dram of evil
Doth all the noble substance often dout
To his own scandal.

Enter Ghost

Horatio
                               Look, my lord, it comes.

Hamlet
Angels and ministers of grace defend us!
40 Be thou a spirit of health or goblin damn'd,
Bring with thee airs from heaven or blasts from hell,
Be thy intents wicked or charitable,

43 *questionable shape*: appearance which invites questioning; Hamlet sheds some of his doubts about the Ghost when he addresses it by name.
47 *canoniz'd bones*: body which has been buried properly (according to canon law of the Christian Church). *hearsed*: hearsèd; coffined.
48 *cerements*: shroud.
49 *inurn'd*: placed in the funeral urn.

52 *complete steel*: còmplete; full armour.
53 *glimpses of the moon*: fitful moonlight.
54 *hideous*: terrifying.
55 *disposition*: nature.

57 *what . . . do*: Hamlet (like Horatio, *1, 1, 133ff*) assumes that the Ghost will demand some action.

59 *some . . . desire*: wanted to tell you something.

62 *removed*: removèd; distant.

65 *I . . . fee*: my life isn't worth a pin to me.

69–78 *What . . . beneath*: Horatio fears that the Ghost is an evil spirit tempting Hamlet to a suicidal madness.
69 *flood*: sea.

Thou com'st in such a questionable shape
That I will speak to thee. I'll call thee Hamlet,
45 King, father, royal Dane. O answer me.
Let me not burst in ignorance, but tell
Why thy canoniz'd bones, hearsed in death,
Have burst their cerements, why the sepulchre
Wherein we saw thee quietly inurn'd
50 Hath op'd his ponderous and marble jaws
To cast thee up again. What may this mean,
That thou, dead corse, again in complete steel
Revisits thus the glimpses of the moon,
Making night hideous and we fools of nature
55 So horridly to shake our disposition
With thoughts beyond the reaches of our souls?
Say why is this? Wherefore? What should we do?

Ghost *beckons*

Horatio
It beckons you to go away with it,
As if it some impartment did desire
60 To you alone.
Marcellus
Look with what courteous action
It waves you to a more removed ground.
But do not go with it.
Horatio
No, by no means.
Hamlet
It will not speak. Then I will follow it.
Horatio
Do not, my lord.
Hamlet
Why, what should be the fear?
65 I do not set my life at a pin's fee,
And for my soul, what can it do to that,
Being a thing immortal as itself?
It waves me forth again. I'll follow it.
Horatio
What if it tempt you toward the flood, my lord,
70 Or to the dreadful summit of the cliff

71 *beetles o'er*: overhangs.

That beetles o'er his base into the sea,
And there assume some other horrible form

73 *deprive . . . reason*: take away the reason that governs you.

Which might deprive your sovereignty of reason
And draw you into madness? Think of it.

75 *toys of desperation*: fancies of despair.

75 The very place puts toys of desperation,
Without more motive, into every brain
That looks so many fathoms to the sea
And hears it roar beneath.

Hamlet
                                It waves me still.
Go on, I'll follow thee.

Marcellus
80 You shall not go, my lord.

Hamlet
                                Hold off your hands.

Horatio
Be rul'd; you shall not go.

Hamlet
                                My fate cries out

82 *artire*: artery; the Elizabethans, not understanding the circulation of the blood, believed that the arteries conducted vital spirits to the brain.

And makes each petty artire in this body
As hardy as the Nemean lion's nerve.

83 *the Nemean lion*: Hercules slew this mythological beast as the first of his great labours.

Still am I call'd. Unhand me, gentlemen.
85 By heaven, I'll make a ghost of him that lets me.

84 *Unhand me*: take your hands off me.
85 *lets*: hinders.

I say away.—Go on, I'll follow thee.
                        [*Exeunt* Ghost *and* Hamlet

Horatio
He waxes desperate with imagination.

87 *waxes*: grows.

Marcellus
Let's follow. 'Tis not fit thus to obey him.

88 *thus*: when he is like this.

Horatio
Have after. To what issue will this come?

89 *Have after*: let's follow him.

Marcellus
90 Something is rotten in the state of Denmark.

Horatio
Heaven will direct it.

Marcellus
                                Nay, let's follow him.   [*Exeunt*

Act 1 Scene 5
Alone with Hamlet, the Ghost tells its story
of adultery and murder for which it
demands revenge.

3 *tormenting flames*: the fires of
Purgatory.

6 *bound*: i.e. by filial duty.

11 *to fast*: The pains endured by
incorporeal spirits can only be
expressed in physical terms.
12 *crimes*: sins.
in . . . nature: when I was alive.

16 *harrow up*: rack.
17 *start from*: fall out of.
spheres: sockets (see *4, 7, 15*).
18 *knotted . . . locks*: whole head of hair.
combined: combinèd.

20 *porpentine*: porcupine.
21 *eternal blazon*: heraldic description of
eternity; the Ghost's vagueness adds
to the terror of his situation.
22 *List*: listen; the incantatory repetitions
compel attention.

SCENE 5

Enter Ghost *and* Hamlet

Hamlet
Whither wilt thou lead me? Speak, I'll go no further.
Ghost
Mark me.
Hamlet
                    I will.
Ghost
                              My hour is almost come
When I to sulph'rous and tormenting flames
Must render up myself.
Hamlet
                                        Alas, poor ghost.
Ghost
5 Pity me not, but lend thy serious hearing
To what I shall unfold.
Hamlet
                                        Speak, I am bound to hear.
Ghost
So art thou to revenge when thou shalt hear.
Hamlet
What?
Ghost
I am thy father's spirit,
10 Doom'd for a certain term to walk the night,
And for the day confin'd to fast in fires,
Till the foul crimes done in my days of nature
Are burnt and purg'd away. But that I am forbid
To tell the secrets of my prison-house,
15 I could a tale unfold whose lightest word
Would harrow up thy soul, freeze thy young blood,
Make thy two eyes like stars start from their spheres,
Thy knotted and combined locks to part,
And each particular hair to stand an end
20 Like quills upon the fretful porpentine.
But this eternal blazon must not be
To ears of flesh and blood. List, list, O list!
If thou didst ever thy dear father love—

'I am thy father's spirit' (*1*, 5, 9). Kenneth Branagh as Hamlet, Royal Shakespeare Company, 1992.

Hamlet
O God!
Ghost
25 Revenge his foul and most unnatural murder.
Hamlet
Murder!
Ghost
Murder most foul, as in the best it is,
But this most foul, strange and unnatural.
Hamlet
Haste me to know't, that I with wings as swift
30 As meditation or the thoughts of love
May sweep to my revenge.
Ghost
                    I find thee apt.
And duller shouldst thou be than the fat weed
That roots itself in ease on Lethe wharf,
Wouldst thou not stir in this. Now, Hamlet, hear.
35 'Tis given out that, sleeping in my orchard,
A serpent stung me—so the whole ear of Denmark
Is by a forged process of my death
Rankly abus'd—but know, thou noble youth,
The serpent that did sting thy father's life
40 Now wears his crown.
Hamlet
O my phophetic soul! My uncle!
Ghost
Ay, that incestuous, that adulterate beast,
With witchcraft of his wit, with traitorous gifts—
O wicked wit, and gifts that have the power
45 So to seduce!—won to his shameful lust
The will of my most seeming-virtuous queen.
O Hamlet, what a falling off was there,
From me, whose love was of that dignity
That it went hand in hand even with the vow
50 I made to her in marriage, and to decline
Upon a wretch whose natural gifts were poor
To those of mine.
But virtue, as it never will be mov'd,
Though lewdness court it in a shape of heaven,
55 So lust, though to a radiant angel link'd,

27 *in the best*: at best.

28 *unnatural*: i.e. because it is a violation of the natural bond of kinship.

30 *meditation*: thought.

32 *fat . . . wharf*: the overgrown wild plants that spread over the banks of the Lethe; to drink the water of this river in the classical underworld brought total oblivion.
35 *orchard*: garden.
36 *the . . . Denmark*: everyone in Denmark who heard this.
37 *forged process*: forged; false account.

42 *adulterate*: adulterous.

48 *of that dignity*: so honourable.

50 *decline*: descend to the level of.
51 *natural gifts*: personal qualities (compared with the 'traitorous gifts' with which he had seduced the queen).
53 *virtue . . . mov'd*: just as virtue will never be shaken.
54 *in . . . heaven*: in the likeness of an angel.

56 *sate itself*: grow tired of gorging itself.

61 *secure*: unsuspecting.

62 *cursed*: cursèd.
 hebenon: This poison has never been identified, but may perhaps be associated with the plant henbane, or with deadly nightshade.

64 *leperous distilment*: leprosy-like distillation (causing an outbreak of scaly eruptions).

66 *courses*: rushes.

68–9 *posset . . . curd*: thicken and curdle.

69 *eager*: acid.

71 *instant . . . about*: fast-spreading scab covered over (like the bark of a tree).

72 *lazar-like*: like a leper.

75 *dispatch'd*: deprived.

76 *even . . . sin*: at the height of my sinfulness (because unconscious).

77 *Unhousel'd . . . unanel'd*: i.e. deprived of all the rites of the Roman Catholic Church (as Hamlet recalls at 3, 3, 80–1).
 Unhousel'd: without receiving the sacrament ('housel') of holy communion.
 disappointed: unprepared (without confessing and being absolved from my sins).
 unanel'd: not anointed with holy oil.

78 *reck'ning*: settling of accounts (with God).
 my account: give an account of my life.

81 *nature*: natural feeling.
 bear it not: do not condone it.

83 *luxury*: lustfulness.
 damned: damnèd.

84 *howsomever*: in whatever way.

85–6 *Taint . . . aught*: do not think ill, or let your mind plot anything against your mother.

86 *heaven*: i.e. God's judgement.

89–90 *The . . . fire*: the dim light of the glow-worm can only be seen in darkness.

89 *matin*: morning.

90 *gins*: begins.

91s.d. *Exit*: The Ghost may disappear through the trap-door in the stage.

93 *couple hell*: invoke the powers of hell.

Will sate itself in a celestial bed
And prey on garbage.
But soft, methinks I scent the morning air:
Brief let me be. Sleeping within my orchard,
60 My custom always of the afternoon,
Upon my secure hour thy uncle stole
With juice of cursed hebenon in a vial,
And in the porches of my ears did pour
The leperous distilment, whose effect
65 Holds such an enmity with blood of man
That swift as quicksilver it courses through
The natural gates and alleys of the body,
And with a sudden vigour it doth posset
And curd, like eager droppings into milk,
70 The thin and wholesome blood. So did it mine,
And a most instant tetter bark'd about,
Most lazar-like, with vile and loathsome crust
All my smooth body.
Thus was I, sleeping, by a brother's hand
75 Of life, of crown, of queen at once dispatch'd,
Cut off even in the blossoms of my sin,
Unhousel'd, disappointed, unanel'd,
No reck'ning made, but sent to my account
With all my imperfections on my head.
80 O horrible! O horrible! most horrible!
If thou has nature in thee, bear it not,
Let not the royal bed of Denmark be
A couch for luxury and damned incest.
But howsomever thou pursuest this act,
85 Taint not thy mind nor let thy soul contrive
Against thy mother aught. Leave her to heaven,
And to those thorns that in her bosom lodge
To prick and sting her. Fare thee well at once:
The glow-worm shows the matin to be near
90 And gins to pale his uneffectual fire.
Adieu, adieu, adieu. Remember me.   [*Exit*

Hamlet
O all you host of heaven! O earth! What else?
And shall I couple hell? O fie! Hold, hold, my heart,
And you, my sinews, grow not instant old,
95 But bear me stiffly up. Remember thee?

whiles: as long as.
97 *distracted globe*: bewildered head.
98 *table*: writing-tablet, notebook.
99 *fond*: foolish.
   records: recòrds; things to be remembered.
100 *saws of books*: quotations from books.
   forms: ideas, shapes.
   pressures: impressions.
101 *youth and observation*: my young observation.
104 *baser*: more commonplace.
105 *most . . . woman*: Hamlet has already forgotten the Ghost's warning of line 85.
106 *damned*: damnèd.
107 *tables*: writing-tablets, notebook.
   Meet it is: it is right and proper.
110 *there you are*: Hamlet refers to his writing.
   to my word: a) to keep my promise; b) as for my motto.

115 *secure*: protect.

116 *So be it*: Hamlet says 'amen' to Horatio's prayer.

117 *Hillo, ho, ho*: Marcellus calls like a falconer—and Hamlet responds in the same way.

Ay, thou poor ghost, whiles memory holds a seat
In this distracted globe. Remember thee?
Yea, from the table of my memory
I'll wipe away all trivial fond records,
100 All saws of books, all forms, all pressures past
That youth and observation copied there,
And thy commandment all alone shall live
Within the book and volume of my brain,
Unmix'd with baser matter. Yes, by heaven!
105 O most pernicious woman!
O villain, villain, smiling damned villain!
My tables. Meet it is I set it down
That one may smile, and smile, and be a villain—
At least I am sure it may be so in Denmark. [*Writes*]
110 So, uncle, there you are. Now to my word.
It is 'Adieu, adieu, remember me.'
I have sworn't.

Enter Horatio *and* Marcellus [*calling*]

Horatio
My lord, my lord.
Marcellus
Lord Hamlet.
Horatio
115 Heavens secure him.
Hamlet
[*Aside*] So be it.
Marcellus
Hillo, ho, ho, my lord.
Hamlet
Hillo, ho, ho, boy. Come, bird, come.
Marcellus
How is't, my noble lord?
Horatio
120 What news, my lord?
Hamlet
O, wonderful!
Horatio
Good my lord, tell it.

Hamlet
No, you will reveal it.
Horatio
Not I, my lord, by heaven.
Marcellus
125   Nor I, my lord.
Hamlet
How say you then, would heart of man once think it—
But you'll be secret?
Horatio and **Marcellus**
Ay, by heaven.
Hamlet
There's never a villain dwelling in all Denmark
130   But he's an arrant knave.
Horatio
There needs no ghost, my lord, come from the grave
To tell us this.
Hamlet
                    Why, right, you are in the right.
And so without more circumstance at all
I hold it fit that we shake hands and part,
135   You as your business and desire shall point you—
For every man hath business and desire,
Such as it is—and for my own poor part,
I will go pray.
Horatio
These are but wild and whirling words, my lord.
Hamlet
140   I am sorry they offend you, heartily—
Yes faith, heartily.
Horatio
                    There's no offence, my lord.
Hamlet
Yes by Saint Patrick but there is, Horatio,
And much offence too. Touching this vision here,
It is an honest ghost, that let me tell you.
145   For your desire to know what is between us,
O'ermaster't as you may. And now, good friends,
As you are friends, scholars, and soldiers,
Give me one poor request.

130   *arrant knave*: utter rascal; Hamlet swerves from a confidence to a jest.

133   *circumstance*: explanation, ceremony.

135   *point*: direct.

139   *whirling*: excited.

140   *heartily*: with all my heart.
141   *faith*: by my faith, sincerely. *There's no offence*: I'm not offended.

142   *Saint Patrick*: The Irish saint was associated, in early Christian tradition, with visions of Purgatory.
143   *Touching*: regarding.
144   *honest*: genuine (i.e. not a devil in the form of the dead king).
146   *O'ermaster't . . . may*: control it any way you can; later in the play (3, 2, 75) it is clear that Hamlet has confided in Horatio.

Horatio

What is't, my lord? We will.

Hamlet

Never make known what you have seen tonight.

Horatio and **Marcellus**

150   My lord, we will not.

Hamlet

Nay, but swear't.

Horatio

In faith, my lord, not I.

Marcellus

Nor I, my lord, in faith.

Hamlet

Upon my sword.

Marcellus

155   We have sworn, my lord, already.

Hamlet

Indeed, upon my sword, indeed.

Ghost

[*Cries under the stage*] Swear.

Hamlet

Ah ha, boy, say'st thou so? Art thou there, truepenny?
Come on, you hear this fellow in the cellarage.

160   Consent to swear.

Horatio

Propose the oath, my lord.

Hamlet

Never to speak of this that you have seen.
Swear by my sword.

Ghost

Swear.

They swear

Hamlet

Hic et ubique? Then we'll shift our ground.

165   Come hither, gentlemen,
And lay your hands again upon my sword.
Swear by my sword
Never to speak of this that you have heard.

154 *sword*: the cross formed by the hilt of the sword.

157s.d. *under the stage*: This 'underground' episode blends grim burlesque humour with a sense of eerie strangeness in a moment of 'comic relief'.

158 *truepenny*: honest fellow.

159 *cellarage*: cellars; here, the space underneath the stage.

164 *Hic et ubique*: here and everywhere; the Latin tag sounds like some description of the omnipresence of God.

Ghost
Swear by his sword.

They swear

Hamlet
170 Well said, old mole. Canst work i'th'earth so fast?
A worthy pioner! Once more remove, good friends.
Horatio
O day and night, but this is wondrous strange.
Hamlet
And therefore as a stranger give it welcome.
There are more things in heaven and earth, Horatio,
175 Than are dreamt of in your philosophy.
But come,
Here, as before, never, so help you mercy,
How strange or odd some'er I bear myself—
As I perchance hereafter shall think meet
180 To put an antic disposition on—
That you, at such time seeing me, never shall,
With arms encumber'd thus, or this head-shake,
Or by pronouncing of some doubtful phrase,
As 'Well, we know', or 'We could and if we would',
185 Or 'If we list to speak', or 'There be and if they might',
Or such ambiguous giving out, to note
That you know aught of me—this do swear,
So grace and mercy at your most need help you.
Ghost
Swear.

They swear

Hamlet
190 Rest, rest, perturbed spirit. So, gentlemen,
With all my love I do commend me to you;
And what so poor a man as Hamlet is
May do t'express his love and friending to you,
God willing, shall not lack. Let us go in together.
195 And still your fingers on your lips, I pray.
The time is out of joint. O cursed spite,
That ever I was born to set it right.
Nay, come, let's go together.   [*Exeunt*

171 *pioner*: miner.

175 *in your philosophy*: by philosophers.

177 *so . . . mercy*: as you hope that God
will have mercy on you; the disordered
syntax reflects Hamlet's state of
excitement.
178 *some'er*: soever.
180 *antic disposition*: strange behaviour.

182 *encumber'd*: folded.
183 *doubtful*: ambiguous, mysterious.
184 *and if*: if only.
185 *list*: wished.
186 *giving out*: indication.
note: suggest.

188 *So . . . you*: in the hope that God's
gracious mercy will help you at the
Day of Judgement.

190 *perturbed*: perturbèd.

193 *friending*: friendship.

195 *still*: always.
196 *out of joint*: completely disordered.
cursed: cursèd.

Act 2 Scene 1
Polonius sends his man to Paris to spy on
Laertes, and Ophelia tells her father about
Hamlet's strange behaviour.

Os.d. *old*: This stage direction gives a
   suggestion of how Shakespeare
   thought of the character of Polonius.
1 *notes*: letters.

3 *shall . . . wisely*: it would be a very
   good thing.
4 *inquire*: inquiry.

7 *Inquire me*: This construction (with
   'me' in the so-called 'ethic dative'
   case) is no longer used in English.
   Danskers: Danish nationals.
8 *what means*: how much money they
   have.
   keep: lodge.
10 *encompassment . . . question*:
   roundabout way of questioning.

SCENE 1

Enter old Polonius, *with his man* Reynaldo

Polonius
Give him this money and these notes, Reynaldo.
   Reynaldo
I will, my lord.
   Polonius
You shall do marvellous wisely, good Reynaldo,
Before you visit him, to make inquire
5 Of his behaviour.
   Reynaldo
              My lord, I did intend it.
   Polonius
Marry, well said, very well said. Look you, sir,
Inquire me first what Danskers are in Paris,
And how, and who, what means, and where they keep,
What company, at what expense; and finding
10 By this encompassment and drift of question

11–12 *come you . . . it*: you will get
   closer than if you ask specific
   questions (about Laertes).
13 *Take you*: assume.

19 *put on him*: charge him with.

20 *forgeries*: false accusations.
   rank: disgraceful.

22 *usual slips*: common faults.

23–4 *noted and most known To*: well
   known and associated with.

26 *drabbing*: frequenting prostitutes.
28 *season*: moderate.
30 *incontinency*: sexual excesses.
31–6 *breathe . . . assault*: Reynaldo
   should imply that Laertes is behaving
   like any young man who has been
   given his freedom.
31 *quaintly*: cunningly.
34 *savageness . . . blood*: wildness of
   untamed youth.
   unreclaimed: unreclaimèd.
35 *Of general assault*: which happens to
   most men.

That they do know my son, come you more nearer
Than your particular demands will touch it.
Take you as 'twere some distant knowledge of him,
As thus, 'I know his father, and his friends,
15 And in part him'—do you mark this, Reynaldo?
   Reynaldo
Ay, very well, my lord.
   Polonius
'And in part him. But', you may say, 'not well;
But if't be he I mean, he's very wild,
Addicted so and so'—and there put on him
20 What forgeries you please—marry, none so rank
As may dishonour him—take heed of that—
But, sir, such wanton, wild, and usual slips
As are companions noted and most known
To youth and liberty.
   Reynaldo
25 As gaming, my lord?
   Polonius
                    Ay, or drinking, fencing, swearing,
Quarrelling, drabbing—you may go so far.
   Reynaldo
My lord, that would dishonour him.
   Polonius
'Faith no, as you may season it in the charge.
You must not put another scandal on him,
30 That he is open to incontinency—
That's not my meaning; but breathe his faults so
   quaintly
That they may seem the taints of liberty,
The flash and outbreak of a fiery mind,
A savageness in unreclaimed blood,
35 Of general assault.
   Reynaldo
But my good lord—
   Polonius
                    Wherefore should you do this?
   Reynaldo
Ay, my lord, I would know that.

38 *drift*: scheme.
39 *fetch of warrant*: legitimate device.
40 *sullies*: stains; this is the Folio reading, but Q2 has 'sallies' (compare *1, 2, 129*).
41 *a little . . . working*: that got grubby while it was being made.
42 *Mark you*: listen to me.
43 *Your . . . converse*: convèrse; the person you are talking to.
would sound: want to question.
44 *prenominate*: already named.
46 *closes . . . consequence*: naturally agrees with you in the following terms.
48 *phrase or the addition*: manner of speaking or form of address.

50 *'a*: he.
58 *o'ertook in's rouse*: the worse for drink.
59 *tennis*: Royal (or real) tennis was a popular game in Paris.
61 *Videlicet*: that is to say.
63 *carp*: a freshwater fish.
64 *we . . . reach*: we wise and experienced men.
65 *windlasses*: roundabout courses.
assays of bias: devious tests. In the game of bowls, a player must not aim directly, but must weigh his bowl's 'bias'.

66 'By indirect methods learn what is the right way.'
67 *lecture*: lesson.
68 *have me*: have understood me.

69 *buy*: be with.

Polonius
Marry, sir, here's my drift,
And I believe it is a fetch of warrant.
40 You laying these slight sullies on my son,
As 'twere a thing a little soil'd i'th' working,
Mark you,
Your party in converse, him you would sound,
Having ever seen in the prenominate crimes
45 The youth you breathe of guilty, be assur'd
He closes with you in this consequence:
'Good sir', or so, or 'friend', or 'gentleman',
According to the phrase or the addition
Of man and country.
        Reynaldo
                        Very good, my lord.
        Polonius
50 And then, sir, does 'a this—'a does—what was I about
to say? By the mass, I was about to say something.
Where did I leave?
        Reynaldo
At 'closes in the consequence'.
        Polonius
At 'closes in the consequence', ay, marry.
55 He closes thus: 'I know the gentleman,
I saw him yesterday', or 'th'other day',
Or then, or then, with such or such, 'and as you say,
There was a gaming', 'there o'ertook in's rouse',
'There falling out at tennis', or perchance
60 'I saw him enter such a house of sale'—
Videlicet a brothel, or so forth.
See you now,
Your bait of falsehood takes this carp of truth;
And thus do we of wisdom and of reach,
65 With windlasses and with assays of bias,
By indirections find directions out.
So by my former lecture and advice
Shall you my son. You have me, have you not?
        Reynaldo
My lord, I have.
        Polonius
                        God buy ye, fare ye well.

Reynaldo

70 Good my lord.

Polonius

Observe his inclination in yourself.

Reynaldo

I shall, my lord.

Polonius

               And let him ply his music.

Reynaldo

Well, my lord.   *[Exit*

Enter Ophelia

Polonius

Farewell. How now, Ophelia, what's the matter?

Ophelia

75 O my lord, my lord, I have been so affrighted.

Polonius

With what, i'th' name of God?

Ophelia

My lord, as I was sewing in my closet,
Lord Hamlet, with his doublet all unbrac'd,
No hat upon his head, his stockings foul'd,

80 Ungarter'd and down-gyved to his ankle,
Pale as his shirt, his knees knocking each other,
And with a look so piteous in purport
As if he had been loosed out of hell
To speak of horrors, he comes before me.

Polonius

85 Mad for thy love?

Ophelia

                 My lord, I do not know,
But truly I do fear it.

Polonius

                 What said he?

Ophelia

He took me by the wrist and held me hard.
Then goes he to the length of all his arm,
And with his other hand thus o'er his brow

90 He falls to such perusal of my face
As 'a would draw it. Long stay'd he so.

---

70 *Good my lord*: Reynaldo humbly accepts the dismissal.

71 'Go along with what he wants to do.'

72 *ply his music*: get on with what he is doing (Polonius may be changing the subject, and referring to his son's education).

73 *Well*: Reynaldo expresses duty as he takes his leave.

77 *closet*: small private room.

78 *unbrac'd*: unfastened. The garment should properly be buttoned down the front.

79 *No hat*: In Elizabethan England, gentlemen wore hats at all times.

80 *down-gyved*: gyvèd; Hamlet's stockings hung around his ankles like prison fetters (gyves).

83 *loosed*: loosèd; released.

88 *goes . . . arm*: backs away, holding me at arm's length.

90 *perusal*: careful scrutiny.

91 *As 'a would*: as though he wanted to.

At last, a little shaking of mine arm,
And thrice his head thus waving up and down,
He rais'd a sigh so piteous and profound
95 As it did seem to shatter all his bulk
And end his being. That done, he lets me go,
And with his head over his shoulder turn'd
He seem'd to find his way without his eyes,
For out o'doors he went without their helps,
100 And to the last bended their light on me.
    Polonius
Come, go with me, I will go seek the king.
This is the very ecstasy of love,
Whose violent property fordoes itself
And leads the will to desperate undertakings
105 As oft as any passion under heaven
That does afflict our natures. I am sorry—
What, have you given him any hard words of late?
    Ophelia
No, my good lord, but as you did command,
I did repel his letters and denied
110 His access to me.
    Polonius
            That hath made him mad.
I am sorry that with better heed and judgement
I had not quoted him. I fear'd he did but trifle
And meant to wrack thee. But beshrew my jealousy!
By heaven, it is as proper to our age
115 To cast beyond ourselves in our opinions
As it is common for the younger sort
To lack discretion. Come, go we to the king.
This must be known, which, being kept close, might move
More grief to hide than hate to utter love.
120 Come.   [*Exeunt*

---

95 *all his bulk*: his whole body.

100 *bended their light*: turned his gaze.

102 *ecstasy*: madness.
103 *property*: nature.
    fordoes: destroys.

108 *as you did command*: i.e. in *Act 1, scene 3*.
109 *repel*: send back.

111 *heed*: attention.
112 *quoted*: observed.
113 *wrack*: ruin.
    beshrew my jealousy: Polonius curses the suspicious fear which has prevented him (he thinks) from understanding Hamlet's behaviour.
114 *proper to our age*: normal for old men.
115 *cast . . . opinions*: get unreasonable ideas (in hunting, a hound is said to *cast* when it searches for a scent).
118 *close*: secret.
118–19 *being . . . love*: might cause more trouble if we keep quiet than anger if we talk about his love.

Act 2 Scene 2
Rosencrantz and Guildenstern are set to spy on Hamlet for the king, and Polonius describes Hamlet's encounter with Ophelia. The players arrive in Elsinore, and Hamlet sees a way to trap the king.

2 *Moreover that*: besides the fact that.

6 *Sith nor . . . nor*: since neither . . . nor.

12 *sith . . . haviour*: since then so closely acquainted with his youthful activities.
13 *vouchsafe your rest*: agree to stay.

16 *occasion*: some chance opportunity. *glean*: pick up.

18 *open'd*: discovered. *remedy*: power to correct.

21 *adheres*: clings to.
22 *gentry*: gentlemanly courtesy.
23 *expend*: spend.
24 *supply and profit*: profitable satisfaction.

26 *fits*: is appropriate for.

27 *by . . . us*: as our ruling monarchs.
28–9 *Put . . . entreaty*: command rather than request us to do your mighty will; Guildenstern seems to have adopted the king's unwieldy language.
30 *in . . . bent*: to the best of our abilities; in archery the 'bent' is the full extent to which the bow can be drawn.

SCENE 2

Flourish. Enter King *and* Queen, Rosencrantz *and* Guildenstern, *with* Attendants

King
Welcome, dear Rosencrantz and Guildenstern.
Moreover that we much did long to see you,
The need we have to use you did provoke
Our hasty sending. Something have you heard
5 Of Hamlet's transformation—so I call it,
Sith nor th'exterior nor the inward man
Resembles that it was. What it should be,
More than his father's death, that thus hath put him
So much from th'understanding of himself
10 I cannot dream of. I entreat you both
That, being of so young days brought up with him,
And sith so neighbour'd to his youth and haviour,
That you vouchsafe your rest here in our court
Some little time, so by your companies
15 To draw him on to pleasures and to gather,
So much as from occasion you may glean,
Whether aught to us unknown afflicts him thus
That, open'd, lies within our remedy.
    Queen
Good gentlemen, he hath much talk'd of you,
20 And sure I am, two men there is not living
To whom he more adheres. If it will please you
To show us so much gentry and good will
As to expend your time with us awhile
For the supply and profit of our hope,
25 Your visitation shall receive such thanks
As fits a king's remembrance.
    Rosencrantz
                                Both your majesties
Might, by the sovereign power you have of us,
Put your dread pleasures more into command
Than to entreaty.
    Guildenstern
                        But we both obey,
30 And here give up ourselves in the full bent

To lay our service freely at your feet
To be commanded.
King
Thanks, Rosencrantz and gentle Guildenstern.
Queen
Thanks, Guildenstern and gentle Rosencrantz.
35 And I beseech you instantly to visit
My too much changed son. Go, some of you,
And bring these gentlemen where Hamlet is.
Guildenstern
Heavens make our presence and our practices
Pleasant and helpful to him.
Queen
                                        Ay, amen.
                    [*Exeunt* Rosencrantz *and* Guildenstern
                                        and an Attendant

Enter Polonius

Polonius
40 Th'ambassadors from Norway, my good lord,
Are joyfully return'd.
King
Thou still hast been the father of good news.
Polonius
Have I, my lord? I assure my good liege
I hold my duty as I hold my soul,
45 Both to my God and to my gracious king;
And I do think—or else this brain of mine
Hunts not the trail of policy so sure
As it hath us'd to do—that I have found
The very cause of Hamlet's lunacy.
King
50 O speak of that: that do I long to hear.
Polonius
Give first admittance to th'ambassadors.
My news shall be the fruit to that great feast.
King
Thyself do grace to them and bring them in.
                                        [*Exit* Polonius

36 *changed*: changèd.

53 *do grace to*: a) welcome; b) speak the
   blessing before the 'feast'.

He tells me, my dear Gertrude, he hath found
55 The head and source of all your son's distemper.

Queen

I doubt it is no other but the main,
His father's death and our o'er-hasty marriage.

King

Well, we shall sift him.

Enter Polonius, Voltemand, *and* Cornelius

                            Welcome, my good friends.
Say, Voltemand, what from our brother Norway?

Voltemand

60 Most fair return of greetings and desires.
Upon our first, he sent out to suppress
His nephew's levies, which to him appear'd
To be a preparation 'gainst the Polack;
But better look'd into, he truly found
65 It was against your highness; whereat griev'd
That so his sickness, age, and impotence
Was falsely borne in hand, sends out arrests
On Fortinbras; which he, in brief, obeys,
Receives rebuke from Norway, and, in fine,
70 Makes vow before his uncle never more
To give th'assay of arms against your majesty:
Whereon old Norway, overcome with joy,
Gives him three thousand crowns in annual fee
And his commission to employ those soldiers
75 So levied, as before, against the Polack,
With an entreaty, herein further shown,
[*Gives a paper*] That it might please you to give quiet
    pass
Through your dominions for this enterprise
On such regards of safety and allowance
80 As therein are set down.

King

                           It likes us well;
And at our more consider'd time we'll read,
Answer, and think upon this business.
Meantime, we thank you for your well-took labour.

---

58 *sift*: thoroughly interrogate.

59 *brother Norway*: brother-king of Norway.

61 *Upon our first*: as soon as we raised the subject—as they had been instructed in *Act 1*, scene 2.
63 *preparation 'gainst*: army raised—levied—to make war on.
    the Polack: the king of Poland.

66 *impotence*: feebleness.
67 *borne in hand*: deceived.
    arrests: prohibitions.

69 *fine*: conclusion.

71 *give . . . against*: challenge.

77 *quiet pass*: safe passage. Shakespeare seems to have thought that Denmark lay between Norway and Poland.

79 *regards . . . allowance*: terms relating to safety and permission.

80 *likes*: pleases. Claudius uses the royal plural.
81 *at . . . time*: when we have more time to think about it.
83 *well-took*: well done, successful.

Go to your rest, at night we'll feast together.

85   Most welcome home.

[*Exeunt* Voltemand *and* Cornelius

Polonius
            This business is well ended.

86 *expostulate*: enquire into.

87 *What . . . duty is*: i.e. the nature of kingship and the duty of a subject.

My liege and madam, to expostulate
What majesty should be, what duty is,
Why day is day, night night, and time is time,
Were nothing but to waste night, day, and time.

90 *wit*: intelligence. Polonius utters a wise maxim—but rarely follows his own advice.

90   Therefore, since brevity is the soul of wit,
And tediousness the limbs and outward flourishes,
I will be brief. Your noble son is mad.
Mad call I it, for to define true madness,
What is't but to be nothing else but mad?

94 *What . . . mad*: it would be mad to try to define madness.
95 *let that go*: drop that subject.
    art: artifice, rhetorical device.

95   But let that go.

Queen
            More matter with less art.

Polonius
Madam, I swear I use no art at all.
That he is mad 'tis true; 'tis true 'tis pity;
And pity 'tis 'tis true. A foolish figure—
But farewell it, for I will use no art.

98 *figure*: figure of speech; Polonius proceeds to use more 'figures' in a speech which is tediously artful.
100 *grant*: allow.

100 Mad let us grant him then. And now remains
That we find out the cause of this effect,
Or rather say the cause of this defect,

103 *effect . . . cause*: defective effect has a cause.
104 *Thus . . . thus*: that's the way it is; and what we must do is this.
105 *Perpend*: pay attention.
106 *while . . . mine*: i.e. until she is married.
108 *gather and surmise*: draw your own conclusions.

For this effect defective comes by cause.
Thus it remains; and the remainder thus:
105 Perpend,
I have a daughter—have while she is mine—
Who in her duty and obedience, mark,
Hath given me this. Now gather and surmise.
[*Reads*] *To the celestial and my soul's idol, the most*

110 *beautified*: made beautiful (perhaps by the use of cosmetics).
111 *these*: these lines.
111–12 *in . . .&c*: The letter ('&c' serves for a formal address) is to be kept next to her heart.

110 *beautified Ophelia*—That's an ill phrase, a vile phrase,
'beautified' is a vile phrase. But you shall hear—*these; in*
her excellent white bosom, these, &c.

Queen
Came this from Hamlet to her?

Polonius
Good madam, stay awhile, I will be faithful.

114 *be faithful*: keep my word.
115 *Doubt thou*: you may doubt.
116 *move*: The old (Ptolemaic) astronomy taught that the sun moved around the earth.

115   *Doubt thou the stars are fire,*
           Doubt that the sun doth move,

119 *ill . . . numbers*: bad at writing poetry like this.
120 *reckon*: count up.

122–3 *this . . . him*: this body belongs to him.

125 *more above*: in addition.
126 *fell out*: happened.

131 *would fain*: wish I could.

136 *table-book*: notebook, writing pad.
137 *given . . . dumb*: let my heart close its eyes in dumb silence.
138 *idle*: careless.
139 *round*: straight, bluntly.

141 *out of thy star*: beyond your (social) sphere.
142 *prescripts*: instructions.
143 *resort*: visitation.

147–50 *Fell . . . raves*: Polonius describes the classical symptoms of love-melancholy: depression ('sadness') with loss of appetite ('a fast') and insomnia ('watch'), bringing weakness and delirium ('lightness') and leading in a downward course ('declension') to insanity.

Doubt truth to be a liar,
But never doubt I love.
O dear Ophelia, I am ill at these numbers. I have not art
120 *to reckon my groans. But that I love thee best, O most*
best, believe it. Adieu.

Thine evermore, most dear lady, whilst this
machine is to him, Hamlet.
This in obedience hath my daughter shown me,
125 And, more above, hath his solicitings,
As they fell out by time, by means, and place,
All given to mine ear.
    King
But how hath she receiv'd his love?
    Polonius
What do you think of me?
    King
130 As of a man faithful and honourable.
    Polonius
I would fain prove so. But what might you think,
When I had seen this hot love on the wing—
As I perceiv'd it, I must tell you that,
Before my daughter told me—what might you
135 Or my dear majesty your queen here think,
If I had play'd the desk or table-book,
Or given my heart a winking mute and dumb,
Or look'd upon this love with idle sight—
What might you think? No, I went round to work,
140 And my young mistress thus I did bespeak:
'Lord Hamlet is a prince out of thy star.
This must not be.' And then I prescripts gave her,
That she should lock herself from his resort,
Admit no messengers, receive no tokens;
145 Which done, she took the fruits of my advice,
And he, repelled—a short tale to make—
Fell into a sadness, then into a fast,
Thence to a watch, thence into a weakness,
Thence to a lightness, and, by this declension,
150 Into the madness wherein now he raves
And all we mourn for.
    King
                Do you think 'tis this?

Queen
It may be; very like.
   Polonius
Hath there been such a time—I would fain know
   that—
That I have positively said ''Tis so',
155 When it prov'd otherwise?
   King
                                    Not that I know.
   Polonius
Take this from this if this be otherwise.

Points to his head and shoulder

If circumstances lead me, I will find
Where truth is hid, though it were hid indeed
Within the centre.
   King
                              How may we try it further?
   Polonius
160 You know sometimes he walks four hours together
Here in the lobby.
   Queen
                              So he does indeed.
   Polonius
At such a time I'll loose my daughter to him.
Be you and I behind an arras then,
Mark the encounter. If he love her not,
165 And be not from his reason fall'n thereon,
Let me be no assistant for a state,
But keep a farm and carters.
   King
                                    We will try it.

Enter Hamlet, reading on a book

   Queen
But look where sadly the poor wretch comes reading.
   Polonius
Away, I do beseech you both, away.
170 I'll board him presently. O give me leave.

159 *centre*: centre of the earth.
160 *four*: several.
162 *loose*: Polonius speaks like a farmer.
163 *arras*: tapestry wall-hanging (named
   after the town of Arras).

165 *thereon*: on account of that.
166 *assistant for a state*: minister of state.
168 *sadly*: seriously.
170 *board*: accost.
   presently: at once.
   give me leave: Polonius hastens the
   departure of Claudius and Gertrude.

171 *does*: is.

172 *God-a-mercy*: A polite response (= God have mercy on you) to the greeting of a social inferior.

174 *a fishmonger*: Hamlet's intention is undoubtedly offensive, although his meaning is obscure. There seems to be sexual innuendo in the lines, which may have some method in their madness—as Polonius suspects (line 203).

181 *sun . . . dog*: Hamlet appears to be reading from his book (which scholars have been unable to identify).
181–2 *a good kissing carrion*: a carcass (like that of the dead dog) that is ripe for the sun to shine on.

184 *walk i'th' sun*: go about in public.

186 *How . . . by that*: what do you think of that. Polonius is triumphant in his exclamation.
still: always.
harping: constantly sounding one note.
187 *'a said*: he said.
189 *near*: like.

192 *matter*: subject. Hamlet wilfully misunderstands.

[*Exeunt* King *and* Queen *and* Attendants

How does my good Lord Hamlet?

Hamlet

Well, God-a-mercy.

Polonius

Do you know me, my lord?

Hamlet

Excellent well. You are a fishmonger.

Polonius

175 Not I, my lord.

Hamlet

Then I would you were so honest a man.

Polonius

Honest, my lord?

Hamlet

Ay sir. To be honest, as this world goes, is to be one man picked out of ten thousand.

Polonius

180 That's very true, my lord.

Hamlet

For if the sun breed maggots in a dead dog, being a good kissing carrion—Have you a daughter?

Polonius

I have, my lord.

Hamlet

Let her not walk i'th' sun. Conception is a blessing, but
185 as your daughter may conceive—friend, look to't.

Polonius

[*Aside*] How say you by that? Still harping on my daughter. Yet he knew me not at first; 'a said I was a fishmonger. 'A is far gone. And truly in my youth I suffered much extremity for love, very near this. I'll
190 speak to him again.—What do you read, my lord?

Hamlet

Words, words, words.

Polonius

What is the matter, my lord?

Hamlet

Between who?

Polonius

I mean the matter that you read, my lord.

195 *satirical rogue*: No particular writer
has been identified; the sentiments
are commonplace.
197 *purging*: exuding.
gum: sap (from the bark of the plum-
tree).
199 *hams*: thighs.
200 *honesty*: decency.
201 *set down*: written down.
old as: as old as.

203 *method*: some kind of sense.

204 *walk out of the air*: come inside.
Polonius treats Hamlet like an invalid
who should avoid cold air.

206 *pregnant*: meaningful. The image is
continued in 'delivered of'.

210 *suddenly*: immediately.

212 *will not*: Such a double negative (with
'cannot') was not uncommon in
Elizabethan usage.

Hamlet

195　Slanders, sir. For the satirical rogue says here that old
men have grey beards, that their faces are wrinkled,
their eyes purging thick amber and plum-tree gum, and
that they have a plentiful lack of wit, together with most
weak hams—all which, sir, though I most powerfully
200　and potently believe, yet I hold it not honesty to have it
thus set down. For yourself, sir, shall grow old as I am—
if like a crab you could go backward.

Polonius

[*Aside*] Though this be madness, yet there is method
in't.—Will you walk out of the air, my lord?

Hamlet

205　Into my grave?

Polonius

Indeed, that's out of the air.—[*Aside*] How pregnant
sometimes his replies are—a happiness that often
madness hits on, which reason and sanity could not so
prosperously be delivered of. I will leave him and
210　suddenly contrive the means of meeting between him
and my daughter.—My lord, I will take my leave of you.

Hamlet

You cannot, sir, take from me anything that I will not
more willingly part withal—except my life, except my
life, except my life.

Polonius

215　Fare you well, my lord.

Hamlet

These tedious old fools.

Enter Rosencrantz *and* Guildenstern

Polonius

You go to seek the Lord Hamlet. There he is.

Rosencrantz

God save you, sir.　　　　　　　　　　　　　[*Exit* Polonius

Guildenstern

My honoured lord.

Rosencrantz

220　My most dear lord.

'My excellent good friends' (2, 2, 221). Peter Stormare as Hamlet, Royal Dramatic Theatre, Stockholm at the National Theatre, 1987.

Hamlet

My excellent good friends. How dost thou, Guildenstern? Ah, Rosencrantz. Good lads, how do you both?

Rosencrantz

As the indifferent children of the earth.

Guildenstern

225 Happy in that we are not over-happy: on Fortune's cap we are not the very button.

Hamlet

Nor the soles of her shoe?

Rosencrantz

Neither, my lord.

Hamlet

Then you live about her waist, or in the middle of her 230 favours?

Guildenstern

Faith, her privates we.

Hamlet

In the secret parts of Fortune? O most true, she is a strumpet. What news?

Rosencrantz

None, my lord, but the world's grown honest.

Hamlet

235 Then is doomsday near. But your news is not true. Let me question more in particular. What have you, my good friends, deserved at the hands of Fortune that she sends you to prison hither?

Guildenstern

Prison, my lord?

Hamlet

240 Denmark's a prison.

Rosencrantz

Then is the world one.

Hamlet

A goodly one, in which there are many confines, wards, and dungeons, Denmark being one o'th' worst.

Rosencrantz

We think not so, my lord.

224 'Like any ordinary men.'

226 *button*: The button at the top of a hat was the highest point.

230 *favours*: i.e. sexual favours.
231 *privates*: private parts (i.e. the sexual organs) of the body.
233 *strumpet*: It was commonplace to speak in such a way of the fickleness of Fortune.
235 *Then . . . near*: then the world must be coming to an end.

242 *confines*: places of confinement. *wards*: cells.

Hamlet

245 Why, then 'tis none to you; for there is nothing either good or bad but thinking makes it so. To me it is a prison.

Rosencrantz

Why, then your ambition makes it one: 'tis too narrow for your mind.

Hamlet

250 O God, I could be bounded in a nutshell and count myself a king of infinite space—were it not that I have bad dreams.

Guildenstern

Which dreams indeed are ambition; for the very substance of the ambitious is merely the shadow of a
255 dream.

Hamlet

A dream itself is but a shadow.

Rosencrantz

Truly, and I hold ambition of so airy and light a quality that it is but a shadow's shadow.

Hamlet

Then are our beggars bodies, and our monarchs and
260 outstretched heroes the beggars' shadows. Shall we to th' court? For by my fay, I cannot reason.

Rosencrantz and **Guildenstern**

We'll wait upon you.

Hamlet

No such matter. I will not sort you with the rest of my servants; for, to speak to you like an honest man, I am
265 most dreadfully attended. But in the beaten way of friendship, what make you at Elsinore?

Rosencrantz

To visit you, my lord, no other occasion.

Hamlet

Beggar that I am, I am even poor in thanks, but I thank you. And sure, dear friends, my thanks are too dear a
270 halfpenny. Were you not sent for? Is it your own inclining? Is it a free visitation? Come, come, deal justly with me. Come, come. Nay, speak.

Guildenstern

What should we say, my lord?

250 *count*: consider.

253–5 *the very substance . . . dream*: all that an ambitious man achieves is no more than a shadow of what he dreamed of.

259–60 *Then . . . shadows*: by that reasoning those we call beggars are men of substance, and those we call successful are only shadows of the beggars; Hamlet pursues the argument to ridiculous excess.
260 *outstretched*: ambitious, overreaching.
261 *fay*: faith.
   reason: carry on this kind of argument.
262 *wait upon*: escort, attend.
263 *sort*: class.
264 *to . . . man*: to tell you the truth.
265 *the beaten way*: Hamlet abandons his verbal tricks and approaches more directly.
266 *make you*: are you doing.

269 *too dear*: not worth.

271 *inclining*: wish.
   free: voluntary.

274 *but*: Hamlet already suspects them, and assumes they will not give him a straight answer.
276 *colour*: disguise.

279 *conjure you*: ask you solemnly.
280 *rights of*: what is due to.
     consonancy: harmonious agreement.
282 *what more dear*: whatever there is that is more precious.
     a better proposer: one more skilled at framing oaths.
286 *have an eye of*: am watching.
286–7 *hold not off*: speak freely.
289–91 *so . . . feather*: in that way my anticipation will forestall your answer, and you will not break your secrecy.
292 *foregone . . . exercises*: neglected my usual occupations.
293 *goes . . . disposition*: my mood is so depressed.
294 *frame*: structure.
294–5 *sterile promontory*: barren outcrop of land stretching out into the sea.
295 *canopy*: Hamlet probably points to the canopy over the stage, painted with sun, moon, and stars for the 'heavens'.

296 *brave*: splendid.
297 *fretted*: decorated.
298 *foul . . . vapours*: It was believed that infections were carried in the air.
300 *express*: direct; the adjective applies to 'moving' rather than 'form'.
302 *apprehension*: power of understanding.
303 *paragon*: perfection.
304 *quintessence*: refined essence (distilled from the other four elements).
     dust: 'dust thou art, and unto dust shalt thou return' (Genesis 3:19).

Hamlet

Anything but to th' purpose. You were sent for, and
275 there is a kind of confession in your looks, which your modesties have not craft enough to colour. I know the good king and queen have sent for you.

Rosencrantz

To what end, my lord?

Hamlet

That, you must teach me. But let me conjure you, by the
280 rights of our fellowship, by the consonancy of our youth, by the obligation of our ever-preserved love, and by what more dear a better proposer can charge you withal, be even and direct with me whether you were sent for or no.

Rosencrantz

285 [*Aside to* Guildenstern] What say you?

Hamlet

Nay, then I have an eye of you. If you love me, hold not off.

Guildenstern

My lord, we were sent for.

Hamlet

I will tell you why; so shall my anticipation prevent your
290 discovery, and your secrecy to the king and queen moult no feather. I have of late, but wherefore I know not, lost all my mirth, forgone all custom of exercises; and indeed it goes so heavily with my disposition that this goodly frame the earth seems to me a sterile
295 promontory, this most excellent canopy the air, look you, this brave o'erhanging firmament, this majestical roof fretted with golden fire, why, it appeareth nothing to me but a foul and pestilent congregation of vapours. What piece of work is a man, how noble in reason, how
300 infinite in faculties, in form and moving how express and admirable, in action how like an angel, in apprehension how like a god: the beauty of the world, the paragon of animals—and yet, to me, what is this quintessence of dust? Man delights not me—nor
305 woman neither, though by your smiling you seem to say so.

311 *Lenten entertainment*: a poor
    reception; Lent is a time of fasting.
312 *coted*: coursed; the metaphor is from
    hunting hares with hounds.
314–19 *his majesty . . . freely*: Hamlet
    describes the characters and
    functions of popular drama.
315 *on*: from.
316 *foil*: rapier.
    target: small shield.
    gratis: for nothing.
317 *humorous*: melancholy.
318 *tickle a th' sear*: easily amused; the
    image is a gun with a sensitive
    ('tickle') trigger ('sear').
319–20 *blank verse*: iambic pentameters—
    the usual medium of dramatic speech.
320 *halt*: a) limp, go lame; b) scan badly.
321 *wont*: accustomed.
322 *tragedians of the city*: he describes a
    company of London actors.
323 *chances it*: does it happen.
    travel: are on tour.
    residence: permanent theatre.
325 *inhibition*: ban, restriction.
325–6 *the late innovation*: the recent
    uprising (i.e. the rebellion led by the
    Earl of Essex in February 1601).
327 *estimation*: popularity.
328 *followed*: frequented.
331 *their . . . pace*: the standard of their
    work is as good as ever.
332–7 *there . . . thither*: Rosencrantz
    describes a company of child actors
    who began performing in London
    towards the end of 1600; their plays
    often made fun of the actors,
    dramatists, and audiences of the
    regular theatres, and initiated a period
    of rivalry, the 'War of the Theatres',
    between public and private
    playhouses.
332 *eyrie*: nestful.
    little eyases: baby hawks.

Rosencrantz
My lord, there was no such stuff in my thoughts.
Hamlet
Why did ye laugh then, when I said man delights not
me?
Rosencrantz
310 To think, my lord, if you delight not in man, what
Lenten entertainment the players shall receive from
you. We coted them on the way, and hither are they
coming to offer you service.
Hamlet
He that plays the king shall be welcome—his majesty
315 shall have tribute on me, the adventurous knight shall
use his foil and target, the lover shall not sigh gratis, the
humorous man shall end his part in peace, the clown
shall make those laugh whose lungs are tickle a th' sear,
and the lady shall say her mind freely—or the blank
320 verse shall halt for't. What players are they?
Rosencrantz
Even those you were wont to take such delight in, the
tragedians of the city.
Hamlet
How chances it they travel? Their residence, both in
reputation and profit, was better both ways.
Rosencrantz
325 I think their inhibition comes by the means of the late
innovation.
Hamlet
Do they hold the same estimation they did when I was
in the city? Are they so followed?
Rosencrantz
No, indeed are they not.
Hamlet
330 How comes it? Do they grow rusty?
Rosencrantz
Nay, their endeavour keeps in the wonted pace; but
there is, sir, an eyrie of children, little eyases, that cry out
on the top of question, and are most tyrannically
clapped for't. These are now the fashion, and so berattle
335 the common stages—so they call them—that many

332–3 *cry . . . question*: squawk louder than anything else.
333 *tyrannically*: excessively.
334 *berattle*: abuse.
335 *common stages*: public theatres; the boy players performed in 'private' playhouses, admission to which was more expensive.
336 *wearing rapiers*: carrying swords.
goose-quills: pens—i.e. the satiric drama written with these.
339 *escotted*: provided for.
quality: profession.
339–40 *no . . . sing*: when their voices break (when they would be dismissed).
342 *if . . . better*: if they have no better way of earning a living.
343–4 *exclaim . . . succession*: insult their own calling.
345 *much to do*: a great argument—i.e. the 'War of the Theatres'.
346 *tar*: incite; the word is used in dog-fighting.
347 *no . . . argument*: no profit to be made from plays.
348 *poet*: writer, dramatist.
went . . . question: came to blows.
350 *throwing . . . brains*: mental activity.
351 *carry it away*: carry off the victor's crown.
352 *Hercules . . . too*: Shakespeare alludes to the emblem of his Globe Theatre, where *Hamlet* was performed; Hercules took the burden of the entire globe from Atlas.

354 *make mouths*: pull faces (in ridicule).
355 *ducats*: gold coins.
356 *little*: miniature.
'Sblood: by Christ's blood.
357 *philosophy*: science, natural philosophy.

wearing rapiers are afraid of goose-quills and dare scarce come thither.

Hamlet
What, are they children? Who maintains 'em? How are they escotted? Will they pursue the quality no longer
340 than they can sing? Will they not say afterwards, if they should grow themselves to common players—as it is most like, if their means are no better—their writers do them wrong to make them exclaim against their own succession?

Rosencrantz
345 Faith, there has been much to do on both sides; and the nation holds it no sin to tar them to controversy. There was for a while no money bid for argument unless the poet and the player went to cuffs in the question.

Hamlet
Is't possible?

Guildenstern
350 O, there has been much throwing about of brains.

Hamlet
Do the boys carry it away?

Rosencrantz
Ay, that they do, my lord, Hercules and his load too.

Hamlet
It is not very strange; for my uncle is King of Denmark, and those that would make mouths at him while my
355 father lived give twenty, forty, fifty, a hundred ducats apiece for his picture in little. 'Sblood, there is something in this more than natural, if philosophy could find it out.

A flourish of trumpets

Guildenstern

There are the players.

Hamlet

360 Gentlemen, you are welcome to Elsinore. Your hands,
come then. Th'appurtenance of welcome is fashion and
ceremony. Let me comply with you in this garb—lest
my extent to the players, which I tell you must show
fairly outwards, should more appear like entertainment
365 than yours. You are welcome. But my uncle-father and
aunt-mother are deceived.

Guildenstern

In what, my dear lord?

Hamlet

I am but mad north-north-west. When the wind is
southerly, I know a hawk from a handsaw.

Enter Polonius

Polonius

370 Well be with you, gentlemen.

Hamlet

Hark you, Guildenstern, and you too—at each ear a
hearer. That great baby you see there is not yet out of his
swaddling-clouts.

Rosencrantz

Happily he is the second time come to them, for they say
375 an old man is twice a child.

Hamlet

I will prophesy he comes to tell me of the players. Mark
it.—You say right, sir, a Monday morning, 'twas then
indeed.

Polonius

My lord, I have news to tell you.

Hamlet

380 My lord, I have news to tell you. When Roscius was an
actor in Rome—

Polonius

The actors are come hither, my lord.

360–5 *Your . . . welcome*: Hamlet will shake hands, disguising his real feelings, with his former school friends.

361 *appurtenance*: proper accompaniment.

361–2 *fashion and ceremony*: fashionable ceremony.

362 *garb*: manner, costume.

363 *my extent*: the welcome I extend.

364 *entertainment*: a friendly reception.

368 *north-north-west*: A madman's moods were thought to be affected by the weather and the direction of the wind; Hamlet warns that he has not completely lost his senses.

369 *handsaw*: hernshaw (= a kind of heron, another bird of prey).

371–2 *at . . . hearer*: both of you listen to me.

373 *swaddling-clouts*: swaddling-clothes, the wrappings of a new-born baby.

374 *Happily*: perhaps.

375 *twice*: for a second time.

377–8 *You . . . indeed*: Hamlet pretends to be carrying on a conversation.

380 *Roscius*: A famous Roman actor.

383 *Buzz, buzz*: A contemptuous dismissal
     of stale news.

386–9 *tragedy . . . unlimited*: Polonius
     lists different kinds of plays, but his
     catalogue develops into self-parody—
     though *Cymbeline*, one of
     Shakespeare's last plays, would fit the
     description of 'tragical-comical-
     historical-pastoral'.
389–90 *Seneca . . . light*: The Roman
     dramatist Seneca had a great
     influence on Shakespeare's own
     tragedies from *Titus Andronicus* to
     King Lear, and *The Comedy of Errors*
     is based on two comedies by Plautus.
390–1 *the law . . . liberty*: Polonius (in a
     phrase never properly explained)
     seems to be commending the actors
     whether they follow the rules or play
     with more licence.
391 *only*: best.
392 *Jephthah*: The story of Jephthah
     (Judges 11:30–40), who sacrificed
     his daughter for political reasons, was
     retold in the popular ballad (*c.* 1567)
     which Hamlet sings.
396 *passing*: exceedingly.
397 *Still*: always.

401 *that follows not*: i.e. that Polonius
     should love his daughter as Jephthah
     did.

404–7 *As . . . more*: Hamlet continues to
     quote the religious ballad ('pious
     chanson'):
     And as by lot, God wot
     It came to pass most like it was
     Great wars there should be,
     And who should be the chief but he.
407 *row*: stanza.
408 *abridgement*: interruption (cutting
     short his speech, and shortening the
     time with entertainment).

Hamlet
Buzz, buzz.
   Polonius
Upon my honour—
   Hamlet
385 Then came each actor on his ass—
   Polonius
The best actors in the world, either for tragedy, comedy,
history, pastoral, pastoral-comical, historical-pastoral,
tragical-historical, tragical-comical-historical-pastoral,
scene individable, or poem unlimited. Seneca cannot be
390 too heavy, nor Plautus too light. For the law of writ, and
the liberty, these are the only men.
   Hamlet
O Jephthah, judge of Israel, what a treasure hadst thou!
   Polonius
What a treasure had he, my lord?
   Hamlet
Why,
395   One fair daughter and no more,
       The which he loved passing well.
   Polonius
[*Aside*] Still on my daughter.
   Hamlet
Am I not i'th' right, old Jephthah?
   Polonius
If you call me Jephthah, my lord, I have a daughter that
400 I love passing well.
   Hamlet
Nay, that follows not.
   Polonius
What follows then, my lord?
   Hamlet
Why,
      As by lot God wot,
405 and then, you know,
      It came to pass, as most like it was.
The first row of the pious chanson will show you more,
for look where my abridgement comes.

Enter the Players

You are welcome, masters. Welcome, all.—I am glad to
410 see thee well.—Welcome, good friends.—O, old friend,
why thy face is valanced since I saw thee last. Com'st
thou to beard me in Denmark?—What, my young lady
and mistress! By'r lady, your ladyship is nearer to
heaven than when I saw you last by the altitude of a
415 chopine. Pray God your voice, like a piece of uncurrent
gold, be not cracked within the ring.—Masters, you are
all welcome. We'll e'en to't like French falconers, fly at
anything we see. We'll have a speech straight. Come,
give us a taste of your quality. Come, a passionate
420 speech.

First Player
What speech, my good lord?
Hamlet
I heard thee speak me a speech once, but it was never
acted, or if it was, not above once—for the play, I
remember, pleased not the million, 'twas caviar to the
425 general. But it was, as I received it—and others, whose
judgements in such matters cried in the top of mine—
an excellent play, well digested in the scenes, set down
with as much modesty as cunning. I remember one said
there were no sallets in the lines to make the matter
430 savoury, nor no matter in the phrase that might indict
the author of affection, but called it an honest method,
as wholesome as sweet, and by very much more
handsome than fine. One speech in't I chiefly loved—
'twas Aeneas' tale to Dido—and thereabout of it
435 especially when he speaks of Priam's slaughter. If it live

411 *valanced*: fringed (with a beard).
412 *beard*: confront.
      my young lady: Hamlet greets the boy
      actor who will play the female roles.
413 *By'r lady*: by Our Lady (the Virgin
      Mary).
413–14 *nearer to heaven*: i.e. taller.
415 *chopine*: Venetian high-heeled fashion
      shoe.
416 *cracked . . . ring*: a) broken;
      b) clipped inside the ring surrounding
      the monarch's head (when a coin
      would cease to be legal tender).
417 *e'en to't*: make a try at it.
418 *straight*: immediately.
419 *quality*: professional skill.

423 *the play*: Hamlet may be recalling
      Dido, Queen of Carthage (*c.* 1587), a
      play by Shakespeare's rival,
      Christopher Marlowe, based on Virgil's
      Aeneid, Book II.
424–5 *caviar . . . general*: a gourmet
      delicacy not appreciated by popular
      taste.
425 *received*: considered.
426 *cried . . . mine*: were better than
      mine.
427 *digested*: organized.
428 *modesty*: restraint.
      cunning: skill.
      one: somebody.
429 *sallets*: tasty bits, dirty jokes.
430 *matter . . . phrase*: fancy language.
431 *affection*: affectation.
432–3 *by . . . fine*: showing much more
      natural ability than acquired
      technique.
434 *Aeneas . . . Dido*: Aeneas recounts the
      story of the sack of Troy in *Act 2* of
      Marlowe's play.
435 *Priam*: the King of Troy.

438 *Pyrrhus*: son of the Greek hero
   Achilles, who led the final attack on
   Troy in revenge for the death of his
   father.
   th' Hyrcanian beast: Tigers of
   Hyrcania (a province of Asia Minor)
   were traditionally famous for ferocity.
440 *sable arms*: black armour.
442 *couched . . . horse*: couchèd. The
   Greeks entered Troy in a wooden
   horse, which proved fateful
   ('ominous') to the city.
443 *complexion*: figure.
445 *total gules*: red all over.
   trick'd: spotted.
447 *Bak'd . . . streets*: baked into a crust
   by the hot air of the burning streets.
450 *o'ersized*: o'ersizèd; smeared over.
451 *carbuncles*: precious stones said to
   glow fiery red in the dark.
452 *grandsire*: grandfather; Priam was
   reputed to have fathered fifty sons.
453 *proceed you*: you continue.

456 *Anon*: soon afterwards.
457 *too short*: with blows that fell too
   short.
   antique sword: The old king was trying
   to wield the sword he had fought with
   in his youth.
459 *Repugnant to command*: refusing to
   obey him.
461 *with . . . sword*: overbalanced by the
   movement of the mighty broadsword.
   fell: cruel.
462 *unnerved*: unnervèd; enfeebled.
   senseless Ilium: the non-human
   citadel of Troy.
463 *flaming top*: burning tower.
464 *his*: its.
465 *Takes . . . ear*: deafens Pyrrhus.
466 *declining*: descending.
   milky: white.
469 *like a neutral*: as though impartial.
471 *against*: just before.
472 *rack*: cloud formations.

474 *hush*: silent.

in your memory, begin at this line—let me see, let me
see—
The rugged Pyrrhus, like th' Hyrcanian beast—
'Tis not so. It begins with Pyrrhus—
440 *The rugged Pyrrhus, he whose sable arms,*
Black as his purpose, did the night resemble
When he lay couched in the ominous horse,
Hath now this dread and black complexion smear'd
With heraldry more dismal. Head to foot
445 *Now is he total gules, horridly trick'd*
With blood of fathers, mothers, daughters, sons,
Bak'd and impasted with the parching streets,
That lend a tyrannous and a damned light
To their lord's murder. Roasted in wrath and fire,
450 *And thus o'ersized with coagulate gore,*
With eyes like carbuncles, the hellish Pyrrhus
Old grandsire Priam seeks.
So proceed you.
   Polonius
'Fore God, my lord, well spoken, with good accent and
455 good discretion.
   First Player
                              Anon he finds him,
Striking too short at Greeks. His antique sword,
Rebellious to his arm, lies where it falls,
Repugnant to command. Unequal match'd,
460 *Pyrrhus at Priam drives, in rage strikes wide;*
But with the whiff and wind of his fell sword
Th'unnerved father falls. Then senseless Ilium,
Seeming to feel this blow, with flaming top
Stoops to his base, and with a hideous crash
465 *Takes prisoner Pyrrhus' ear. For lo, his sword,*
Which was declining on the milky head
Of reverend Priam, seem'd i'th' air to stick;
So, as a painted tyrant, Pyrrhus stood,
And like a neutral to his will and matter,
470 *Did nothing.*
But as we often see against some storm
A silence in the heavens, the rack stand still,
The bold winds speechless, and the orb below
As hush as death, anon the dreadful thunder

'But who—ah, woe!—had seen the mobled queen—' (2, 2, 490), Frank Middlemiss as Polonius, Roger Rees as Hamlet, Dexter Fletcher as the Player Queen, Stephen Simms and Derek Crewe as Players, and Bernard Horsfall as First Player, Royal Shakespeare Company, 1984.

475 *region*: skies.
476 *Aroused*: arousèd.
477 *Cyclops*: mythological giant
    blacksmiths who made armour for the
    gods.
478 *Mars*: the god of war.
    forg'd . . . eterne: made permanently
    resistant.
479 *remorse*: pity.
481 *strumpet*: faithless prostitute.
482 *synod*: assembly.
483 *fellies*: curved pieces forming rim of
    wheel.
    her wheel: Fortune is traditionally
    represented controlling a wheel,
    emblem of inconstancy.

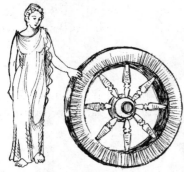

484 *nave*: hub.
489 *Hecuba*: Priam's wife, epitome of
    suffering womanhood.
490 *mobbled*: muffled (though Hamlet
    questions the obscure word).
494 *bisson rheum*: blinding tears.
    clout: piece of old cloth.
495 *late*: recently.
496 *all o'erteemed*: o'erteemèd; thoroughly
    exhausted with child-bearing.
498 *with . . . steep'd*: speaking bitter
    words.

505 *made milch*: milked down tears from.

507 *whe'er*: whether.

475 *Doth rend the region; so after Pyrrhus' pause*
    Aroused vengeance sets him new awork,
    And never did the Cyclops' hammers fall
    On Mars's armour, forg'd for proof eterne,
    With less remorse than Pyrrhus' bleeding sword
480 *Now falls on Priam.*
    Out, out, thou strumpet Fortune! All you gods
    In general synod take away her power,
    Break all the spokes and fellies from her wheel,
    And bowl the round nave down the hill of heaven
485 *As low as to the fiends.*

Polonius
This is too long.

Hamlet
It shall to the barber's with your beard.—Prithee say on.
He's for a jig or a tale of bawdry, or he sleeps. Say on,
come to Hecuba.

First Player
490 *But who—ah, woe!—had seen the mobbled queen—*

Hamlet
'The mobbled queen'.

Polonius
That's good.

First Player
Run barefoot up and down, threat'ning the flames
With bisson rheum, a clout upon that head
495 *Where late the diadem stood, and, for a robe,*
    About her lank and all o'erteemed loins
    A blanket, in th'alarm of fear caught up—
    Who this had seen, with tongue in venom steep'd,
    'Gainst Fortune's state would treason have pronounc'd.
500 *But if the gods themselves did see her then,*
    When she saw Pyrrhus make malicious sport
    In mincing with his sword her husband's limbs,
    The instant burst of clamour that she made,
    Unless things mortal move them not at all,
505 *Would have made milch the burning eyes of heaven*
    And passion in the gods.

Polonius
Look whe'er he has not turned his colour and has tears
in's eyes. Prithee no more.

510 *bestowed*: accommodated.
511 *used*: treated.
512 *abstract*: summary.
513 *you were better*: it would be better for you.

515 *their desert*: what they deserve.

516 *God's bodkin*: by God's precious body. *after*: according to.
517 *scape whipping*: avoid being whipped—a penalty to which travelling players were especially liable unless they were protected by some nobleman.

525 *for a need*: if necessary. *study*: learn.

534 *God buy*: goodbye.
535 *peasant*: base.

537 *But*: merely. *dream*: pretence.

Hamlet
'Tis well. I'll have thee speak out the rest of this soon.—

510 Good my lord, will you see the players well bestowed?
Do you hear, let them be well used, for they are the abstract and brief chronicles of the time. After your death you were better have a bad epitaph than their ill report while you live.

Polonius

515 My lord, I will use them according to their desert.

Hamlet
God's bodkin, man, much better. Use every man after his desert, and who shall scape whipping? Use them after your own honour and dignity: the less they deserve, the more merit is in your bounty. Take them in.

Polonius

520 Come, sirs.

Hamlet
Follow him, friends. We'll hear a play tomorrow. [*To* First Player] Dost thou hear me, old friend? Can you play *The Murder of Gonzago*?

First Player
Ay, my lord.

Hamlet

525 We'll ha't tomorrow night. You could for a need study a speech of some dozen or sixteen lines, which I would set down and insert in't, could you not?

First Player
Ay, my lord.

Hamlet
Very well. [*To all the* Players] Follow that lord, and look

530 you mock him not.   [*Exeunt* Polonius *and* Players
[*To* Rosencrantz *and* Guildenstern] My good friends, I'll leave you till night. You are welcome to Elsinore.

Rosencrantz
Good my lord.

                    [*Exeunt* Rosencrantz *and* Guildenstern

Hamlet
Ay, so, God buy to you. Now I am alone.

535 O what a rogue and peasant slave am I!
Is it not monstrous that this player here,
But in a fiction, in a dream of passion,

538–42 *force . . . conceit*: Hamlet praises
the actor's skill, which controls his
whole body and expresses his feigned
emotion.
538 *conceit*: imagination.
539 *her*: i.e. the soul's.
his visage wann'd: his face turned
pale.
540 *aspect*: looks (the word is accented on
the second syllable).
541 *function*: energy.
542 *forms*: gestures.

548 *cleave the general ear*: burst
everyone's ears.
horrid: horrifying.
549 *free*: innocent.
550 *amaze*: bewilder.

553 *muddy-mettled*: dull-spirited.
peak: mope.
554 *John-a-dreams*: a dreamer.
unpregnant of: not stirred to action by.
556 *property*: body (his proper person).
557 *defeat*: destruction.
558 *pate*: head.
559 *Plucks . . . face*: A great insult.
560–1 *gives . . . lungs*: calls me a
downright liar, making me swallow the
insult.
561 *me*: to me.
563 *'Swounds*: by God's wounds.
take it: accept the insult.
564 *am . . . gall*: have no more anger
(thought to be secreted in the gall-
bladder) in me than a pigeon.
565 *To . . . bitter*: to make me resent such
tyranny.
566 *region kites*: kites in the sky.
568 *Remorseless*: pitiless.
kindless: unnatural (see *1, 2, 65*).
569 *brave*: admirable.

573 *drab*: prostitute.
574 *scullion*: kitchen servant.
575 *About*: get to work.

577 *cunning of the scene*: art of the
presentation.
578 *presently*: instantly.

Could force his soul so to his own conceit
That from her working all his visage wann'd,
540   Tears in his eyes, distraction in his aspect,
A broken voice, and his whole function suiting
With forms to his conceit? And all for nothing!
For Hecuba!
What's Hecuba to him, or he to her,
545   That he should weep for her? What would he do
Had he the motive and the cue for passion
That I have? He would drown the stage with tears,
And cleave the general ear with horrid speech,
Make mad the guilty and appal the free,
550   Confound the ignorant, and amaze indeed
The very faculties of eyes and ears.
Yet I,
A dull and muddy-mettled rascal, peak
Like John-a-dreams, unpregnant of my cause,
555   And can say nothing—no, not for a king,
Upon whose property and most dear life
A damn'd defeat was made. Am I a coward?
Who calls me villain, breaks my pate across,
Plucks off my beard and blows it in my face,
560   Tweaks me by the nose, gives me the lie i'th' throat
As deep as to the lungs—who does me this?
Ha!
'Swounds, I should take it: for it cannot be
But I am pigeon-liver'd and lack gall
565   To make oppression bitter, or ere this
I should ha' fatted all the region kites
With this slave's offal. Bloody, bawdy villain!
Remorseless, treacherous, lecherous, kindless villain!
Why, what an ass am I! This is most brave,
570   That I, the son of a dear father murder'd,
Prompted to my revenge by heaven and hell,
Must like a whore unpack my heart with words
And fall a-cursing like a very drab,
A scullion! Fie upon't! Foh!
575   About, my brains. Hum—I have heard
That guilty creatures sitting at a play
Have, by the very cunning of the scene,
Been struck so to the soul that presently

583 *Before*: in front of. Hamlet seems to
be guiding the audience's attention.
584 *tent*: probe—as with a surgical
instrument.
blench: flinch.

585–90 *The spirit . . . me*: Hamlet voices
his doubts about the nature of the
Ghost; compare *1, 5, 144*.
589 *potent . . . spirits*: powerful with such
moods.
591 *relative*: substantial.

They have proclaim'd their malefactions.
580 For murder, though it have no tongue, will speak
With most miraculous organ. I'll have these players
Play something like the murder of my father
Before mine uncle. I'll observe his looks;
I'll tent him to the quick. If 'a do blench,
585 I know my course. The spirit that I have seen
May be a devil, and the devil hath power
T'assume a pleasing shape, yea, and perhaps,
Out of my weakness and my melancholy,
As he is very potent with such spirits,
590 Abuses me to damn me. I'll have grounds
More relative than this. The play's the thing
Wherein I'll catch the conscience of the king.   [*Exit*

1 *by no . . . conference*: not in the
course of conversation.
2 *puts on*: assumes. The king appears to
suspect Hamlet's 'antic disposition'.

5 *distracted*: mentally confused.

7 *forward*: willing.
sounded: questioned.

12 *disposition*: behaviour.

13 *Niggard*: reluctant. Rosencrantz seems
to contradict the description given by
Guildenstern in line 7.

14 *assay*: persuade.

16 *fell out*: happened.
17 *o'erraught*: overtook.

Scene 1

Enter King, Queen, Polonius, Ophelia, Rosencrantz,
Guildenstern

King
And can you by no drift of conference
Get from him why he puts on this confusion,
Grating so harshly all his days of quiet
With turbulent and dangerous lunacy?
   Rosencrantz
5 He does confess he feels himself distracted,
But from what cause 'a will by no means speak.
   Guildenstern
Nor do we find him forward to be sounded,
But with a crafty madness keeps aloof
When we would bring him on to some confession
10 Of his true state.
   Queen
                    Did he receive you well?
   Rosencrantz
Most like a gentleman.
   Guildenstern
But with much forcing of his disposition.
   Rosencrantz
Niggard of question, but of our demands
Most free in his reply.
   Queen
                    Did you assay him
15 To any pastime?
   Rosencrantz
Madam, it so fell out that certain players
We o'erraught on the way. Of these we told him,
And there did seem in him a kind of joy
To hear of it. They are here about the court,

20 And, as I think, they have already order
   This night to play before him.
            Polonius
                              'Tis most true,
   And he beseech'd me to entreat your Majesties
   To hear and see the matter.
            King
   With all my heart; and it doth much content me
25 To hear him so inclin'd.
   Good gentlemen, give him a further edge,
   And drive his purpose into these delights.
            Rosencrantz
   We shall, my lord.
                    [*Exeunt* Rosencrantz *and* Guildenstern
            King
                         Sweet Gertrude, leave us too,
   For we have closely sent for Hamlet hither
30 That he, as 'twere by accident, may here
   Affront Ophelia.
   Her father and myself, lawful espials,
   We'll so bestow ourselves that, seeing unseen,
   We may of their encounter frankly judge,
35 And gather by him, as he is behav'd,
   If't be th'affliction of his love or no
   That thus he suffers for.
            Queen
                         I shall obey you.
   And for your part, Ophelia, I do wish
   That your good beauties be the happy cause
40 Of Hamlet's wildness; so shall I hope your virtues
   Will bring him to his wonted way again,
   To both your honours.
            Ophelia
                         Madam, I wish it may.
                              [*Exit* Queen
            Polonius
   Ophelia, walk you here.—Gracious, so please you,
   We will bestow ourselves.—Read on this book,
45 That show of such an exercise may colour
   Your loneliness.—We are oft to blame in this,
   'Tis too much prov'd, that with devotion's visage

26 *edge*: encouragement.
27 *drive his purpose*: stimulate his interest.
29 *closely*: privately.
32 *lawful espials*: licensed (by himself) spies.
33 *bestow*: hide.
35 *gather . . . behav'd*: see from the way he acts.
38 *for your part*: so far as you are concerned; Ophelia's role in this deception is probably wholly innocent.
40 *wildness*: disorder.
41 *wonted*: accustomed.
42 *both your honours*: the best for both of you (see *5*, 1, 228–30).
43 *Gracious*: Your Majesty.
45 *exercise*: religious duty.
   colour: explain.
46 *loneliness*: being alone.
   in this: for doing things like this.
47 *prov'd*: found.
   visage: outward appearance.

48 *action*: behaviour.

50–4 *How . . . burden*: Claudius confirms
the truth of the Ghost's accusation.
51 *plast'ring art*: cosmetic camouflage.
52 *the thing . . . it*: the cosmetic paint.
53 *painted*: hypocritical.

56–88 *To be . . . action*: Hamlet debates
with himself whether patient
endurance of wrong is more
honourable than courageous
opposition.
56 *be*: live, exist.
58 *outrageous*: wilful.
59 *take . . . them*: The mixed metaphors
aptly express Hamlet's sense of
futility.
61 *No more*: that is all.
63 *consummation*: final completion.
65 *rub*: catch, snag; in the game of
bowls, the 'rub' is anything that
impedes the bowl's movement.
67 *shuffled off*: got free from.
mortal coil: business of humanity.
68 *give us pause*: make us stop to think.
68–9 *there's . . . life*: that's why
misfortune endures so long.
70 *time*: this temporal world.

72 *dispriz'd*: unrequited.

74 *merit*: the deserving man.
of: from.
75 *quietus*: final reckoning.
76 *bodkin*: needle, small dagger.
fardels: burdens.

79 *bourn*: frontier.

And pious action we do sugar o'er
The devil himself.

King

[*Aside*]   O 'tis too true.
50 How smart a lash that speech doth give my conscience.
The harlot's cheek, beautied with plast'ring art,
Is not more ugly to the thing that helps it
Than is my deed to my most painted word.
O heavy burden!

Polonius

55 I hear him coming. Let's withdraw, my lord.

[*Exeunt* King *and* Polonius

Enter Hamlet

Hamlet

To be, or not to be, that is the question:
Whether 'tis nobler in the mind to suffer
The slings and arrows of outrageous fortune,
Or to take arms against a sea of troubles
60 And by opposing end them. To die—to sleep,
No more; and by a sleep to say we end
The heart-ache and the thousand natural shocks
That flesh is heir to: 'tis a consummation
Devoutly to be wish'd. To die, to sleep;
65 To sleep, perchance to dream—ay, there's the rub:
For in that sleep of death what dreams may come,
When we have shuffled off this mortal coil,
Must give us pause—there's the respect
That makes calamity of so long life.
70 For who would bear the whips and scorns of time,
Th'oppressor's wrong, the proud man's contumely,
The pangs of dispriz'd love, the law's delay,
The insolence of office, and the spurns
That patient merit of th'unworthy takes,
75 When he himself might his quietus make
With a bare bodkin? Who would fardels bear,
To grunt and sweat under a weary life,
But that the dread of something after death,
The undiscover'd country, from whose bourn
80 No traveller returns, puzzles the will,

'To be, or not to be, that is the question:' (*3*, 1, 56), Alan Rickman as Hamlet, Riverside Studios, 1992.

And makes us rather bear those ills we have
Than fly to others that we know not of?
Thus conscience does make cowards of us all,
And thus the native hue of resolution
85 Is sicklied o'er with the pale cast of thought,
And enterprises of great pitch and moment
With this regard their currents turn awry
And lose the name of action. Soft you now,
The fair Ophelia! Nymph, in thy orisons
90 Be all my sins remember'd.

Ophelia
                              Good my lord,
How does your honour for this many a day?

Hamlet
I humbly thank you, well.

Ophelia
My lord, I have remembrances of yours
That I have longed long to redeliver.
95 I pray you now receive them.

Hamlet
                              No, not I.
I never gave you aught.

Ophelia
My honour'd lord, you know right well you did,
And with them words of so sweet breath compos'd
As made the things more rich. Their perfume lost,
100 Take these again; for to the noble mind
Rich gifts wax poor when givers prove unkind.
There, my lord.

Hamlet
Ha, ha! Are you honest?

Ophelia
My lord?

Hamlet
105 Are you fair?

Ophelia
What means your lordship?

Hamlet
That if you be honest and fair, your honesty should
admit no discourse to your beauty.

109 *commerce*: business dealings.

113 *his*: its.
114 *sometime*: once.
paradox: something contrary to reason.
gives it proof: proves it to be true. Hamlet seems to be alluding to his mother.

117–18 *virtue . . . stock*: virtue cannot be implanted like this into our human nature: 'inoculate' (= graft) is used horticulturally.
118 *relish of it*: taste of it—i.e. the original sin of human nature.

121 *nunnery*: a) convent (to protect her chastity); b) brothel (a slang term).
122 *indifferent*: moderately.

125 *at my beck*: waiting to be committed by me.

128 *We*: we men—see 'you' (= you women) at line 139; Hamlet ceases to think of either himself or Ophelia as individuals.

138 *wilt needs*: are determined to.

Ophelia
Could beauty, my lord, have better commerce than with
110 honesty?
Hamlet
Ay, truly, for the power of beauty will sooner transform honesty from what it is to a bawd than the force of honesty can translate beauty into his likeness. This was sometime a paradox, but now the time gives it proof. I
115 did love you once.
Ophelia
Indeed, my lord, you made me believe so.
Hamlet
You should not have believed me; for virtue cannot so inoculate our old stock but we shall relish of it. I loved you not.
Ophelia
120 I was the more deceived.
Hamlet
Get thee to a nunnery. Why, wouldst thou be a breeder of sinners? I am myself indifferent honest, but yet I could accuse me of such things that it were better my mother had not borne me. I am very proud, revengeful,
125 ambitious, with more offences at my beck than I have thoughts to put them in, imagination to give them shape, or time to act them in. What should such fellows as I do crawling between earth and heaven? We are arrant knaves all, believe none of us. Go thy ways to a
130 nunnery. Where's your father?
Ophelia
At home, my lord.
Hamlet
Let the doors be shut upon him, that he may play the fool nowhere but in's own house. Farewell.
Ophelia
O help him, you sweet heavens.
Hamlet
135 If thou dost marry, I'll give thee this plague for thy dowry: be thou as chaste as ice, as pure as snow, thou shalt not escape calumny. Get thee to a nunnery, farewell. Of if thou wilt needs marry, marry a fool; for

'Get thee to a nunnery.' (*3*, 1, 121), Tara Fitzgerald as Ophelia and Ralph Fiennes as Hamlet, Hackney Empire, 1995.

139 *monsters*: i.e. horned cuckolds (the implication is that all wives will sooner or later be unfaithful).

142 *paintings*: use of cosmetics.

144 *jig . . . lisp*: walk and talk affectedly.
nickname: give new name to.
145 *make . . . ignorance*: pretend that these seductive wiles are done because you know no better.
147 *mo*: more.

150ff. The return to regular verse restores a kind of normality after Hamlet's disjointed prose.
152 *expectancy and rose*: finest hope.
153 *glass*: looking-glass.
154 *observ'd*: honoured, respected.
155 *deject*: dejected.
156 *music*: i.e. which were like music to her ears.
157 *most sovereign*: ruling over all other faculties.
159 *feature*: figure.
blown: flowering.
160 *ecstasy*: madness.

162 *affections*: feelings.
165 *sits on brood*: is brooding over. The image is continued with 'hatch'.
166 *doubt*: fear.
169 *set it down*: decided. The king's plot against Hamlet's life is already set in motion.
170 *tribute*: At the time of Elizabeth I the Danes made a fresh attempt to claim the tribute ('Danegeld') which the English had paid in self-protection since the tenth century.
171 *Haply*: perhaps.
the seas: sea voyages were a recognized treatment for depression.
172 *variable objects*: different sights.

wise men know well enough what monsters you make
140 of them. To a nunnery, go—and quickly too. Farewell.

Ophelia
Heavenly powers, restore him.

Hamlet
I have heard of your paintings well enough. God hath
given you one face and you make yourselves another.
You jig and amble, and you lisp, you nickname God's
145 creatures, and make your wantonness your ignorance.
Go to, I'll no more on't, it hath made me mad. I say we
will have no mo marriage. Those that are married
already—all but one—shall live; the rest shall keep as
they are. To a nunnery, go.   [*Exit*

Ophelia
150 O, what a noble mind is here o'erthrown!
The courtier's, soldier's, scholar's, eye, tongue, sword,
Th'expectancy and rose of the fair state,
The glass of fashion and the mould of form,
Th'observ'd of all observers, quite, quite down!
155 And I, of ladies most deject and wretched,
That suck'd the honey of his music vows,
Now see that noble and most sovereign reason
Like sweet bells jangled out of tune and harsh,
That unmatch'd form and feature of blown youth
160 Blasted with ecstasy. O woe is me
T'have seen what I have seen, see what I see.

Enter King *and* Polonius

King
Love? His affections do not that way tend,
Nor what he spake, though it lack'd form a little,
Was not like madness. There's something in his soul
165 O'er which his melancholy sits on brood,
And I do doubt the hatch and the disclose
Will be some danger; which for to prevent,
I have in quick determination
Thus set it down: he shall with speed to England
170 For the demand of our neglected tribute.
Haply the seas and countries different,
With variable objects, shall expel

173 *This . . . heart*: this business that's
     weighing on his mind.
174 *still*: constantly.
175 *fashion of himself*: his normal
     behaviour.

178 *neglected*: rejected.

183 *be round with*: speak plainly to.
184 *in the ear*: where I can listen to.
185 *find him*: find out what's wrong with
     him.

This something settled matter in his heart,
Whereon his brains still beating puts him thus
175 From fashion of himself. What think you on't?
　　　Polonius
It shall do well. But yet do I believe
The origin and commencement of his grief
Sprung from neglected love. How now, Ophelia?
You need not tell us what Lord Hamlet said,
180 We heard it all. My lord, do as you please,
But if you hold it fit, after the play
Let his queen-mother all alone entreat him
To show his grief, let her be round with him,
And I'll be plac'd, so please you, in the ear
185 Of all their conference. If she find him not,
To England send him; or confine him where
Your wisdom best shall think.
　　　King
　　　　　　　　　　　　It shall be so.
Madness in great ones must not unwatch'd go.

　　　　　　　　　　　　　　　　[Exeunt

Act 3 Scene 2
Hamlet lectures the players before their performance—which is interrupted by the king's guilty alarm. Hamlet is summoned to an interview with his mother.

1 *the speech*: Hamlet refers at first to the lines he has just written (see *2, 2, 525–7*), but soon proceeds to comment on the whole art of acting.
3 *your players*: these actors. *had as lief*: would rather.
5 *use all gently*: be moderate in everything you do (like gentlemen).
7 *acquire and beget*: learn and develop.
9 *periwig-pated*: with a wig on his head. Wigs were not generally worn at this time.
10 *groundlings*: those who stood around the stage, in the cheapest area.
12 *inexplicable*: incomprehensible. (Ophelia is puzzled by the players' mime).
13 *Termagant*: a noisy heathen god, represented in medieval drama.
13–14 *out-Herods Herod*: exceeds the biblical tyrant (Matthew 2:16) in his angry raging; Herod was a popular, semi-comic character in the medieval drama.
16–17 *let . . . tutor*: judge for yourselves.

SCENE 2

Enter Hamlet *and three of the* Players

Hamlet
Speak the speech, I pray you, as I pronounced it to you, trippingly on the tongue; but if you mouth it as many of your players do, I had as lief the town-crier spoke my lines. Nor do not saw the air too much with your hand, 5 thus, but use all gently; for in the very torrent, tempest, and, as I may say, whirlwind of your passion, you must acquire and beget a temperance that may give it smoothness. O, it offends me to the soul to hear a robustious periwig-pated fellow tear a passion to 10 tatters, to very rags, to split the ears of the groundlings, who for the most part are capable of nothing but inexplicable dumb-shows and noise. I would have such a fellow whipped for o'erdoing Termagant. It out-Herods Herod. Pray you avoid it.

First Player
15 I warrant your honour.

Hamlet
Be not too tame neither, but let your own discretion be your tutor. Suit the action to the word, the word to the action, with this special observance, that you o'erstep

20 *from . . . playing*: contrary to the aims of drama.
21–2 *hold . . . nature*: show life as it really is.
22 *feature*: appearance.
scorn: that which is scorned.
23 *the very . . . time*: things as they really are at the time.
his: its.
24 *pressure*: shape (as an impression on wax).
come tardy off: done badly.
25 *unskilful*: uneducated.
26 *censure*: criticism.
the which one: the one judicious man.
27 *allowance*: estimation.
29 *profanely*: blasphemously.
30 *Christians*: ordinary decent people.
31 *man*: any human being.
33 *journeymen*: hired labourers.

35 *indifferently*: fairly well.

37 *set down*: written. Comic actors were notorious for their freedom with the author's text.

46 *presently*: at once.

not the modesty of nature. For anything so o'erdone is
20 from the purpose of playing, whose end, both at the
first and now, was and is to hold as 'twere the mirror up
to nature; to show virtue her feature, scorn her own
image, and the very age and body of the time his form
and pressure. Now this overdone or come tardy off,
25 though it makes the unskilful laugh, cannot but make
the judicious grieve, the censure of the which one must
in your allowance o'erweigh a whole theatre of others.
O, there be players that I have seen play—and heard
others praise, and that highly—not to speak it profanely,
30 that neither having th'accent of Christians, nor the gait
of Christian, pagan, nor man, have so strutted and
bellowed that I have thought some of Nature's
journeymen had made men, and not made them well,
they imitated humanity so abominably.

First Player
35 I hope we have reformed that indifferently with us.

Hamlet
O reform it altogether. And let those that play your
clowns speak no more than is set down for them—for
there be of them that will themselves laugh, to set on
some quantity of barren spectators to laugh too, though
40 in the meantime some necessary question of the play be
then to be considered. That's villainous, and shows a
most pitiful ambition in the fool that uses it. Go make
you ready.   [*Exeunt* Players

Enter Polonius, Rosencrantz, *and* Guildenstern

How now, my lord? Will the king hear this piece of
45 work?

Polonius
And the queen too, and that presently.

Hamlet
Bid the players make haste.   [*Exit* Polonius
Will you two help to hasten them?

Rosencrantz
Ay, my lord.   [*Exeunt* Rosencrantz *and* Guildenstern

Hamlet
50 What ho, Horatio!

Enter Horatio

Horatio

Here, sweet lord, at your service.

Hamlet

Horatio, thou art e'en as just a man

As e'er my conversation cop'd withal.

Horatio

O my dear lord.

Hamlet

                              Nay, do not think I flatter,

55 For what advancement may I hope from thee

That no revenue hast but thy good spirits

To feed and clothe thee? Why should the poor be

        flatter'd?

No, let the candied tongue lick absurd pomp,

And crook the pregnant hinges of the knee

60 Where thrift may follow fawning. Dost thou hear?

Since my dear soul was mistress of her choice,

And could of men distinguish her election,

Sh'ath seal'd thee for herself; for thou hast been

As one, in suff'ring all, that suffers nothing,

65 A man that Fortune's buffets and rewards

Hast ta'en with equal thanks; and blest are those

Whose blood and judgement are so well commeddled

That they are not a pipe for Fortune's finger

To sound what stop she please. Give me that man

70 That is not passion's slave, and I will wear him

In my heart's core, ay, in my heart of heart,

As I do thee. Something too much of this.

There is a play tonight before the king:

One scene of it comes near the circumstance

75 Which I have told thee of my father's death.

I prithee, when thou seest that act afoot,

Even with the very comment of thy soul

Observe my uncle. If his occulted guilt

Do not itself unkennel in one speech,

80 It is a damned ghost that we have seen,

And my imaginations are as foul

As Vulcan's stithy. Give him heedful note;

For I mine eyes will rivet to his face,

52 *e'en*: indeed.
     just: well-balanced; Horatio is exactly
     the kind of friend that Hamlet needs.
53 *my . . . withal*: I had any dealings
     with.

58–60 *let . . . fawning*: Shakespeare
     imagines flattery as a grovelling
     spaniel, licking his master's face in
     the hope of reward.
58 *candied*: sweetened, flattering.
59 *pregnant*: ready to bow or kneel.
60 *thrift*: profit.
     fawning: flattery.
61–3 *Since . . . herself*: The Elizabethans
     had a high regard for male friendship,
     considering it a more spiritual
     relationship and a higher good than
     heterosexual love.
61 *mistress . . . choice*: could choose for
     itself; the soul (Latin *anima*) is
     traditionally female.
62 *distinguish her election*: discriminate
     in her selection.
63 *seal'd*: claimed.
64 *one . . . nothing*: someone who shows
     no effect however much he endures.
65 *buffets*: blows.
67 *blood*: passion.
     commeddled: mixed evenly together.
68 *pipe*: The image of the recorder
     (where different notes are produced by
     stopping up the holes) is developed in
     lines 349–56.

70 *wear*: hold.
76 *act*: episode.
77 *very comment*: closest scrutiny.
78 *occulted*: secret.
79 *unkennel*: break from cover.
80 *damned*: damnèd.
82 *Vulcan's stithy*: the underground forge
     of the classical god of blacksmiths.
     heedful note: careful observation.

85 *censure . . . seeming*: assessing his
behaviour.

86 *'a steal aught*: he gets away with
anything.
87 *pay the theft*: answer for it.

88 *be idle*: look as though I am not doing
anything.

90 *fares*: The king means 'does'; but
Hamlet takes up the sense 'eats'.

91 *chameleon's dish*: It was believed that
the chameleon (a lizard that changes
colour to match its background) fed
on air.
92 *promise-crammed*: stuffed full of
promises. We hear Claudius's
promises to Hamlet, in *1, 2, 108–9*,
and later in *3, 2, 325–7*.
capons: chickens which are fattened
for the table.
93 *have nothing with*: don't understand.
94 *are not mine*: don't answer my
question.

101 Hamlet's reply depends largely upon
puns for its wit: 'brute' develops from
'Brutus', who killed Caesar in the
Roman Capitol; and the killing (in
jest) of a calf was part of traditional
mumming entertainment; 'calf' also
means 'fool'.

And after we will both our judgements join
85 In censure of his seeming.
    Horatio
                    Well, my lord.
If 'a steal aught the whilst this play is playing
And scape detecting, I will pay the theft.

Enter Trumpets *and* Kettle-drums *and sound a
flourish*

    Hamlet
They are coming to the play. I must be idle.
Get you a place.

Enter King, Queen, Polonius, Ophelia, Rosencrantz,
Guildenstern, *and other* Lords *attendant, with the*
King's Guard *carrying torches*

    King
90 How fares our cousin Hamlet?
    Hamlet
Excellent, i'faith, of the chameleon's dish. I eat the air,
promise-crammed. You cannot feed capons so.
    King
I have nothing with this answer, Hamlet. These words
are not mine.
    Hamlet
95 No, nor mine now.—[*To* Polonius] My lord, you played
once i'th'university, you say?
    Polonius
That did I, my lord, and was accounted a good actor.
    Hamlet
What did you enact?
    Polonius
I did enact Julius Caesar. I was killed i'th'Capitol. Brutus
100 killed me.
    Hamlet
It was a brute part of him to kill so capital a calf there.
Be the players ready?
    Rosencrantz
Ay, my lord, they stay upon your patience.

Queen
Come hither, my dear Hamlet, sit by me.
Hamlet

105 *attractive*: with magnetic powers.

105 No, good mother, here's metal more attractive.

Turns to Ophelia

Polonius
[*Aside to the* King] O ho! do you mark that?
Hamlet

106–7 *lie in your lap*: The sexual innuendo is clear—although Hamlet denies it in line 110. In the Morality Plays the youth, by lying in the lap of the temptress, puts himself in her power.

[*Lying down at* Ophelia's *feet*] Lady, shall I lie in your lap?
Ophelia
No, my lord.
Hamlet

110 I mean, my head upon your lap.
Ophelia
Ay, my lord.
Hamlet

112 *country matters*: sexual intercourse.

Do you think I meant country matters?
Ophelia
I think nothing, my lord.

116 *Nothing*: i.e. her virginity. See *Hero & Leander* by Christopher Marlowe:
    maids are nothing then,
  Without the sweet society of men.
        (255–6)

120 *your only jig-maker*: the best maker of comedies.

122 *within's*: within this.

123 *twice two months*: Ophelia's remark indicates—perhaps not accurately—that some time has passed between *Acts 1* and *2*.

125 *sables*: luxurious dark furs, traditionally worn in mourning.

127 *by'r lady*: by Our Lady (the Virgin Mary).
128–9 *'a suffer not thinking on*: he will have to put up with being forgotten.
129 *hobby-horse*: This was a traditional feature of the morris dance; Hamlet proceeds to sing (or quote) a line from a popular song.
130s.d. *dumb-show*: mime; such performances sometimes preceded the main action of pre-Shakespearean tragedies for the instruction of audiences unfamiliar with the play—though some spectators, like Claudius here, probably ignored them.

Hamlet
That's a fair thought to lie between maids' legs.
 Ophelia
115 What is, my lord?
 Hamlet
Nothing.
 Ophelia
You are merry, my lord.
 Hamlet
Who, I?
 Ophelia
Ay, my lord.
 Hamlet
120 O God, your only jig-maker. What should a man do but be merry? For look you how cheerfully my mother looks and my father died within's two hours.
 Ophelia
Nay, 'tis twice two months, my lord.
 Hamlet
So long? Nay then, let the devil wear black, for I'll have
125 a suit of sables. O heavens, die two months ago and not forgotten yet! Then there's hope a great man's memory may outlive his life half a year. But by'r lady 'a must build churches then, or else shall 'a suffer not thinking on, with the hobby-horse, whose epitaph is 'For O, for
130 O, the hobby-horse is forgot'.

The trumpets sound. A dumb-show follows

Enter a King *and a* Queen, *the* Queen *embracing him and he her. She kneels, and makes a show of protestation unto him. He takes her up, and declines his head upon her neck. He lies him down upon a bank of flowers. She, seeing him asleep, leaves him. Anon comes in another* Man, *takes off his crown, kisses it, pours poison in the sleeper's ears, and leaves him. The* Queen *returns, finds the* King *dead, makes passionate action. The* Poisoner *with some* Three *or* Four *comes in again. They seem to condole with her. The dead body is carried away. The* Poisoner *woos the* Queen *with gifts. She seems harsh awhile, but in the end accepts his love.* [*Exeunt*

132 *miching malicho*: sneaking mischief.

Ophelia
What means this, my lord?
Hamlet
Marry, this is miching malicho. It means mischief.
Ophelia
Belike this show imports the argument of the play.

133 *argument*: plot.

Enter Prologue

134 *this fellow*: The dumb-shows were often accompanied by a presenter whose function was to explain their meaning to the audiences—although the present one is not very helpful.
135 *counsel*: secrets.

137 *any show*: Ophelia's reaction insists on Hamlet's indecency.

Hamlet
We shall know by this fellow. The players cannot keep
135 counsel: they'll tell all.
Ophelia
Will 'a tell us what this show meant?
Hamlet
Ay, or any show that you will show him. Be not you ashamed to show, he'll not shame to tell you what it means.
Ophelia
140 You are naught, you are naught. I'll mark the play.

140 *naught*: rubbish, offensive.

Prologue
For us and for our tragedy,
Here stooping to your clemency,
We beg your hearing patiently.   [*Exit*
Hamlet
Is this a prologue, or the posy of a ring?
Ophelia
145 'Tis brief, my lord.
Hamlet
As woman's love.

144 *posy for a ring*: motto engraved inside a ring.

Enter the Player King *and* Queen

147 *Phoebus' cart*: the chariot of the sun-god.
148 *Neptune's salt wash*: the sea, ruled by the god Neptune.
Tellus' orbed ground: orbèd; the rounded sphere of the earth, dominion of Tellus.
149 *borrow'd sheen*: brightness reflected from the sun.
151 *Hymen*: the classical god of marriage.
152 *bands*: bonds.

Player King
Full thirty times hath Phoebus' cart gone round
Neptune's salt wash and Tellus' orbed ground,
And thirty dozen moons with borrow'd sheen
150 *About the world have times twelve thirties been*
Since love our hearts and Hymen did our hands
Unite commutual in most sacred bands.

Player Queen

So many journeys may the sun and moon
Make us again count o'er ere love be done.
155 *But woe is me, you are so sick of late,*
So far from cheer and from your former state,
That I distrust you. Yet though I distrust,
Discomfort you, my lord, it nothing must;
For women's fear and love hold quantity,
160 *In neither aught, or in extremity.*
Now what my love is, proof hath made you know,
And as my love is siz'd, my fear is so.
Where love is great, the littlest doubts are fear;
Where little fears grow great, great love grows there.

Player King

165 *Faith, I must leave thee, love, and shortly too:*
My operant powers their functions leave to do;
And thou shalt live in this fair world behind,
Honour'd, belov'd; and haply one as kind
For husband shalt thou—

Player Queen

O confound the rest.
170 *Such love must needs be treason in my breast.*
In second husband let me be accurst;
None wed the second but who kill'd the first.

Hamlet

[*Aside*] That's wormwood.

Player Queen

The instances that second marriage move
175 *Are base respects of thrift, but none of love.*
A second time I kill my husband dead,
When second husband kisses me in bed.

Player King

I do believe you think what now you speak;
But what we do determine, oft we break.
180 *Purpose is but the slave to memory,*
Of violent birth but poor validity,
Which now, the fruit unripe, sticks on the tree,
But fall unshaken when they mellow be.
Most necessary 'tis that we forget
185 *To pay ourselves what to ourselves is debt.*
What to ourselves in passion we propose,

157 *distrust*: am worried about.

159–60 *hold . . . extremity*: are in proportion to each other: there is nothing of either or else too much of both.
162 *siz'd*: measured.

166 *operant powers*: faculties.
leave to do: cease to work.

172 *but who*: except those who.

173 *wormwood*: bitter medicine.

174 *instances*: motives, causes.
175 *base . . . thrift*: mean considerations of worldly advantages.
178 *think*: mean.
180 *Purpose*: what we decide to do. The speech of the Player King is a mere sequence of platitudes, not always readily intelligible; consequently Shakespeare's audience need not deflect the focus of their attention from Claudius.
slave to memory: depends on what we remember.
181 *validity*: staying power.
184–5 'It is inevitable ('necessary') that we should forget to pay the debts that we owe only to ourselves.'
186–7 *What . . . lose*: what we plan to do in the heat of emotion is forgotten when the emotion passes.

The passion ending, doth the purpose lose.
The violence of either grief or joy
Their own enactures with themselves destroy.
190 Where joy most revels grief doth most lament;
Grief joys, joy grieves, on slender accident.
This world is not for aye, nor 'tis not strange
That even our loves should with our fortunes change,
For 'tis a question left us yet to prove,
195 Whether love lead fortune or else fortune love.
The great man down, you mark his favourite flies;
The poor advanc'd makes friends of enemies;
And hitherto doth love on fortune tend:
For who not needs shall never lack a friend,
200 And who in want a hollow friend doth try
Directly seasons him his enemy.
But orderly to end where I begun,
Our wills and fates do so contrary run
That our devices still are overthrown:
205 Our thoughts are ours, their ends none of our own.
So think thou wilt no second husband wed,
But die thy thoughts when thy first lord is dead.

    Player Queen
Nor earth to me give food, nor heaven light,
Sport and repose lock from me day and night,
210 To desperation turn my trust and hope,
An anchor's cheer in prison be my scope,
Each opposite, that blanks the face of joy,
Meet what I would have well and it destroy,
Both here and hence pursue me lasting strife,
215 If, once a widow, ever I be a wife.

    Hamlet
If she should break it now.

    Player King
'Tis deeply sworn. Sweet, leave me here awhile.
My spirits grow dull, and fain I would beguile
The tedious day with sleep.

    [*He sleeps*]

---

191 *slender accident*: the slightest occasion.
192 *aye*: ever.

196 *down*: displaced.
197 *advanc'd*: put in a high position.
198 *hitherto*: up to this point. He is debating the 'question' stated in line 199.
199 *who not needs*: the person who has no need of help.
200 *in want*: in trouble.
  hollow: insincere.
  try: put to the test.
201 *seasons him*: turns him into.
203 *wills and fates*: desires and destinies.
204 *devices*: designs.
  still: always.
205 *ends*: results.

211 *anchor's cheer*: the living of a hermit (anchorite).
  my scope: all that I ask for.
212–13 'May everything turn out opposite to my desires, wiping out my delight.'
214 *here and hence*: in this life and the next.

216 *break*: reveal; 'she' may refer either to the Player Queen or to Gertrude. Hamlet's interjection is timely, breaking into the hypnotic rhythms of the players.

220 *mischance*: ill-fortune.

222 *protest too much*: is making too many promises.

224 *Have . . . argument*: do you know what it is about. Claudius is getting suspicious.
no offence: anything objectionable. Hamlet deliberately mistakes the meaning when he repeats the word.

225 *jest*: pretend, make believe.
offence: crime.

228 *The Mousetrap*: Hamlet invents a new title for his altered version of 'The Murder of Gonzago' (see *2, 2, 523*).
tropically: metaphorically. A 'trope' is a figure of speech.

229 *a murder done in Vienna*: The play does in fact 'image' something of a murder done in Urbino in 1538.

232 *free*: guiltless.

233 *the galled jade*: the horse which has a sore (usually caused by an ill-fitting saddle).
withers: shoulders (of a horse).

234 *nephew to the king*: Hamlet seems to declare himself as a threat to his uncle.

235 *chorus*: In early drama the figure of the Chorus was used to explain or 'interpret' the action of the play.

236–7 'I could supply words ('interpret') for you and your lover if I could see what was going on between you.' Hamlet could act as the 'interpreter' who supplies the words in a puppet-show.

238 *keen*: sharp.

239 *cost you a groaning*: make you cry.
edge: sharp sexual desire.

240 *better, and worse*: more keen, and more objectionable.

Player Queen
        Sleep rock thy brain,
220 *And never come mischance between us twain.*   [*Exit*

Hamlet
Madam, how like you this play?

Queen
The lady doth protest too much, methinks.

Hamlet
O, but she'll keep her word.

King
Have you heard the argument? Is there no offence in't?

Hamlet
225 No, no, they do but jest—poison in jest. No offence i'th'world.

King
What do you call the play?

Hamlet
The Mousetrap—marry, how tropically! This play is the image of a murder done in Vienna—Gonzago is the
230 duke's name, his wife Baptista—you shall see anon. 'Tis a knavish piece of work, but what o' that? Your Majesty, and we that have free souls, it touches us not. Let the galled jade wince, our withers are unwrung.

Enter Lucianus

This is one Lucianus, nephew to the king.

Ophelia
235 You are as good as a chorus, my lord.

Hamlet
I could interpret between you and your love if I could see the puppets dallying.

Ophelia
You are keen, my lord, you are keen.

Hamlet
It would cost you a groaning to take off my edge.

Ophelia
240 Still better, and worse.

Hamlet

So you mis-take your husbands.—Begin, murderer.
Leave thy damnable faces and begin. Come, the
croaking raven doth bellow for revenge.

Lucianus

Thoughts black, hands apt, drugs fit, and time agreeing,
245 *Confederate season, else no creature seeing,*
Thou mixture rank, of midnight weeds collected,
With Hecate's ban thrice blasted, thrice infected,
Thy natural magic and dire property
On wholesome life usurps immediately.

[*Pours the poison in the sleeper's ears*]

Hamlet

250 'A poisons him i'th' garden for his estate. His name's
Gonzago. The story is extant, and written in very choice
Italian. You shall see anon how the murderer gets the
love of Gonzago's wife.

Ophelia

The king rises.

Hamlet

255 What, frighted with false fire?

Queen

How fares my lord?

Polonius

Give o'er the play.

King

Give me some light. Away.

Polonius

Lights, lights, lights.

[*Exeunt all but* Hamlet *and* Horatio

Hamlet

260   Why, let the strucken deer go weep,
   The hart ungalled play;
  For some must watch while some must sleep,
   Thus runs the world away.
Would not this, sir, and a forest of feathers, if the rest of
265 my fortunes turn Turk with me, with Provincial roses

241 *So . . . husbands*: that's not how you women take your husbands (i.e. 'for better, for worse', as in the marriage service).

242-3 *the . . . revenge*: Hamlet, impatient for the next stage in his plot, misquotes lines from an old play, the anonymous *True Tragedy of Richard III*.

244-9 Some critics assume this to be the speech written by Hamlet.

244 *apt*: ready.

245 *Confederate season*: the right time.

246 *midnight weeds collected*: herbs gathered at midnight.

248 *Hecate*: Hecate was the classical goddess of witchcraft, traditionally represented in three forms—hence 'thrice'.
ban: curse.

249 *usurps*: takes possession of.

250 *His name*: i.e. the sleeper's name.

251 *The story is extant*: Hamlet is probably correct—but Shakespeare's source has not been found.

254 *rises*: Court protocol demands that the courtiers should also stand up, and the confusion of the scene is heightened by the calls for 'Lights'. The whole action of the play pivots on this point.

255 *false fire*: the report of guns firing blank cartridges.

260 *strucken*: wounded. Hamlet quotes— or perhaps sings—a popular ballad.

261 *ungalled*: ungallèd.

262 *watch*: keep awake.

263 'That's how it is in life.'

264 *this*: i.e. the success of his theatrical venture.
forest of feathers: mass of feathers in my hat (a fashion favoured by actors).

265 *turn Turk with me*: let me down.
Provincial roses: rosettes from Provins (N. France).

266 *razed*: slashed (as decoration).
cry: company (the word usually
describes a pack of hounds).
268 *share*: A Shareholder was part-owner
of the theatrical company's assets and
took a share of its profits;
Shakespeare was one of the sharers of
his own company, the King's Men.
270–3 *For . . . pajock*: Hamlet improvises
extra lines for his ballad: 'Damon' was
a faithful shepherd friend in pastoral
poetry; 'Jove' = Hamlet's father, of
whom the realm has been deprived
('dismantled'); 'pajock' = a low,
dishonest fellow.

on my razed shoes, get me a fellowship in a cry of
players?
Horatio
Half a share.
Hamlet
A whole one, I.

270   For thou dost know, O Damon dear,
                This realm dismantled was
        Of Jove himself, and now reigns here
                A very, very—pajock.

Horatio
You might have rhymed.
Hamlet
275 O good Horatio, I'll take the ghost's word for a
thousand pound. Didst perceive?
Horatio
Very well, my lord.
Hamlet
Upon the talk of the poisoning?
Horatio
I did very well note him.
Hamlet
280 Ah ha! Come, some music; come, the recorders.
        For if the king like not the comedy,
                Why then, belike he likes it not, perdie.
Come, some music.

281–2 Hamlet parodies lines from a well-
known revenge play, Kyd's *The
Spanish Tragedy*.
282 *perdie*: by God (French *pardieu*).

Enter Rosencrantz *and* Guildenstern

Guildenstern
Good my lord, vouchsafe me a word with you.
Hamlet
285 Sir, a whole history.
Guildenstern
The king, sir—
Hamlet
Ay, sir, what of him?
Guildenstern
Is in his retirement marvellous distempered.
Hamlet
With drink, sir?

288 *marvellous distempered*: extremely
upset. Hamlet deliberately
misunderstands.

290 *choler*: anger. Hamlet again misunderstands, and takes the sense 'bile'.

292 *put . . . purgation*: attempt to treat his disorder (physically, with laxatives or bloodletting; spiritually, by urging confession of his guilt).

294 *put . . . frame*: talk sense.

295 *start . . . affair*: don't change the subject so suddenly.

301 *breed*: kind.
wholesome: sensible.

303 *your pardon*: your permission to depart.

314 *admiration*: astonishment.

316 *closet*: private chamber. Rosencrantz and Guildenstern activate the plot proposed by Polonius in *Act 3, Scene 1*, 180ff.

Guildenstern

290 No, my lord, with choler.

Hamlet

Your wisdom should show itself more richer to signify this to the doctor, for for me to put him to his purgation would perhaps plunge him into more choler.

Guildenstern

Good my lord, put your discourse into some frame, and
295 start not so wildly from my affair.

Hamlet

I am tame, sir. Pronounce.

Guildenstern

The queen your mother, in most great affliction of spirit, hath sent me to you.

Hamlet

You are welcome.

Guildenstern

300 Nay, good my lord, this courtesy is not of the right breed. If it shall please you to make me a wholesome answer, I will do your mother's commandment; if not, your pardon and my return shall be the end of my business.

Hamlet

305 Sir, I cannot.

Rosencrantz

What, my lord?

Hamlet

Make you a wholesome answer. My wit's diseased. But sir, such answer as I can make, you shall command—or rather, as you say, my mother. Therefore no more, but to
310 the matter. My mother, you say—

Rosencrantz

Then thus she says: your behaviour hath struck her into amazement and admiration.

Hamlet

O wonderful son, that can so stonish a mother! But is there no sequel at the heels of this mother's admiration?
315 Impart.

Rosencrantz

She desires to speak with you in her closet ere you go to bed.

319 *trade*: business; Hamlet is
contemptuous.

Hamlet
We shall obey, were she ten times our mother.
Have you any further trade with us?
Rosencrantz
320 My lord, you once did love me.
Hamlet
And do still, by these pickers and stealers.
Rosencrantz
Good my lord, what is your cause of distemper? You do
surely bar the door upon your own liberty if you deny
your griefs to your friend.
Hamlet
325 Sir, I lack advancement.
Rosencrantz
How can that be, when you have the voice of the king
himself for your succession in Denmark?
Hamlet
Ay, sir, but while the grass grows—the proverb is
something musty.

Enter the Players *with recorders*

330 O, the recorders. Let me see one.—To withdraw with
you, why do you go about to recover the wind of me, as
if you would drive me into a toil?
Guildenstern
O my lord, if my duty be too bold, my love is too
unmannerly.
Hamlet
335 I do not well understand that. Will you play upon this
pipe?
Guildenstern
My lord, I cannot.
Hamlet
I pray you.
Guildenstern
Believe me, I cannot.
Hamlet
340 I do beseech you.
Guildenstern
I know no touch of it, my lord.

321 *pickers and stealers*: i.e. hands. The
Church catechism teaches the duty 'to
keep (one's) hands from picking and
stealing'.
323 *bar . . . liberty*: shut yourself up in
your own trouble. Rosencrantz's
advice might also be a threat.
deny: refuse to confide.
325 *advancement*: promotion.

326 *voice*: support (see *1, 2, 109*).

328 *the proverb*: i.e. 'while the grass
grows, the horse starves'.
329 *something musty*: rather stale.

329s.d. *Players*: actors.

330 *withdraw*: have a private word (with
Rosencrantz and Guildenstern).
331–2 'Why do you go such a roundabout
way, like hunters who get upwind in
order to drive their quarry into a snare
('toil').'
333–4 Guildenstern's smoothly evasive
answer is not easily understandable;
he seems to be saying that his great
love for Hamlet is responsible for any
apparent discourtesy.
335 *that*: i.e. how love can be
'unmannerly'.

341 *I know . . . it*: I don't know how to play
it.

342 *ventages*: stops, air-holes.

Hamlet

It is as easy as lying. Govern these ventages with your fingers and thumb, give it breath with your mouth, and it will discourse most eloquent music. Look you, these
345 are the stops.

Guildenstern

But these cannot I command to any utterance of harmony. I have not the skill.

Hamlet

Why, look you now, how unworthy a thing you make of me. You would play upon me, you would seem to know
350 my stops, you would pluck out the heart of my mystery, you would sound me from my lowest note to the top of my compass; and there is much music, excellent voice, in this little organ, yet cannot you make it speak. 'Sblood, do you think I am easier to be played on than a
355 pipe? Call me what instrument you will, though you fret me, you cannot play upon me.

Enter Polonius

God bless you, sir.

Polonius

My lord, the queen would speak with you, and presently.

Hamlet

360 Do you see yonder cloud that's almost in shape of a camel?

Polonius

By th' mass and 'tis—like a camel indeed.

Hamlet

Methinks it is like a weasel.

Polonius

It is backed like a weasel.

Hamlet

365 Or like a whale.

Polonius

Very like a whale.

351 *sound*: fathom (with a pun on 'make sound').
352 *compass*: range.
353 *organ*: instrument.

355 *fret*: irritate: 'frets' are also the finger-positions on some stringed instruments.

359 *presently*: immediately.

368 *to the top of my bent*: as far as I can go. The 'bent' is the full stretch of a bow.

372 *witching time*: the time when witches appear.
373 *yawn*: gape. The graves open for the ghosts to walk out.
374 *drink hot blood*: i.e. in diabolic parody of the action of the mass.
377 *nature*: natural feeling.
378 *Nero*: the ancient Roman emperor who killed his mother after she had poisoned her husband.
firm: steadfast.
380 *speak daggers*: wound her with words.
381 *My . . . hypocrites*: let my voice not speak my mind.
382 *How . . . shent*: she may be reproached ('shent') by my words.
383 *seals*: authorization (like the seals on a legal document).

Act 3 Scene 3
The king plans to send Hamlet away from Denmark, and tries to ease his guilty conscience in prayer, presenting Hamlet with an unexpected opportunity to avenge his father.

3 *dispatch*: deal with.
4 *shall along*: shall go along.
5 *terms of our estate*: my position (as king).

7 *brows*: threatening looks.
provide: equip.

9 *bodies*: i.e. the lives of the king's subjects.

Hamlet
Then I will come to my mother by and by.— [*Aside*]
They fool me to the top of my bent.—I will come by and by.
Polonius
370 I will say so.   [*Exit*
Hamlet
'By and by' is easily said.—Leave me, friends.
                                          [*Exeunt all but* Hamlet
'Tis now the very witching time of night,
When churchyards yawn and hell itself breathes out
Contagion to this world. Now could I drink hot blood,
375 And do such bitter business as the day
Would quake to look on. Soft, now to my mother.
O heart, lose not thy nature. Let not ever
The soul of Nero enter this firm bosom;
Let me be cruel, not unnatural.
380 I will speak daggers to her, but use none.
My tongue and soul in this be hypocrites:
How in my words somever she be shent,
To give them seals never my soul consent.   [*Exit*

SCENE 3

Enter King, Rosencrantz, *and* Guildenstern

King
I like him not, nor stands it safe with us
To let his madness range. Therefore prepare you.
I your commission will forthwith dispatch,
And he to England shall along with you.
5 The terms of our estate may not endure
Hazard so near us as doth hourly grow
Out of his brows.
Guildenstern
                              We will ourselves provide.
Most holy and religious fear it is
To keep those many many bodies safe
10 That live and feed upon your Majesty.

Rosencrantz

The single and peculiar life is bound
With all the strength and armour of the mind
To keep itself from noyance; but much more
That spirit upon whose weal depends and rests

15 The lives of many. The cess of majesty
Dies not alone, but like a gulf doth draw
What's near it with it. Or it is a massy wheel
Fix'd on the summit of the highest mount,
To whose huge spokes ten thousand lesser things

20 Are mortis'd and adjoin'd, which when it falls,
Each small annexment, petty consequence,
Attends the boist'rous ruin. Never alone
Did the king sigh, but with a general groan.

King

Arm you, I pray you, to this speedy voyage,

25 For we will fetters put about this fear
Which now goes too free-footed.

Rosencrantz

We will haste us.

[*Exeunt* Rosencrantz *and* Guildenstern

Enter Polonius

Polonius

My lord, he's going to his mother's closet.
Behind the arras I'll convey myself
To hear the process. I'll warrant she'll tax him home,

30 And as you said—and wisely was it said—
'Tis meet that some more audience than a mother,
Since nature makes them partial, should o'erhear
The speech of vantage. Fare you well, my liege.
I'll call upon you ere you go to bed,

35 And tell you what I know.

King

Thanks, dear my lord.

[*Exit* Polonius

O, my offence is rank, it smells to heaven;
It hath the primal eldest curse upon't—
A brother's murder. Pray can I not,
Though inclination be as sharp as will,

11–23 *The single . . . groan*: The speech of Rosencrantz is characteristically pompous and imprecise in meaning.

13 *noyance*: harm.

14 *weal*: well-being.

15 *cess of majesty*: cessation of rule (when the monarch dies or is dethroned).

16 *gulf*: whirlpool.

17 *massy wheel*: There are many pictures which show the monarch at the top of Fortune's wheel.

19 *lesser things*: e.g. courtiers and statesmen.

20 *mortis'd and adjoin'd*: closely joined (the image is from carpentry).

21 *annexment*: thing which is joined on.

22 *Attends the boist'rous ruin*: accompanies the major disaster.

24 'Get ready to travel quickly.'

25 *this fear*: this cause of fear.

28 *convey*: secrete, hide.

29 *process*: what goes on.
tax him home: speak plainly to him.

30 *as you said*: the suggestion in fact came from Polonius himself (see 3, 1, 184–5).

31 *meet*: suitable.

33 *of vantage*: in addition; *or* from a good (concealed) position.

36 *rank*: rotten; at last Claudius reveals his thoughts to the audience.

37 *primal eldest curse*: the curse of Cain, who became the world's first murderer by killing his brother (Genesis, 4:11–12).

39 *inclination*: natural desire.
will: determination.

41 *double business bound*: with two jobs
to do.
42 *in pause . . . begin*: still wondering
which to do first.
43 *cursed*: cursèd.

46 *wash . . . snow*: Compare 'though your
sins be scarlet, they shall be as white
as snow' (Isaiah 1:18).
47 *to confront . . . offence*: meet sin face
to face.
48 *twofold force*: Claudius remembers the
petitions of the Lord's prayer: 'Lead us
not into temptation' *and* 'deliver us
from evil'—*both* 'prevent us from
sinning', *and* 'forgive us for the wrong
we have already done'.
49 *forestalled*: forestallèd.
51 *My fault is past*: Claudius's sin has
already been committed—he must
pray for forgiveness now.
56 *retain th'offence*: keep the results of
the sin.
57 *currents*: courses of events.
58 *gilded*: a) touched by gold; b) guilty.

61 *There*: i.e. 'above'—in heaven.
shuffling: tricky dealing.
61–2 *lies In his true nature*: is seen for
what it really is.
62–4 *we ourselves . . . evidence*: when we
are confronted with our sins, we are
compelled to give evidence against
ourselves.
64 *What rests*: what's the alternative.
65 *can*: can do.
68 *limed*: limèd; trapped. Birds were
caught by liming the branches where
they perched.
69 *engag'd*: entangled.
Make assay: come to my aid.
70 *strings of steel*: hardened (because of
what he has done).

40 My stronger guilt defeats my strong intent,
And, like a man to double business bound,
I stand in pause where I shall first begin,
And both neglect. What if this cursed hand
Were thicker than itself with brother's blood,
45 Is there not rain enough in the sweet heavens
To wash it white as snow? Whereto serves mercy
But to confront the visage of offence?
And what's in prayer but this twofold force,
To be forestalled ere we come to fall
50 Or pardon'd being down? Then I'll look up.
My fault is past—but O, what form of prayer
Can serve my turn? 'Forgive me my foul murder?'
That cannot be, since I am still possess'd
Of those effects for which I did the murder—
55 My crown, mine own ambition, and my queen.
May one be pardon'd and retain th'offence?
In the corrupted currents of this world
Offence's gilded hand may shove by justice,
And oft 'tis seen the wicked prize itself
60 Buys out the law. But 'tis not so above:
There is no shuffling, there the action lies
In his true nature, and we ourselves compell'd
Even to the teeth and forehead of our faults
To give in evidence. What then? What rests?
65 Try what repentance can. What can it not?
Yet what can it, when one cannot repent?
O wretched state! O bosom black as death!
O limed soul, that struggling to be free
Art more engag'd! Help, angels! Make assay.
70 Bow, stubborn knees; and heart with strings of steel,
Be soft as sinews of the new-born babe.
All may be well.

He kneels

Enter Hamlet

Hamlet

Now might I do it pat, now 'a is a-praying.
And now I'll do't.

Draws his sword

         And so 'a goes to heaven;

75 And so am I reveng'd. That would be scann'd:
A villain kills my father, and for that
I, his sole son, do this same villain send
To heaven.
Why, this is hire and salary, not revenge.

80 'A took my father grossly, full of bread,
With all his crimes broad blown, as flush as May;
And how his audit stands who knows save heaven?
But in our circumstance and course of thought
'Tis heavy with him. And am I then reveng'd,

85 To take him in the purging of his soul,
When he is fit and season'd for his passage?
No.
Up, sword, and know thou a more horrid hent:
When he is drunk asleep, or in his rage,

90 Or in th'incestuous pleasure of his bed,
At game a-swearing, or about some act
That has no relish of salvation in't,
Then trip him, that his heels may kick at heaven
And that his soul may be as damn'd and black

95 As hell, whereto it goes. My mother stays.
This physic but prolongs thy sickly days.   [*Exit*
    King
My words fly up, my thoughts remain below.
Words without thoughts never to heaven go.   [*Exit*

73 *pat*: smartly.

74 *'a goes to heaven*: Hamlet assumes that his uncle, being able to pray, must be in a state of grace and will not suffer like his father's ghost.
75 *scann'd*: interpreted.
77 *sole*: only.

79 *hire and salary*: i.e. payment (not punishment) for the deed.
80 *grossly*: unprepared for death; compare *1*, 5, 77.
81 *crimes*: sins.
broad blown: in full blossom.
flush: full of life.
82 *audit*: reckoning.
83 *in . . . thought*: in the way that we on earth think about it.
84 *'Tis heavy with him*: things are bad for him.
85 *him*: i.e. Claudius.
86 *fit and season'd*: thoroughly prepared.
passage: journey.
88 *Up*: away.
know . . . hent: wait until you find a more fearful opportunity.
91 *game*: gambling.
92 *relish*: taste.
93 *heels . . . heaven*: i.e. fall headlong into hell.
95 *stays*: is waiting.
96 *physic*: i.e. the praying.

'And so 'a goes to heaven; And so am I reveng'd, (*3*, 3, 74–5), Roger Rees as Hamlet and Brian Blessed as Claudius, Royal Shakespeare Company, 1984.

Act 3 Scene 4
Polonius hides behind the arras to overhear
Hamlet's conversation with his mother—
and pays with his life. Hamlet confronts
Gertrude with her guilt, and only the Ghost
can put an end to his tirade of abuse.

1 *straight*: immediately.
  lay home to him: speak firmly to him
  (see 'tax him home' *3*, 3, 29).
2 *pranks*: rude behaviour.
  broad: outrageous.
4 *silence me*: hide myself in silence.
5 *be round*: speak plainly.
  war'nt: promise (warrant).

SCENE 4

Enter Queen *and* Polonius

Polonius
'A will come straight. Look you lay home to him,
Tell him his pranks have been too broad to bear with
And that your Grace hath screen'd and stood between
Much heat and him. I'll silence me even here.
5 Pray you be round.
    Queen
                      I'll war'nt you, fear me not.
Withdraw, I hear him coming.

Polonius hides behind the arras

Enter Hamlet

Hamlet
Now, mother, what's the matter?
    Queen
Hamlet, thou hast thy father much offended.
    Hamlet
Mother, you have my father much offended.
    Queen
10 Come, come, you answer with an idle tongue.
    Hamlet
Go, go, you question with a wicked tongue.
    Queen
Why, how now, Hamlet?
    Hamlet
                    What's the matter now?
    Queen
Have you forgot me?
    Hamlet
                    No, by the rood, not so.
You are the queen, your husband's brother's wife,
15 And, would it were not so, you are my mother.
    Queen
Nay, then I'll set those to you that can speak.

13 *forgot me*: forgotten who I am.
  by the rood: by the cross on which
  Christ was crucified.

14 *husband's brother's wife*: Such a
  marriage was forbidden by the church
  laws of that time as stated in *The
  Book of Common Prayer*.
15 *would*: I wish.

Hamlet
Come, come, and sit you down, you shall not budge.
You go not till I set you up a glass
Where you may see the inmost part of you.
    Queen
20 What wilt thou do? Thou wilt not murder me?
Help, ho!
    Polonius
[*Behind the arras*] What ho! Help!
    Hamlet
How now? A rat! Dead for a ducat, dead.

Thrusts his rapier through the arras

    Polonius
[*Behind*] O, I am slain.
    Queen
25 O me, what hast thou done?
    Hamlet
                           Nay, I know not.
Is it the king?

Lifts up the arras and discovers Polonius, *dead*

    Queen
O what a rash and bloody deed is this!
    Hamlet
A bloody deed. Almost as bad, good mother,
As kill a king and marry with his brother.
    Queen
30 As kill a king?
    Hamlet
                  Ay, lady, it was my word.—
Thou wretched, rash, intruding fool, farewell.
I took thee for thy better. Take thy fortune:
Thou find'st to be too busy is some danger.—
Leave wringing of your hands. Peace, sit you down,
35 And let me wring your heart; for so I shall
If it be made of penetrable stuff,
If damned custom have not braz'd it so,
That it be proof and bulwark against sense.

23 *A rat*: rats are well-known for drawing attention to themselves by squeaking. *Dead for a ducat*: I'll bet a ducat I've killed it.

29 *kill a king*: Gertrude's reaction declares her innocence of the murder.

32 *thy better*: i.e. Claudius.
33 *too busy*: interfering.

37 *custom*: habit. *braz'd*: brazened—hardened like brass.
38 *proof*: impenetrable (like armour). *sense*: feeling.

Queen
What have I done, that thou dar'st wag thy tongue
40 In noise so rude against me?
　　Hamlet
　　　　　　　　　　Such an act
That blurs the grace and blush of modesty,
Call virtue hypocrite, takes off the rose
From the fair forehead of an innocent love
And sets a blister there, makes marriage vows
45 As false as dicers' oaths—O, such a deed
As from the body of contraction plucks
The very soul, and sweet religion makes
A rhapsody of words. Heaven's face does glow
O'er this solidity and compound mass
50 With tristful visage, as against the doom,
Is thought-sick at the act.
　　Queen
　　　　　　　　　Ay me, what act
That roars so loud and thunders in the index?
　　Hamlet
Look here upon this picture, and on this,
The counterfeit presentment of two brothers.
55 See what a grace was seated on this brow,
Hyperion's curls, the front of Jove himself,
An eye like Mars to threaten and command,
A station like the herald Mercury
New-lighted on a heaven-kissing hill,
60 A combination and a form indeed
Where every god did seem to set his seal
To give the world assurance of a man.
This was your husband. Look you now what follows.
Here is your husband, like a mildew'd ear
65 Blasting his wholesome brother. Have you eyes?
Could you on this fair mountain leave to feed
And batten on this moor? Ha, have you eyes?
You cannot call it love; for at your age
The heyday in the blood is tame, it's humble,
70 And waits upon the judgement, and what judgement
Would step from this to this? Sense sure you have,
Else could you not have motion; but sure that sense
Is apoplex'd, for madness would not err

---

42 *rose*: perfection.

44 *blister*: brand of a whore.
45 *dicers*: gamblers.
46-7 *from . . . soul*: takes the spiritual heart out of a marriage.
48 *rhapsody of words*: mere verbal outpouring.
48-51 *Heaven's . . . act*: the sky blushes gloomily over the entire world ('this . . . mass') as if just before doomsday, and is sick at the thought of what has been done; Hamlet's vision almost cracks his syntax.
52 *index*: opening, table of contents.

53 *Look . . . this*: Hamlet may produce two miniatures, or point to portraits on the wall.

56-9 *Hyperion . . . hill*: Hamlet gives his father all the attributes of the classical gods.
56 *Hyperion*: god of the sun.
　　front of Jove: Jupiter's forehead.
58-9 *station . . . hill*: stance like that of the winged messenger of the gods alighting on some hill-top.
61 *set his seal*: stamp his likeness.

64 *mildew'd ear*: mouldy ear of corn.
65 *Blasting*: infecting.

67 *batten*: gorge yourself.

69 *heyday . . . blood*: passionate sexual period.
70 *waits upon*: is controlled by.
71-2 *Sense . . . motion*: Aristotle taught that all beings capable of perception through some sense must have some power of movement.
73 *apoplex'd*: paralysed.

'Look here upon this picture, and on this' (*3*, 4, 53), Marty Cruikshank as Gertrude and Samuel West as Hamlet, Royal Shakespeare Company, 2001.

74 *sense . . . thrall'd*: reason was never so captivated by passion.

76 *difference*: distinction.

79 *sans all*: without any of the other senses.

81 *mope*: be unaware.

82 *Rebellious hell*: hellish sexual rebellion.

83 *mutine*: mutiny.
matron: mature woman.

84–5 *wax . . . fire*: a candle's wax melting in the flame it feeds.

86 *compulsive ardour*: irresistible passion.
gives the charge: makes the attack.

87 *frost*: i.e. the cooler desires of the 'matron'.

88 *panders will*: is put to the service of passion.

90 *grained*: grainèd; ingrained.

91 *will . . . tinct*: will not lose their colour (e.g. when washed).

92 *enseamed*: enseamèd; greasy.

93 *Stew'd*: steeped, soaked. Hamlet's disgust comes to its climax—characteristically, with a pun ('stews' = brothels).

95 *like daggers*: i.e. just as Hamlet promised at 3, 2, 380.

97 *tithe*: tenth part.

98 *precedent lord*: previous husband.
vice: parody; the vice in the Morality Plays was a comic villain.

99 *cutpurse*: thief.

103 *of shreds and patches*: made of bits and pieces.

Nor sense to ecstasy was ne'er so thrall'd
75 But it reserv'd some quantity of choice
To serve in such a difference. What devil was't
That thus hath cozen'd you at hoodman-blind?
Eyes without feeling, feeling without sight,
Ears without hands or eyes, smelling sans all,
80 Or but a sickly part of one true sense
Could not so mope. O shame, where is thy blush?
Rebellious hell,
If thou canst mutine in a matron's bones,
To flaming youth let virtue be as wax
85 And melt in her own fire; proclaim no shame
When the compulsive ardour gives the charge,
Since frost itself as actively doth burn
And reason panders will.

Queen

O Hamlet, speak no more.
Thou turn'st my eyes into my very soul,
90 And there I see such black and grained spots
As will not leave their tinct.

Hamlet

Nay, but to live
In the rank sweat of an enseamed bed,
Stew'd in corruption, honeying and making love
Over the nasty sty!

Queen

O speak to me no more.
95 These words like daggers enter in my ears.
No more, sweet Hamlet.

Hamlet

A murderer and a villain,
A slave that is not twentieth part the tithe
Of your precedent lord, a vice of kings,
A cutpurse of the empire and the rule,
100 That from a shelf the precious diadem stole
And put it in his pocket—

Queen

No more.

Hamlet

A king of shreds and patches—

'Look you how pale he glares.' (3, 4, 125), Sara Kestelman as Gertrude, Simon Russell Beale as Hamlet, and Sylvester Morand as the Ghost, Royal National Theatre, 2000.

Enter Ghost

Save me and hover o'er me with your wings,
105 You heavenly guards! What would your gracious
    figure?

Queen

Alas, he's mad.

Hamlet

Do you not come your tardy son to chide,
That, laps'd in time and passion, lets go by
Th'important acting of your dread command?
110 O say.

Ghost

    Do not forget. This visitation
Is but to whet thy almost blunted purpose.
But look, amazement on thy mother sits.
O step between her and her fighting soul.
Conceit in weakest bodies strongest works.
115 Speak to her, Hamlet.

Hamlet

How is it with you, lady?

Queen

              Alas, how is't with you,
That you do bend your eye on vacancy,
And with th'incorporal air do hold discourse?
Forth at your eyes your spirits wildly peep,
120 And, as the sleeping soldiers in th'alarm,
Your bedded hair, like life in excrements,
Start up and stand an end. O gentle son,
Upon the heat and flame of thy distemper
Sprinkle cool patience. Where do you look?

Hamlet

125 On him, on him. Look you how pale he glares.
His form and cause conjoin'd, preaching to stones,
Would make them capable.—Do not look upon me,
Lest with this piteous action you convert
My stern effects. Then what I have to do
130 Will want true colour—tears perchance for blood.

Queen

To whom do you speak this?

---

107 *chide*: reproach.
108 *laps'd . . . passion*: having lost time and vengeful impulse.
109 *important*: urgent.

110 *Do not forget*: Once again (see *1, 5, 91*) the Ghost stirs Hamlet's memory.
111 *whet*: sharpen (like a knife).
112 *amazement*: bewilderment. Gertrude is unaware of the Ghost's presence.
114 *Conceit*: imagination.

117 *bend your eye*: fix your gaze.
118 *incorporal*: empty.
119 *Forth . . . peep*: your eyes stare wildly.
120 *in th'alarm*: when the alarm is sounded.
121 *excrements*: outgrowths (which have no life in them).
122 *an*: on.

126 *His form and cause*: his appearance and the reason he has for appearing. *conjoin'd*: joined together.
127 *capable*: sensible, able to respond.
128 *action*: movement.
129 *effects*: purposes.
130 *want true colour*: not look right—be done for the wrong reason.
    tears . . . blood: perhaps tears will be shed rather than blood.

Hamlet
Do you see nothing there?
    Queen
Nothing at all; yet all that is I see.
    Hamlet
Nor did you nothing hear?
    Queen
135 No, nothing but ourselves.
    Hamlet
Why, look you there, look how it steals away.
My father, in his habit as he liv'd!
Look where he goes even now out at the portal.
                    [*Exit* Ghost
    Queen
This is the very coinage of your brain.
140 This bodiless creation ecstasy
Is very cunning in.
    Hamlet
My pulse as yours doth temperately keep time,
And makes as healthful music. It is not madness
That I have utter'd. Bring me to the test,
145 And I the matter will re-word, which madness
Would gambol from. Mother, for love of grace,
Lay not that flattering unction to your soul,
That not your trespass but my madness speaks.
It will but skin and film the ulcerous place,
150 Whiles rank corruption, mining all within,
Infects unseen. Confess yourself to heaven,
Repent what's past, avoid what is to come;
And do not spread the compost on the weeds
To make them ranker. Forgive me this my virtue;
155 For in the fatness of these pursy times
Virtue itself of vice must pardon beg,
Yea, curb and woo for leave to do him good.
    Queen
O Hamlet, thou hast cleft my heart in twain.
    Hamlet
O throw away the worser part of it
160 And live the purer with the other half.
Good night. But go not to my uncle's bed.
Assume a virtue if you have it not.

137 *in his habit as he liv'd*: wearing the clothes he wore when alive; Q1, perhaps reflecting stage practice, directs the Ghost to enter 'in his night gown' (= dressing gown).
138 *portal*: doorway.
139 *coinage*: invention.
140 *bodiless creation*: making something out of nothing.
    ecstasy: madness.
141 *cunning in*: clever at.
142 *temperately keep time*: beats regularly.
143 *makes . . . music*: sounds as healthy.

145 *re-word*: repeat.
146 *gambol from*: shy away from, refuse to do.
147 *Lay*: apply.
    flattering unction: soothing ointment.
149 *skin and film*: put a skin over.

152 *what is to come*: future opportunities of sin.

154 *ranker*: grow even more. Hamlet develops the 'unweeded garden' metaphor from *1, 2, 135–7*.
155 *fatness*: grossness.
    pursy: (morally) flabby.
157 *curb*: bow.
    him: i.e. vice.

162 *Assume*: pretend.

163–4 *all . . . evil*: destroys all
understanding of the evil of bad
habits.

166 *gives . . . livery*: creates a habit (like a
servant's uniform).
167 *aptly*: readily.
168 *shall*: i.e. must necessarily.

170 *use*: habitual practice.
stamp of nature: inborn
characteristics.
171 *[lodge]*: Modern editors must supply
some word meaning 'entertain
hospitably' to balance 'or throw him
out'.
173–4 *when . . . you*: when you ask for
God's blessing, I (like an obedient
son) will ask for yours.
174 *lord*: i.e. Polonius. Hamlet appears to
believe that the murder of Polonius
was ordained by Providence.
177 *their scourge and minister*: i.e. the
instrument of divine power.
178 *bestow*: dispose of.
answer well: atone for, justify.
181 *This*: i.e. the death of Polonius.
remains behind: is still to come.

184 *bloat*: flabby.
185 *wanton*: sexily.
186 *a pair . . . kisses*: a few filthy kisses.
187 *paddling in*: pawing over.
188 *ravel . . . out*: disentangle everything
for him.

190 *in craft*: in cunning.
190–8 *'Twere good . . . down*: Hamlet,
speaking ironically, warns his mother
not to reveal his confidences.
192 *paddock . . . gib*: toad, bat, or tomcat
(the familiar spirits of witchcraft).
193 *dear concernings*: matters intimately
concerning him.
195 *Unpeg*: open up.
196–8 *like . . . down*: This allusion has not
been traced: presumably the ape
hoped to imitate the birds in flying
when they had been confined in the
basket.
197 *try conclusions*: test his theories.

That monster, custom, who all sense doth eat
Of habits evil, is angel yet in this,
165 That to the use of actions fair and good
He likewise gives a frock or livery
That aptly is put on. Refrain tonight,
And that shall lend a kind of easiness
To the next abstinence, the next more easy;
170 For use almost can change the stamp of nature,
And either [lodge] the devil or throw him out
With wondrous potency. Once more, good night,
And when you are desirous to be blest,
I'll blessing beg of you. For this same lord
175 I do repent; but heaven hath pleas'd it so,
To punish me with this and this with me,
That I must be their scourge and minister.
I will bestow him, and will answer well
The death I gave him. So, again, good night.
180 I must be cruel only to be kind.
This bad begins, and worse remains behind.
One word more, good lady.
   Queen
               What shall I do?
   Hamlet
Not this, by no means, that I bid you do:
Let the bloat king tempt you again to bed,
185 Pinch wanton on your cheek, call you his mouse,
And let him, for a pair of reechy kisses,
Or paddling in your neck with his damn'd fingers,
Make you to ravel all this matter out
That I essentially am not in madness,
190 But mad in craft. 'Twere good you let him know,
For who that's but a queen, fair, sober, wise,
Would from a paddock, from a bat, a gib,
Such dear concernings hide? Who would do so?
No, in despite of sense and secrecy,
195 Unpeg the basket on the house's top,
Let the birds fly, and like the famous ape,
To try conclusions, in the basket creep,
And break your own neck down.

Queen
Be thou assur'd, if words be made of breath,
200 And breath of life, I have no life to breathe
What thou hast said to me.
    Hamlet
I must to England, you know that?
    Queen
                                     Alack,
I had forgot. 'Tis so concluded on.
    Hamlet
There's letters seal'd, and my two schoolfellows,
205 Whom I will trust as I will adders fang'd—
They bear the mandate, they must sweep my way
And marshal me to knavery. Let it work;
For 'tis the sport to have the enginer
Hoist with his own petard, and't shall go hard
210 But I will delve one yard below their mines
And blow them at the moon. O, 'tis most sweet
When in one line two crafts directly meet.
This man shall set me packing.
I'll lug the guts into the neighbour room.
215 Mother, good night indeed. This counsellor
Is now most still, most secret, and most grave,
Who was in life a foolish prating knave.
Come, sir, to draw toward an end with you.
Good night, mother.   [*Exit lugging in* Polonius

The Queen *remains*

203 *concluded*: decided.

205 *fang'd*: with venomous fangs.
206 *sweep my way*: escort me.
207 *marshal . . . knavery*: lead me into some trap.
208 *enginer*: maker of military 'engines'.
209 *Hoist . . . petard*: blown up with his own bomb.
    and . . . hard: unless I'm very unlucky.
210 *delve . . . mines*: dig a countermine a whole yard deeper.
212 'When two plots meet head-on.'
213 *set me packing*: start off my plotting.
214 *lug*: Perhaps Hamlet drags Polonius by the heels.
    neighbour: adjoining.
215 *indeed*: for the last time.
217 *prating*: chattering; the couplet forms an epitaph for Polonius.
218 *draw toward an end*: finish my business.

ACT 4

Claudius, expecting to hear about the
outcome of his plot, learns instead of the
death of Polonius.

SCENE 1

Enter King, *with* Rosencrantz *and* Guildenstern, *to*
the Queen

  King
There's matter in these sighs, these profound heaves,
You must translate. 'Tis fit we understand them.
Where is your son?
  Queen
Bestow this place on us a little while.
               [*Exeunt* Rosencrantz *and* Guildenstern
5 Ah, mine own lord, what have I seen tonight!
  King
What, Gertrude, how does Hamlet?
  Queen
Mad as the sea and wind when both contend
Which is the mightier. In his lawless fit,
Behind the arras hearing something stir,
10 Whips out his rapier, cries 'A rat, a rat',
And in this brainish apprehension kills
The unseen good old man.
  King
             O heavy deed!
It had been so with us had we been there.
His liberty is full of threats to all—
15 To you yourself, to us, to everyone.
Alas, how shall this bloody deed be answer'd?
It will be laid to us, whose providence
Should have kept short, restrain'd, and out of haunt
This mad young man. But so much was our love,
20 We would not understand what was most fit,
But like the owner of a foul disease,
To keep it from divulging, let it feed
Even on the pith of life. Where is he gone?

1 *matter in*: a reason for.
  heaves: sighs.
2 *translate*: put it into words.

4 *Bestow this place*: leave us alone. The
brief appearance of Rosencrantz and
Guildenstern is a useful reminder of
their part in the king's plot.

8 *lawless*: uncontrollable.

11 *brainish apprehension*: mental
seizure.

13 *had been*: would have been.
  us: The king (using the royal plural)
thinks first of his own safety.

16 *answer'd*: explained.

18 *short*: under control.
  haunt: circulation.

22 *divulging*: being known.
23 *pith*: essential substance.

25–7 *O'er . . . done*: Gertrude invents a
story to demonstrate the truth of
Hamlet's madness.
like . . . pure: as true gold shines out
in a mine of base metals.

29 *The . . . touch*: at early daybreak;
Claudius reminds us that it is still late
at night.

32 *countenance*: accept responsibility for.

33 *join . . . aid*: get some more
assistance.

38–44 *we'll . . . air*: Claudius will spread
about his own account of the affair, so
that no suspicious rumour can
implicate him.
40 *untimely*: unfortunately.
[So . . . slander]: Half a line is
missing from this speech.
41 *o'er . . . diameter*: across the world.
42–3 *As . . . shot*: as directly as a cannon
fires its deadly shot at the target.
44 *woundless*: invulnerable.

Queen
To draw apart the body he hath kill'd,
25 O'er whom—his very madness, like some ore
Among a mineral of metals base,
Shows itself pure—'a weeps for what is done.
  King
O Gertrude, come away.
The sun no sooner shall the mountains touch
30 But we will ship him hence; and this vile deed
We must with all our majesty and skill
Both countenance and excuse.—Ho, Guildenstern!

Enter Rosencrantz *and* Guildenstern

Friends, both, go join you with some further aid.
Hamlet in madness hath Polonius slain,
35 And from his mother's closet hath he dragg'd him.
Go seek him out—speak fair—and bring the body
Into the chapel. I pray you haste in this.
          [Exeunt Rosencrantz *and* Guildenstern
Come, Gertrude, we'll call up our wisest friends,
And let them know both what we mean to do
40 And what's untimely done. [So envious slander],
Whose whisper o'er the world's diameter,
As level as the cannon to his blank,
Transports his poison'd shot, may miss our name
And hit the woundless air. O come away,
45 My soul is full of discord and dismay.   *[Exeunt*

Act 4 Scene 2
Hamlet refuses to tell Rosencrantz and
Guildenstern where he has hidden the body
of Polonius.

1 *stowed*: stowed away, hidden.

5 *Compounded . . . kin*: 'dust thou art,
and unto dust shalt thou return'
(Genesis 3:19).

10 *counsel*: secret.
11 *demanded of*: questioned by.
replication: reply (a legal term).

14 *countenance*: favour.
15 *authorities*: powers.

17 *mouthed*: put into the mouth.
18 *gleaned*: picked up.

21 *A knavish . . . fools*: irony is wasted on
fools.

SCENE 2

Enter Hamlet

Hamlet
Safely stowed.

Calling within

But soft, what noise? Who calls on Hamlet? O, here they
come.

Enter Rosencrantz, Guildenstern, *and* Others

Rosencrantz
What have you done, my lord, with the dead body?
Hamlet
5 Compounded it with dust, whereto 'tis kin.
Rosencrantz
Tell us where 'tis, that we may take it thence and bear it
to the chapel.
Hamlet
Do not believe it.
Rosencrantz
Believe what?
Hamlet
10 That I can keep your counsel and not mine own.
Besides, to be demanded of a sponge—what replication
should be made by the son of a king?
Rosencrantz
Take you me for a sponge, my lord?
Hamlet
Ay, sir, that soaks up the king's countenance, his
15 rewards, his authorities. But such officers do the king
best service in the end: he keeps them, like an ape, in the
corner of his jaw—first mouthed, to be last swallowed.
When he needs what you have gleaned, it is but
squeezing you and, sponge, you shall be dry again.
Rosencrantz
20 I understand you not, my lord.
Hamlet
I am glad of it. A knavish speech sleeps in a foolish ear.

Rosencrantz

My lord, you must tell us where the body is and go with us to the king.

Hamlet

The body is with the king, but the king is not with the
25 body. The king is a thing—

Guildenstern

A thing, my lord?

Hamlet

Of nothing. Bring me to him.   [*Exeunt*

SCENE 3

Enter King *and two or three* Lords

King

I have sent to seek him and to find the body.
How dangerous is it that this man goes loose!
Yet must not we put the strong law on him:
He's lov'd of the distracted multitude,
5 Who like not in their judgement but their eyes,
And where 'tis so, th'offender's scourge is weigh'd,
But never the offence. To bear all smooth and even,
This sudden sending him away must seem
Deliberate pause. Diseases desperate grown
10 By desperate appliance are reliev'd,
Or not at all.

Enter Rosencrantz *and* Others

              How now, what hath befall'n?

Rosencrantz

Where the dead body is bestow'd, my lord,
We cannot get from him.

King

                      But where is he?

Rosencrantz

Without, my lord, guarded, to know your pleasure.

King

15 Bring him before us.

Side notes:

24–5 *The body . . . body*: the corpse is in the king's palace, but the king is not where Polonius is (i.e. in heaven).

27 *Of nothing*: of no importance.

Act 4 Scene 3
Hamlet is brought before the king, and tells Claudius where he may find the body of Polonius. Claudius, who is now very worried about his nephew, tells Hamlet that he must leave immediately for England.

4 *distracted*: unreasoning.

5 *like*: choose.

6–7 *th'offender's scourge . . . the offence*: they criticize the punishment and never think about the crime.

7 *To bear . . . even*: to keep everything quiet.

9 *Deliberate pause*: a calculated consideration.

9–10 *Diseases . . . reliev'd*: A proverb: serious illnesses need drastic treatment.

11s.d. Apparently Guildenstern is absent.

Rosencrantz

Ho! Bring in the lord.

Enter Hamlet *with* Guards

King

Now, Hamlet, where's Polonius?

Hamlet

At supper.

King

At supper? Where?

Hamlet

20 *convocation*: assembly. Hamlet proceeds to a clever play with words and ideas, combining a familiar aphorism observing that even an emperor must become a meal for worms, and an allusion to the Diet (= council) held by the Emperor Charles V in the German city of Worms (which was especially famous for its treatment of Luther in 1521). *politic*: scheming.

23 *variable service*: different courses at a meal.

Not where he eats, but where 'a is eaten. A certain
20 convocation of politic worms are e'en at him. Your
worm is your only emperor for diet: we fat all creatures
else to fat us, and we fat ourselves for maggots. Your fat
king and your lean beggar is but variable service—two
dishes, but to one table. That's the end.

King

25 Alas, alas.

Hamlet

A man may fish with the worm that hath eat of a king,
and eat of the fish that hath fed of that worm.

King

What dost thou mean by this?

Hamlet

29 *progress*: state journey, royal tour.

Nothing but to show you how a king may go a progress
30 through the guts of a beggar.

King

Where is Polonius?

Hamlet

33 *th'other place*: hell.

35 *nose*: smell.

In heaven. Send thither to see. If your messenger find
him not there, seek him i'th'other place yourself. But if
indeed you find him not within this month, you shall
35 nose him as you go up the stairs into the lobby.

King

[*To some* Attendants] Go seek him there.

Hamlet

'A will stay still you come.   [*Exeunt* Attendants

King

Hamlet, this deed, for thine especial safety—

39 *tender*: have a care for.

42 *bark*: ship.
at help: in the right quarter.
43 *Th'associates tend*: your companions
wait.
bent: directed.

45 *For England*: Hamlet is not
surprised—he told his mother his
destination in *3, 4, 202*.

49 *cherub*: The Old Testament prophet
Ezekiel described the celestial
Cherubim as being 'full of eyes'
(Ezekiel, 10:12).

52 *man and wife*: see St Mark, 10:8:
'they twain shall be one flesh'.

54 *at foot*: closely.
56–7 'Everything else connected with this
business has been got ready.'
58 *England*: i.e. King of England;
Claudius addresses himself to the
monarch.
hold'st at aught: value at all.
59–62 'Our power should have taught you
to value us, since you are still
smarting from the wounds inflicted on
you, and you are still paying tribute
(the Danegeld) to us.'
60 *cicatrice*: scar.
61 *free awe*: respect given willingly.
62 *coldly set*: value lightly.
63 *sovereign process*: royal command.
imports at full: gives full directions.
64 *congruing to*: in accordance with.
65 *present death*: immediate execution.
The king's purpose is now revealed.
66 *hectic*: fever.
68 *Howe'er my haps*: whatever else
happens.

Which we do tender, as we dearly grieve
40 For that which thou hast done—must send thee hence
With fiery quickness. Therefore prepare thyself.
The bark is ready, and the wind at help,
Th'associates tend, and everything is bent
For England.
    Hamlet
45 For England?
    King
Ay, Hamlet.
    Hamlet
Good.
    King
So is it, if thou knew'st our purposes.
    Hamlet
I see a cherub that sees them. But come, for England.
50 Farewell, dear mother.
    King
Thy loving father, Hamlet.
    Hamlet
My mother. Father and mother is man and wife, man
and wife is one flesh; so my mother. Come, for England.
                        [Exit
    King
Follow him at foot. Tempt him with speed aboard,
55 Delay it not—I'll have him hence tonight.
Away, for everything is seal'd and done
That else leans on th'affair. Pray you make haste.
                  [Exeunt all but the King
And England, if my love thou hold'st at aught—
As my great power thereof may give thee sense,
60 Since yet thy cicatrice looks raw and red
After the Danish sword, and thy free awe
Pays homage to us—thou mayst not coldly set
Our sovereign process, which imports at full,
By letters congruing to that effect,
65 The present death of Hamlet. Do it, England;
For like the hectic in my blood he rages,
And thou must cure me. Till I know 'tis done,
Howe'er my haps, my joys were ne'er begun.   *[Exit*

Act 4 Scene 4
A change of mood and location as an army of Norwegian soldiers marches across the stage. At their head is young Fortinbras, brisk and purposeful; and the watching Hamlet is moved to further meditation on his own inactivity.

2 *by his licence*: see *2, 2, 77–8.*

3 *conveyance*: safe conduct.

6 *express . . . eye*: pay our respects to his person.

8 *softly*: quietly. The soldiers are to behave respectfully.

9 *powers*: soldiers.

12 *Against*: to attack.

14 *old Norway*: the old King of Norway.

15 *the main*: the central part.
16 *frontier*: fortress on the boundary.

17 *addition*: exaggeration.

19 *the name*: i.e. of conqueror. Fortinbras is fighting just for the sake of his reputation.
20 *farm*: rent.

SCENE 4

Enter Fortinbras *with his* Army, *marching over the stage*

Fortinbras
Go, captain, from me greet the Danish king.
Tell him that by his licence Fortinbras
Craves the conveyance of a promis'd march
Over his kingdom. You know the rendezvous.
5 If that his Majesty would aught with us,
We shall express our duty in his eye;
And let him know so.
Captain
                I will do't, my lord.
Fortinbras
Go softly on.   *[Exeunt all but the* Captain

Enter Hamlet, Rosencrantz, *and* Others

Hamlet
Good sir, whose powers are these?
Captain
10 They are of Norway, sir.
Hamlet
How purpos'd, sir, I pray you?
Captain
Against some part of Poland.
Hamlet
Who commands them, sir?
Captain
The nephew to old Norway, Fortinbras.
Hamlet
15 Goes it against the main of Poland, sir,
Or for some frontier?
Captain
Truly to speak, and with no addition,
We go to gain a little patch of ground
That hath in it no profit but the name.
20 To pay five ducats—five—I would not farm it;

22 *ranker*: better interest.
  in fee: outright.

23 *the Polack*: the King of Poland.

25 Hamlet estimates the cost—in lives and money—of this expedition.
26 'Will not settle this trivial matter.'
27 *th'impostume . . . peace*: the abscess which results from peacetime affluence.
28 *without*: externally.

32–3 Hamlet muses on the chance happenings—the encounter with the players, and now the meeting with Fortinbras—which seem to reproach him for his indecisiveness.
34 *his chief . . . time*: all he does with his time.
36 *large discourse*: fine power of reasoning.
37 *Looking before and after*: i.e. learning from the past and planning for the future.
38 *godlike reason*: The power of reasoning is what separates man from the rest of creation.
39 *fust*: go mouldy.
40 *Bestial oblivion*: an animal's forgetfulness.
41 *Of*: resulting from.
  too precisely: in too much detail.
  event: the outcome.
44 *To do*: to be done.
45 *Sith*: since.
  cause: motive.
46 *gross*: as weighty.
47 *mass and charge*: size and expense.
48 *delicate*: sensitive.
  tender: young.
49 *puff'd*: blown up.
50 *Makes mouths at*: pulls faces at, scorns.
  the invisible event: unpredictable outcome.

Nor will it yield to Norway or the Pole
A ranker rate should it be sold in fee.
    Hamlet
Why, then the Polack never will defend it.
    Captain
Yes, it is already garrison'd.
    Hamlet
25 Two thousand souls and twenty thousand ducats
Will not debate the question of this straw!
This is th'impostume of much wealth and peace,
That inward breaks, and shows no cause without
Why the man dies. I humbly thank you, sir.
    Captain
30 God buy you, sir.   [*Exit*
    Rosencrantz
                    Will't please you go, my lord?
    Hamlet
I'll be with you straight. Go a little before.
                    [*Exeunt all but* Hamlet
How all occasions do inform against me,
And spur my dull revenge. What is a man
If his chief good and market of his time
35 Be but to sleep and feed? A beast, no more.
Sure he that made us with such large discourse,
Looking before and after, gave us not
That capability and godlike reason
To fust in us unus'd. Now whether it be
40 Bestial oblivion, or some craven scruple
Of thinking too precisely on th'event—
A thought which, quarter'd, hath but one part wisdom
And ever three parts coward—I do not know
Why yet I live to say this thing's to do,
45 Sith I have cause, and will, and strength, and means
To do't. Examples gross as earth exhort me,
Witness this army of such mass and charge,
Led by a delicate and tender prince,
Whose spirit, with divine ambition puff'd,
50 Makes mouths at the invisible event,
Exposing what is mortal and unsure
To all that fortune, death, and danger dare,

53–6 *Rightly . . . stake*: the reputation of greatness comes not by waiting for a great cause to fight for, but fighting nobly over a trivial matter when it's a matter of honour.

58 *Excitements of*: incentives for. In Hamlet's case, both mind and emotions should be affected.
60 *twenty thousand men*: The numbers of ducats and of men (estimated in line 25) have got confused.
61 *fantasy and trick*: trifling illusion.
62 *like beds*: i.e. willingly.
63 'Not big enough to hold those who are fighting for it.'
64 *tomb . . . continent*: a big enough grave and container.

Even for an eggshell. Rightly to be great
Is not to stir without great argument,
55 But greatly to find quarrel in a straw
When honour's at the stake. How stand I then,
That have a father kill'd, a mother stain'd,
Excitements of my reason and my blood,
And let all sleep, while to my shame I see
60 The imminent death of twenty thousand men
That, for a fantasy and trick of fame,
Go to their graves like beds, fight for a plot
Whereon the numbers cannot try the cause,
Which is not tomb enough and continent
65 To hide the slain? O, from this time forth
My thoughts be bloody or be nothing worth.   [*Exit*

Act 4 Scene 5
Ophelia is crazy with grief for her father's death, and Claudius fears that the murder will have serious consequences. Laertes demands retribution, and his distress is redoubled when he sees his sister.

2 *distract*: distracted.
mood: state of mind.
will needs be: must be.
3 *would she have*: does she want.

Scene 5

Enter Queen, Horatio, *and a* Gentleman

Queen
I will not speak with her.
Gentleman
                          She is importunate,
Indeed distract. Her mood will needs be pitied.
Queen
What would she have?

5 *tricks i'th' world*: strange dealings about.
hems: says 'Mmm'.
6 *Spurns . . . straws*: takes offence at the least little thing.
in doubt: ambiguously.
7 *nothing*: nonsense.
8 *unshaped use*: unshapèd; disorganized manner.
9 *collection*: try to sort it out.
aim: guess.
11 *Which*: i.e. her words.
yield: represent.
12 'Although we cannot be certain, there may be such that is dangerous.'

15 *ill-breeding*: mischief-making.

17 *sick*: guilty. Hamlet's reproaches have had the desired effect.
18 *toy*: trifle.
amiss: misfortune. The rhymed couplets here mark off the proverbial nature of the thought or *sententia*.
19 *artless jealousy*: uncontrolled suspicion.
20 *spills*: destroys.
21 *beauteous Majesty*: Presumably Ophelia refers to the queen.
23s.d. Ophelia's songs, snatches of old ballads, mourn both her father's death and Hamlet's unkindness.

25–6 The lover is depicted as a pilgrim, wearing in his hat a 'cockle' or scallop shell, carrying a pilgrim's walking-staff, and clad in sandalled shoes.
28 *mark*: listen.

Gentleman
She speaks much of her father, says she hears
5   There's tricks i'th' world, and hems, and beats her heart,
Spurns enviously at straws, speaks things in doubt
That carry but half sense. Her speech is nothing,
Yet the unshaped use of it doth move
The hearers to collection. They aim at it,
10 And botch the words up fit to their own thoughts,
Which, as her winks and nods and gestures yield them,
Indeed would make one think there might be thought,
Though nothing sure, yet much unhappily.
    Horatio
'Twere good she were spoken with, for she may strew
15 Dangerous conjectures in ill-breeding minds.
    Queen
Let her come in.   [*Exit* Gentleman
[*Aside*] To my sick soul, as sin's true nature is,
Each toy seems prologue to some great amiss.
So full of artless jealousy is guilt,
20 It spills itself in fearing to be spilt.

Enter Ophelia

    Ophelia
Where is the beauteous Majesty of Denmark?
    Queen
How now, Ophelia?

    Ophelia
[*Sings*] *How should I your true love know*
              From another one?
25   *By his cockle hat and staff*
              And his sandal shoon.
    Queen
Alas, sweet lady, what imports this song?
    Ophelia
Say you? Nay, pray you mark.
[*Sings*] *He is dead and gone, lady,*
30   *He is dead and gone,*
            At his head a grass-green turf,
            At his heels a stone.
O ho!

Queen
Nay, but Ophelia—
Ophelia
35 Pray you mark.
[*Sings*] *White his shroud as the mountain snow—*

Enter King

Queen
Alas, look here, my lord.
Ophelia
[*Sings*] *Larded with sweet flowers*
Which bewept to the grave did not go
40   *With true-love showers.*
King
How do you, pretty lady?
Ophelia
Well, good dild you. They say the owl was a baker's
daughter. Lord, we know what we are, but know not
what we may be. God be at your table.
King
45 Conceit upon her father.
Ophelia
Pray let's have no words of this, but when they ask you
what it means, say you this.
[*Sings*] *Tomorrow is Saint Valentine's day,*
All in the morning betime,
And I a maid at your window,
50   *To be your Valentine.*
Then up he rose, and donn'd his clo'es,
And dupp'd the chamber door,
Let in the maid that out a maid
55   *Never departed more.*
King
Pretty Ophelia—

38 *Larded*: sprinkled all over.

39 *did not go*: Ophelia stumbles in her
song, violating its rhythm but
describing the burial of Polonius more
exactly (see lines 83, 209–11).

42 *good dild you*: may God yield (i.e.
reward) you.
the owl: A folk-tale tells of a baker's
daughter turned into an owl because
she gave short weight.

43–4 *we know . . . we may be*: See
1 John, 3:2: 'Now are we the sons of
God, and it doth not yet appear what
we may be.'

44 *at your table*: with you.

45 *Conceit upon*: distressed about.

48 *St Valentine's day*: 14 February.
Tradition held that young men and
women alike would find a true lover in
the first person of the opposite sex to
be encountered on this day.

49 *betime*: early.

52 *clo'es*: clothes.

53 *dupp'd*: opened.

'*Larded with sweet flowers Which bewept to the grave did not go*' (4, 5, 38–9) Marianne Faithfull as Ophelia, Round House, London, 1969.

Ophelia

Indeed, without an oath, I'll make an end on't.

> *By Gis and by Saint Charity,*
> *Alack and fie for shame,*
> *Young men will do't if they come to't—*
> *By Cock, they are to blame.*
> *Quoth she, 'Before you tumbled me,*
> *You promis'd me to wed.'*

He answers

> *'So would I a done, by yonder sun,*
> *And thou hadst not come to my bed.'*

King

How long hath she been thus?

Ophelia

I hope all will be well. We must be patient. But I cannot choose but weep to think they would lay him i'th' cold ground. My brother shall know of it. And so I thank you for your good counsel. Come, my coach. Good night, ladies, good night. Sweet ladies, good night, good night.

[*Exit*

King

Follow her close; give her good watch, I pray you.

[*Exit* Horatio

O, this is the poison of deep grief: it springs
All from her father's death. And now behold—
O Gertrude, Gertrude,
When sorrows come, they come not single spies,
But in battalions. First, her father slain;
Next, your son gone, and he most violent author
Of his own just remove; the people muddied,
Thick and unwholesome in their thoughts and whispers
For good Polonius' death—and we have done but greenly
In hugger-mugger to inter him; Poor Ophelia
Divided from herself and her fair judgement,
Without the which we are pictures, or mere beasts;
Last, and as much containing as all these,
Her brother is in secret come from France,
Feeds on this wonder, keeps himself in clouds,
And wants not buzzers to infect his ear

Line numbers: 60, 65, 70, 75, 80, 85

---

58 *Gis*: Jesus.
Charity: the personification of the virtue.
60 *do't . . . to't*: take advantage of a girl if they are given the chance.
61 *Cock*: God—but there is also a pun on 'cock' = penis.
62 *tumbled me*: i.e. took my virginity.

65 *a done*: have done.

66 *And*: if.

73 *close*: immediately.
give her good watch: watch her carefully.
77–8 *When . . . battalions*: i.e. it never rains but it pours. Claudius offers a variant on a common saying; 'spies' were single soldiers sent ahead of the general army to reconnoitre.
80 *his . . . remove*: Claudius shifts the blame for the prince's departure on to Hamlet himself.
muddied: confused—like water in a stream or fountain that has been stirred up.
81 *Thick and unwholesome*: troubled and suspicious.
82 *we*: I. Again Claudius uses the royal plural.
greenly: foolishly.
83 *hugger-mugger*: secretly and in haste.
84 'Beside herself, out of her mind.'
85 *which*: i.e. judgement.
pictures: only images of men.
86 *as much containing*: just as serious.
88 *Feeds on this wonder*: broods over his bewilderment.
keeps . . . clouds: holds himself aloof.
89 *wants not*: does not lack.
buzzers: scandal-mongers.

91 *necessity*: the need to blame
someone.
of matter beggar'd: being short of hard
facts.
92 'Won't hesitate to accuse me.'
93 *In ear and ear*: to one person after
another.
this: this whole business.
94 *murd'ring-piece*: gun (e.g. cannon)
which scatters its shot and kills many
at once.
94–5 *in . . . death*: is killing me several
times over.
96 *Switzers*: Swiss bodyguard.

98–107 *The . . . king*: Messengers in
classical tragedy were allowed a
certain poetic licence.
98 *overpeering*: rising above.
his list: its limits.
99 *flats*: low-lying coastal area, where the
rising tide races inland.
impetuous: violent.
100 *in a riotous head*: advancing with a
gang of rebels.
102–4 'As if a new world was just about to
begin, rejecting the traditions and
established customs which are
essential to support "every word" of
civilized rule.'
105 *Choose we*: let *us* choose. Denmark
was an elective monarchy—in which
the king, though nominated by his
predecessor, had to be ratified in his
election by the voice of the people.
106 *Caps*: i.e. thrown in the air.
108 *cry*: give voice (like hounds that have
picked up a scent).
109 *counter*: the wrong way.
110 *broke*: forced open.

111 *this*: Laertes is contemptuous.

90 With pestilent speeches of his father's death,
Wherein necessity, of matter beggar'd,
Will nothing stick our person to arraign
In ear and ear. O my dear Gertrude, this,
Like to a murd'ring-piece, in many places
95 Gives me superfluous death.

A noise within

                              Attend!
Where is my Switzers? Let them guard the door.

Enter a Messenger

What is the matter?
Messenger
                    Save yourself, my lord.
The ocean, overpeering of his list,
Eats not the flats with more impetuous haste
100 Than young Laertes, in a riotous head,
O'erbears your officers. The rabble call him lord,
And, as the world were now but to begin,
Antiquity forgot, custom not known—
The ratifiers and props of every word—
105 They cry, 'Choose we! Laertes shall be king.'
Caps, hands, and tongues applaud it to the clouds,
'Laertes shall be king, Laertes king.'
    Queen
How cheerfully on the false trail they cry.
O, this is counter, you false Danish dogs.

A noise within

    King
110 The doors are broke.

Enter Laertes *with* Followers

    Laertes
Where is this king?—Sirs, stand you all without.

Followers

No, let's come in.

Laertes   I pray you give me leave.

Followers

We will, we will.

Laertes

I thank you. Keep the door.   [*Exeunt* Followers

                                    O thou vile king,

115 Give me my father.

Queen

[*Holding him*]   Calmly, good Laertes.

Laertes

That drop of blood that's calm proclaims me bastard,

Cries cuckold to my father, brands the harlot

Even here between the chaste unsmirched brow

Of my true mother.

King

                            What is the cause, Laertes,

120 That thy rebellion looks so giant-like?—

Let him go, Gertrude. Do not fear our person.

There's such divinity doth hedge a king

That treason can but peep to what it would,

Acts little of his will.—Tell me, Laertes,

125 Why thou art thus incens'd.—Let him go, Gertrude.

—Speak, man.

Laertes

Where is my father?

King

                            Dead.

Queen

                                    But not by him.

King

Let him demand his fill.

Laertes

How came he dead? I'll not be juggled with.

130 To hell, allegiance! Vows to the blackest devil!

Conscience and grace, to the profoundest pit!

I dare damnation. To this point I stand,

That both the worlds I give to negligence,

Let come what comes, only I'll be reveng'd

---

112 *give me leave*: if you don't mind. Laertes is politely dismissive.

117 *brands the harlot*: See *3*, 4, 42–4.

118 *Even here*: i.e. here of all places. *unsmirched*: unsmirchèd.

120 *looks so giant-like*: makes such a show of violence. The classical rebellion myth describes how the giants, by piling Mt Pelion on top of Mt Ossa, assailed the Greek gods in heaven.

121 *fear*: be afraid for.

122 *such divinity . . . a king*: The Elizabethans believed that the king was God's representative on earth, and was protected in his function by the power of the Almighty; Claudius is never more regal than at this moment.

123 *but peep . . . would*: only gets a glimpse of what it would like to do.

124 *his will*: what it wants.

129 *juggled with*: played with.

131 *grace*: Laertes forswears the love of God, necessary for salvation. *profoundest pit*: hell. For the 'bottomless pit' see Revelation, 9:1.

132 *To this point I stand*: I have reached this position.

133 *both . . . negligence*: I don't care what happens to me in this world or the next.

135   *throughly*: thoroughly.
        stay: prevent.

136   *the world's*: i.e. the world's will.
137   *husband*: manage, take care of.
138   *go far with little*: A commonplace
        saying: 'make a little go a long way.'

140   *writ*: laid down, prescribed.
141   *swoopstake*: as in a sweepstake—
        where the winner takes all the stakes.
        Claudius asks if Laertes will use no
        discrimination.
        draw: take from.

143   *Will you*: do you want to.

145–6   The pelican, showing natural feeling
        ('kind') was thought to nourish
        ('Repast') its brood ('kind') with its
        own blood. The extravagant image is
        typical of the inflated sentiments of
        Laertes.

149   *sensibly*: feelingly.
150   *level*: plainly.
        'pear: appear.

153–4   Laertes would willingly (in his
        characteristic exaggeration) lose his
        mind and his sight.
154   *virtue*: power.
156   *turn the beam*: tilt the balance; i.e.
        his revenge will exceed the injury.

135   Most throughly for my father.
              King
                                    Who shall stay you?
        Laertes
        My will, not all the world's.
        And for my means, I'll husband them so well,
        They shall go far with little.
              King
                          Good Laertes,
        If you desire to know the certainty
140   Of your dear father, is't writ in your revenge
        That, swoopstake, you will draw both friend and foe,
        Winner and loser?
              Laertes
        None but his enemies.
              King
                                    Will you know them then?
        Laertes
        To his good friends thus wide I'll ope my arms,
145   And, like the kind life-rend'ring pelican,
        Repast them with my blood.
              King
                                Why, now you speak
        Like a good child and a true gentleman.
        That I am guiltless of your father's death
        And am most sensibly in grief for it,
150   It shall as level to your judgement 'pear
        As day does to your eye.

              A noise within. Ophelia *is heard singing*

                                Let her come in.
        Laertes
        How now, what noise is that?

              Enter Ophelia

        O heat, dry up my brains. Tears seven times salt
        Burn out the sense and virtue of mine eye.
155   By heaven, thy madness shall be paid with weight
        Till our scale turn the beam. O rose of May!

Dear maid—kind sister—sweet Ophelia—
O heavens, is't possible a young maid's wits
Should be as mortal as an old man's life?
160 Nature is fine in love, and where 'tis fine
It sends some precious instance of itself
After the thing it loves.

Ophelia

[*Sings*] *They bore him bare-fac'd on the bier,*
And in his grave rain'd many a tear—
165 Fare you well, my dove.

Laertes

Hadst thou thy wits and didst persuade revenge,
It could not move thus.

Ophelia

You must sing *A-down a-down,* and you *Call him*
a-down-a. O, how the wheel becomes it! It is the false
170 steward that stole his master's daughter.

Laertes

This nothing's more than matter.

Ophelia

There's rosemary, that's for remembrance—pray you,
love, remember. And there is pansies, that's for
thoughts.

Laertes

175 A document in madness: thoughts and remembrance
fitted.

Ophelia

There's fennel for you, and columbines. There's rue for
you. And here's some for me. We may call it herb of
grace a Sundays. You must wear your rue with a
180 difference. There's a daisy. I would give you some
violets, but they withered all when my father died. They
say 'a made a good end.
[*Sings*] *For bonny sweet Robin is all my joy.*

Laertes

Thought and affliction, passion, hell itself
185 She turns to favour and to prettiness.

Ophelia

[*Sings*] *And will 'a not come again?*
And will 'a not come again?
No, no, he is dead,

160–2 'The sensitivity of human love is such that it sends something of itself (which is precious) after the beloved who has gone away.'
161 *instance*: token.

164 For the songs, see p.159.

166 *persuade*: urge me to.
167 *move*: persuade.
168–9 *You . . . down-a*: Ophelia instructs the bystanders to sing refrains to her song.
169 *wheel*: change in rhythm.
169–70 *false . . . daughter*: No such ballad has been found.
171 *This . . . matter*: this nonsense speaks more than words.
172–81 *There's . . . died*: Ophelia distributes her flowers (probably imaginary) according to their symbolic associations.

175 *document*: lesson.
176 *fitted*: suited.
177 *fennel . . . columbines*: flattery . . . marital infidelity.
rue: the herb of repentance.
179 *a*: on.
179–80 *with a difference*: with heraldic variation.
184 *Thought*: sadness.
passion: suffering.
185 *favour*: charm.

Go to thy death-bed,
190 *He never will come again.*

His beard was as white as snow,
All flaxen was his poll.
He is gone, he is gone,
And we cast away moan.
195 *God a mercy on his soul.*
And of all Christian souls. God buy you.   [*Exit*
    Laertes
Do you see this, O God?
    King
Laertes, I must commune with your grief,
Or you deny me right. Go but apart,
200 Make choice of whom your wisest friends you will,
And they shall hear and judge 'twixt you and me.
If by direct or by collateral hand
They find us touch'd, we will our kingdom give,
Our crown, our life, and all that we call ours
205 To you in satisfaction; but if not,
Be you content to lend your patience to us,
And we shall jointly labour with your soul
To give it due content.
    Laertes
                              Let this be so.
His means of death, his obscure funeral—
210 No trophy, sword, nor hatchment o'er his bones,
No noble rite, nor formal ostentation—
Cry to be heard, as 'twere from heaven to earth,
That I must call't in question.
    King
                              So you shall.
And where th'offence is, let the great axe fall.
215 I pray you go with me.   [*Exeunt*

---

192 *All . . . poll*: his hair was white as flax.

194 *we . . . moan*: we waste our grief.

196 *God buy you*: may God be with you.

198 *commune with*: share in.
199 *Go but apart*: just wait a moment.
200 *whom*: whichever.
202 *direct . . . hand*: our own hand, or the hand of an agent.
203 *touch'd*: guilty.
205 *satisfaction*: recompense.
209 *obscure*: secret.
210 *trophy*: memorial.
    hatchment o'er his bones: painting of coat-of-arms displayed outside the house of mourning, and later over the tomb.

211 *ostentation*: ceremony.
213 *That*: so that.
    call't in question: demand an explanation.
215 *go with me*: Claudius has made an ally of the rebel.

Act 4 Scene 6
Horatio is approached by sailors, who bring letters from Hamlet.

SCENE 6

Enter Horatio *and a* Servant

Horatio
What are they that would speak with me?
Servant
Seafaring men, sir. They say they have letters for you.
Horatio
Let them come in.   [*Exit* Servant
I do not know from what part of the world
5 I should be greeted, if not from Lord Hamlet.

Enter Sailors

First Sailor
God bless you, sir.
Horatio
Let him bless thee too.
First Sailor
'A shall, sir, and please him. There's a letter for you, sir.
It came from th'ambassador that was bound for
10 England—if your name be Horatio, as I am let to know
it is.
Horatio
[*Reads the letter*] *Horatio, when thou shalt have
overlooked this, give these fellows some means to the king.
They have letters for him. Ere we were two days old at sea,*
15 *a pirate of very warlike appointment gave us chase.
Finding ourselves too slow of sail, we put on a compelled
valour, and in the grapple I boarded them. On the instant
they got clear of our ship, so I alone became their prisoner.
They have dealt with me like thieves of mercy. But they*
20 *knew what they did: I am to do a turn for them. Let the
king have the letters I have sent, and repair thou to me
with as much speed as thou wouldest fly death. I have
words to speak in thine ear will make thee dumb; yet are
they much too light for the bore of the matter. These good*
25 *fellows will bring thee where I am. Rosencrantz and
Guildenstern hold their course for England; of them I have
much to tell thee. Farewell.*

> *He that thou knowest thine,*
> *Hamlet.*

8 *and*: if it.
9 *th'ambassador*: Apparently Hamlet did not disclose his real identity to the sailors.
13 *overlooked*: read through.
means: i.e. means of access.
14 *Ere . . . sea*: before we had been two days at sea.
15 *warlike appointment*: prepared to do battle. In Shakespeare's day the seas around Denmark were infested with pirates.
16–17 *put on . . . valour*: we were forced to fight them.
17 *in the grapple*: The pirates would have thrown grappling irons to draw alongside the Danish ship—thus allowing Hamlet to cross over easily (and in fact escape from Rosencrantz and Guildenstern).
19 *thieves of mercy*: Hamlet adapts the familiar expression 'angels of mercy' to suit his present need.
20 *what they did*: what they were doing—i.e. they had their own reasons for treating him well.
a turn: a service.
21 *repair*: come and join.
24 *too . . . matter*: not strong enough for their subject; Hamlet's metaphor is of a shot too small for the bore of the gun.

30 *way*: access.

30   Come, I will give you way for these your letters,
    And do't the speedier that you may direct me
    To him from whom you brought them.   [*Exeunt*

Act 4 Scene 7
Claudius learns that Hamlet has returned to
Denmark and encourages Laertes to get his
revenge. The queen describes Ophelia's
death.

1 *my acquittance seal*: agree that I am
not guilty.

3 *Sith*: since.
knowing: knowledgeable.

5 *Pursu'd my life*: tried to kill me (see
4, 1, 13).

6 *proceeded not*: did not do something
about.
feats: wicked deeds.
7 *crimeful*: criminal.
capital: punishable by death.
8 *safety*: care for your own safety.
9 *mainly*: mightily.

10 *much unsinew'd*: very feeble.

13 *be it either which*: whichever it is.
14 *conjunctive*: closely linked.
15–16 *as . . . her*: just as each planet
(according to Ptolemaic astronomy)
moves around the earth in its own
crystalline sphere, so I can only live
and move within her orb.
17 *count*: reckoning.
18 *the general gender*: the common
people.
20 *the spring . . . stone*: In certain
springs there are rich mineral deposits
that petrify all objects placed in their
waters.
21 *gyves*: deformities (literally, shackles).
The hard *g* is alliterative with 'graces'.
22 *Too slightly timber'd*: with too light a
shaft.
26 *desp'rate terms*: a condition of
desperation.

SCENE 7

Enter King *and* Laertes

King
Now must your conscience my acquittance seal,
And you must put me in your heart for friend,
Sith you have heard, and with a knowing ear,
That he which hath your noble father slain
5 Pursu'd my life.
    Laertes
             It well appears. But tell me
Why you proceeded not against these feats
So crimeful and so capital in nature,
As by your safety, wisdom, all things else
You mainly were stirr'd up.
    King
             O, for two special reasons,
10 Which may to you perhaps seem much unsinew'd,
But yet to me th'are strong. The queen his mother
Lives almost by his looks, and for myself—
My virtue or my plague, be it either which—
She is so conjunctive to my life and soul
15 That, as the star moves not but in his sphere,
I could not but by her. The other motive
Why to a public count I might not go
Is the great love the general gender bear him,
Who, dipping all his faults in their affection,
20 Work like the spring that turneth wood to stone,
Convert his gyves to graces; so that my arrows,
Too slightly timber'd for so loud a wind,
Would have reverted to my bow again,
But not where I had aim'd them.
    Laertes
25 And so have I a noble father lost,
    A sister driven into desp'rate terms,

27 *go back again*: i.e. to what she used to be.
28 'Was easily able to beat anyone now living.'
   on mount: conspicuously (like the king on top of a mountain).
30 *Break not your sleeps*: don't lose any sleep.
32 *let . . . danger*: allow ourselves to be insulted with threats.
33 *hear more*: Perhaps Claudius expects news from England—but not the letters that have just arrived.

Whose worth, if praises may go back again,
Stood challenger on mount of all the age
For her perfections. But my revenge will come.
    King
30 Break not your sleeps for that. You must not think
That we are made of stuff so flat and dull
That we can let our beard be shook with danger
And think it pastime. You shortly shall hear more.
I lov'd your father, and we love ourself,
35 And that, I hope, will teach you to imagine—

Enter a Messenger *with letters*

    Messenger
These to your Majesty, this to the queen.
    King
From Hamlet! Who brought them?
    Messenger
Sailors, my lord, they say. I saw them not.
They were given me by Claudio. He received them
40 Of him that brought them.
    King
                    Laertes, you shall hear them.—
Leave us.   [*Exit* Messenger

42 *High and mighty*: Hamlet's form of address is correct, although the phraseology lends itself to sarcasm.
   naked: stripped of belongings.
43–4 *your kingly eyes*: your Majesty in person.

[*Reads*] *High and mighty, you shall know I am set naked on your kingdom. Tomorrow shall I beg leave to see your kingly eyes, when I shall, first asking your pardon,*
45 *thereunto recount the occasion of my sudden and more strange return.*
        Hamlet
What should this mean? Are all the rest come back?
Or is it some abuse, and no such thing?

48 *abuse*: deception.

    Laertes
50 Know you the hand?
    King
                   'Tis Hamlet's character.

50 *character*: handwriting.

'Naked'—
And in a postscript here he says 'Alone'.
Can you devise me?

53 *devise me*: explain this to me.

Laertes
I am lost in it, my lord. But let him come.
55 It warms the very sickness in my heart
That I shall live and tell him to his teeth,
'Thus diest thou'.
      King
                        If it be so, Laertes—
As how should it be so, how otherwise?—
Will you be rul'd by me?
      Laertes
                              Ay, my lord,
60 So you will not o'errule me to a peace.
      King
To thine own peace. If he be now return'd,
As checking at his voyage, and that he means
No more to undertake it, I will work him
To an exploit, now ripe in my device,
65 Under the which he shall not choose but fall;
And for his death no wind of blame shall breathe,
But even his mother shall uncharge the practice
And call it accident.
      Laertes
                              My lord, I will be rul'd,
The rather if you could devise it so
70 That I might be the organ.
            King
                                    It falls right.
You have been talk'd of since your travel much,
And that in Hamlet's hearing, for a quality
Wherein they say you shine. Your sum of parts
Did not together pluck such envy from him
75 As did that one, and that, in my regard,
Of the unworthiest siege.
      Laertes
                              What part is that, my lord?
      King
A very ribbon in the cap of youth—
Yet needful too, for youth no less becomes
The light and careless livery that it wears
80 Than settled age his sables and his weeds
Importing health and graveness. Two months since

58 The king seems momentarily baffled, but immediately regains his composure as he sets to work to flatter and persuade Laertes.

62 *checking at*: stopping in the course of (shying like a horse).

64 *now . . . device*: which I have just thought out.

67 *uncharge the practice*: make excuses for the trick.

73 *your sum of parts*: all your accomplishments taken together.

75–6 *in my regard . . . siege*: which I do not rate very highly ('siege' = rank, status).

77 *very ribbon*: mere decoration.
78–81 'It is good to see young men appearing *as* young men, just as it is appropriate for older men to show their maturity.'
79 *careless*: carefree.
     livery: uniform.
80 *sables . . . weeds*: furred clothing in sober colours.
81 *health*: well-being.

83 *serv'd*: fought.

84 *can well*: have great skill.

85 *Had witchcraft*: was a magician.
grew unto his seat: sat so well on
horseback.

87 *incorps'd and demi-natur'd*: made into
one body and possessed of half the
nature—i.e. like a centaur.

88–90 'He was so much better than I
would ever have thought possible, that
I could not even imagine the
movements he performed.' The
mysterious Lamord seems to have
been demonstrating dressage.

93 *brooch*: jewel (usually worn in the
hat).

95 *made confession of you*: said he knew
you.

97 *defence*: fencing.

98 *rapier*: The weapon favoured by
gentlemen.

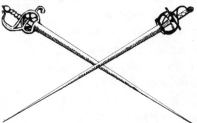

100 *If one could match you*: if there were
anyone capable of giving you a match.
scrimers: fencers (French *escrimeurs*).

101 *motion*: action.

105 *sudden*: immediate.
play: fight a duel.

Here was a gentleman of Normandy—
I have seen myself, and serv'd against, the French,
And they can well on horseback, but this gallant
85 Had witchcraft in't. He grew unto his seat,
And to such wondrous doing brought his horse
As had he been incorps'd and demi-natur'd
With the brave beast. So far he topp'd my thought
That I in forgery of shapes and tricks
90 Come short of what he did.

Laertes

                A Norman was't?

King

A Norman.

Laertes

Upon my life, Lamord.

King

              The very same.

Laertes

I know him well. He is the brooch indeed
And gem of all the nation.

King

95 He made confession of you,
And gave you such a masterly report
For art and exercise in your defence,
And for your rapier most especial,
That he cried out 'twould be a sight indeed
100 If one could match you. The scrimers of their nation
He swore had neither motion, guard, nor eye,
If you oppos'd them. Sir, this report of his
Did Hamlet so envenom with his envy
That he could nothing do but wish and beg
105 Your sudden coming o'er to play with you.
Now out of this—

Laertes

            What out of this, my lord?

King

Laertes, was your father dear to you?
Or are you like the painting of a sorrow,
A face without a heart?

Laertes

            Why ask you this?

110–23 The king's speech, with its observations on the effects of time, develops a dominant theme in the play (see the reflections of the Player King, *3, 2, 179–91*).

111 *begun by time*: i.e. created by circumstances.

112 *passages of proof*: good examples.

113 *qualifies*: modifies, diminishes.

115 *snuff . . . it*: dead portion that will kill the flame.

116 *still*: constantly.

117 *pleurisy*: excess; the word was wrongly believed to derive from Latin *plus*.

118–19 *That . . . would*: whatever we want to do should be done immediately.

119 *would*: desire.

121 *tongues . . . accidents*: i.e. impediments.

122 *this . . . sigh*: to say 'should' is as wasteful as sighing (which was thought to draw blood away from the heart).

123 *quick*: heart.

127 *sanctuarize*: give sanctuary to.

129 *Will you*: if you will.
keep close: stay hidden.

131 *put on*: appoint.

132 *varnish*: polish.

133 *in fine*: finally.

134 *wager . . . heads*: lay bets on you.
remiss: carelessly trusting.

135 *generous*: magnanimous.
contriving: deceitful practices.

136 *peruse the foils*: inspect the weapons.

137 *shuffling*: underhand dealing.

138 *unbated*: not tipped, unblunted.
pass of practice: Claudius seems to be recommending some foul play.

141 *unction*: ointment.
mountebank: quack doctor.

142 *mortal*: deadly.

143 *cataplasm*: plaster.

144 *simples*: medicinal herbs (thought to have more power—'virtue'—when gathered by moonlight).

King

110 Not that I think you did not love your father,
But that I know love is begun by time,
And that I see, in passages of proof,
Time qualifies the spark and fire of it.
There lives within the very flame of love
115 A kind of wick or snuff that will abate it;
And nothing is at a like goodness still,
For goodness, growing to a pleurisy,
Dies in his own too-much. That we would do,
We should do when we would: for this 'would' changes
120 And hath abatements and delays as many
As there are tongues, are hands, are accidents,
And then this 'should' is like a spendthrift sigh
That hurts by easing. But to the quick of th'ulcer:
Hamlet comes back; what would you undertake
125 To show yourself in deed your father's son
More than in words?

Laertes
                                        To cut his throat i'th' church.

King
No place indeed should murder sanctuarize;
Revenge should have no bounds. But good Laertes,
Will you do this, keep close within your chamber;
130 Hamlet, return'd, shall know you are come home;
We'll put on those shall praise your excellence,
And set a double varnish on the fame
The Frenchman gave you, bring you, in fine, together,
And wager o'er your heads. He, being remiss,
135 Most generous, and free from all contriving,
Will not peruse the foils, so that with ease—
Or with a little shuffling—you may choose
A sword unbated, and in a pass of practice
Requite him for your father.

Laertes
                                        I will do't.
140 And for that purpose, I'll anoint my sword.
I bought an unction of a mountebank
So mortal that but dip a knife in it,
Where it draws blood, no cataplasm so rare,
Collected from all simples that have virtue

147 *gall*: graze.

150 *shape*: part.
151 *drift*: scheme, intention.
   look: be visible.

153 *back*: back-up.
154 *blast in proof*: fail when put to the
   test.
155 *your cunnings*: your respective skills.

157 *motion*: action.

160 *A chalice for the nonce*: a cup of wine
   specially for this purpose.
161 *stuck*: thrust (a fencing term).

166 *There is a willow*: The emblem of
   rejected or forsaken lovers. The
   queen's speech has a detached
   eloquence which divides the message
   from the messenger.
   askant: slanting over.
167 *his*: its.
   hoary: The grey underside of the
   leaves of the green willow is reflected
   in the water.
168 *Therewith*: i.e. using the leaves of the
   willow tree.
   fantastic: cleverly made.
169 *crow-flowers*: pink campion.
   long purples: the flowers of the wild
   orchis, which has a purple spike and
   long pale tubers.
170 *liberal*: loose-tongued.
   grosser: cruder.
171 *cold*: chaste.
172 *crownet weeds*: weeds made into a
   wreath.
173 *envious*: malicious.
177 *lauds*: songs of praise.

145 Under the moon, can save the thing from death
That is but scratch'd withal. I'll touch my point
With this contagion, that if I gall him slightly,
It may be death.
      King
                      Let's further think of this,
Weigh what convenience both of time and means
150 May fit us to our shape. If this should fail,
And that our drift look through our bad performance,
'Twere better not essay'd. Therefore this project
Should have a back or second that might hold
If this did blast in proof. Soft, let me see.
155 We'll make a solemn wager on your cunnings—
I ha't!
When in your motion you are hot and dry—
As make your bouts more violent to that end—
And that he calls for drink, I'll have prepar'd him
160 A chalice for the nonce, whereon but sipping,
If he by chance escape your venom'd stuck,
Our purpose may hold there. But stay, what noise?

Enter Queen

Queen
One woe doth tread upon another's heel,
So fast they follow. Your sister's drown'd, Laertes.
      Laertes
165 Drown'd? O, where?
      Queen
There is a willow grows askant the brook
That shows his hoary leaves in the glassy stream.
Therewith fantastic garlands did she make
Of crow-flowers, nettles, daisies, and long purples,
170 That liberal shepherds give a grosser name,
But our cold maids do dead men's fingers call them.
There on the pendent boughs her crownet weeds
Clamb'ring to hang, an envious sliver broke,
When down her weedy trophies and herself
175 Fell in the weeping brook. Her clothes spread wide,
And mermaid-like awhile they bore her up,
Which time she chanted snatches of old lauds,

178 *incapable*: insensible.

179–80 *native . . . element*: born and
equipped to live in water.

186 *forbid*: restrain.

187 *our trick*: only natural.

188 *Let . . . will*: however embarrassing it
may be.
these: i.e. his tears.

189 *The woman will be out*: I shall have no
more of woman's weakness in me.

191 *douts*: quenches.

As one incapable of her own distress,
Or like a creature native and indued
180 Unto that element. But long it could not be
Till that her garments, heavy with their drink,
Pull'd the poor wretch from her melodious lay
To muddy death.

Laertes
                              Alas, then she is drown'd.

Queen
Drown'd, drown'd.

Laertes
185 Too much of water hast thou, poor Ophelia,
And therefore I forbid my tears. But yet
It is our trick; nature her custom holds,
Let shame say what it will. [*Weeps*] When these are
        gone,
The woman will be out. Adieu, my lord,
190 I have a speech o' fire that fain would blaze
But that this folly douts it.   [*Exit*

King
                              Let's follow, Gertrude.
How much I had to do to calm his rage.
Now fear I this will give it start again.
Therefore let's follow.   [*Exeunt*

ACT 5

Act 5 Scene 1

Hamlet and Horatio interrupt two gravediggers at their work. Ophelia's funeral procession approaches, and Hamlet bursts out among the mourners to declare his love in a confrontation with Laertes.

s.d. *two Clowns*: The scene is written for a comic actor and a 'straight man'.

1 *Christian burial*: Christian funeral rites were denied to suicides.

2 *salvation*: damnation; such verbal mistaking ('malapropism') is characteristic of Shakespeare's clowns.

3 *straight*: immediately.

4 *crowner*: coroner.
sat on her: passed judgement on her death.

5–6 *her own defence*: self-defence.

8 *se offendendo*: (*se defendendo*) self-defence.

10 *branches*: divisions.

11 *argal*: (Latin *ergo*) therefore.

12 *Goodman*: Master.

15 *will he nill he*: willy-nilly, like it or not.

20 *quest*: inquest.

SCENE 1

Enter two Clowns [*—the* Gravedigger *and* Another]

Gravedigger
Is she to be buried in Christian burial, when she wilfully seeks her own salvation?
Other
I tell thee she is, therefore make her grave straight. The crowner hath sat on her and finds it Christian burial.
Gravedigger
5 How can that be, unless she drowned herself in her own defence?
Other
Why, 'tis found so.
Gravedigger
It must be *se offendendo*, it cannot be else. For here lies the point: if I drown myself wittingly, it argues an act, and an act hath three branches—it is to act, to do, to perform; argal, she drowned herself wittingly.
Other
Nay, but hear you, Goodman Delver—
Gravedigger
Give me leave. Here lies the water—good. Here stands the man—good. If the man go to this water and drown himself, it is, will he nill he, he goes, mark you that. But if the water come to him and drown him, he drowns not himself. Argal, he that is not guilty of his own death shortens not his own life.
Other
But is this law?
Gravedigger
20 Aye, marry is't, crowner's quest law.

21 *an't*: of it.

Other

Will you ha' the truth an't? If this had not been a
gentlewoman, she should have been buried out o'
Christian burial.

Gravedigger

Why, there thou say'st. And the more pity that great folk

25 *countenance*: privilege.

25 should have countenance in this world to drown or
hang themselves more than their even-Christen. Come,

26 *even-Christen*: fellow-Christians (who
are all equal in the sight of God).

my spade. There is no ancient gentlemen but gardeners,

27 *my spade*: i.e. give me my spade.

ditchers, and gravemakers—they hold up Adam's

28 *hold up*: carry on.

profession.

28–9 *Adam's profession*: Adam had to
care for the garden of Eden (Genesis,
3:23).

He digs

Other

30 Was he a gentleman?

Gravedigger

'A was the first that ever bore arms.

31 *bore arms*: had a gentleman's coat of
arms. The Gravedigger enjoys his joke.

Other

Why, he had none.

Gravedigger

What, art a heathen? How dost thou understand the
Scripture? The Scripture says Adam digged. Could he

35–6 *If . . . thyself*: if you can't give me
the answer, admit that I have beaten
you. The common saying was 'Confess
and be hanged'.

35 dig without arms? I'll put another question to thee. If
thou answerest me not to the purpose, confess thyself—

37 *Go to*: get on with it.

Other

Go to.

Gravedigger

What is he that builds stronger than either the mason,
the shipwright, or the carpenter?

Other

40 *frame*: structure.

40 The gallows-maker, for that frame outlives a thousand
tenants.

Gravedigger

42 *does well*: is a good answer.

I like thy wit well in good faith, the gallows does well.
But how does it well? It does well to those that do ill.
Now, thou dost ill to say the gallows is built stronger

45 than the church; argal, the gallows may do well to thee.
To't again, come.

Other
Who builds stronger than a mason, a shipwright, or a
carpenter?
Gravedigger
Ay, tell me that and unyoke.
Other
50 Marry, now I can tell.
Gravedigger
To't.
Other
Mass, I cannot tell.
Gravedigger
Cudgel thy brains no more about it, for your dull ass
55 will not mend his pace with beating. And when you are
asked this question next, say 'A gravemaker'. The houses
he makes lasts till doomsday. Go, get thee to Yaughan;
fetch me a stoup of liquor.   [*Exit the* Other Clown

The Gravedigger *continues digging*

[*Sings*] *In youth when I did love, did love,*
            Methought it was very sweet:
60 *To contract—O—the time for—a—my behove,*
   O methought there—a—was nothing—a—meet.

Enter Hamlet *and* Horatio

Hamlet
Has this fellow no feeling of his business 'a sings in
grave-making?
Horatio
Custom hath made it in him a property of easiness.
Hamlet
65 'Tis e'en so, the hand of little employment hath the
daintier sense.
Gravedigger
[*Sings*] *But age with his stealing steps*
            Hath claw'd me in his clutch,
            And hath shipp'd me intil the land,
70   *As if I had never been such.*

[*He throws up a skull*]

---

49 *unyoke*: have done with it (like oxen
freed from the yoke at the end of the
day).

52 *Mass*: by the mass.

54 *mend his pace*: go any better.

56 *Yaughan*: perhaps the name [?Johan]
of the local publican.
57 *stoup*: flagon.

58–61 *In . . . meet*: The gravedigger
punctuates his singing with the
grunts—'O . . . a'—of his labours.
60 *contract*: pass.
behove: advantage.

62 *feeling of his business*: respect for his
occupation.
'a: that he.

64 'He is accustomed to the job.'

66 *daintier sense*: more sensitive feeling.

69 *intil*: to.

72 *jowls*: dashes.
72–3 *Cain's . . . murder*: Compare
      3, 3, 37.

74 *politician*: schemer.
   o'er-offices: lords it over.
75 *circumvent God*: cheat even God.

Hamlet

That skull had a tongue in it, and could sing once. How
the knave jowls it to th' ground, as if 'twere Cain's
jawbone, that did the first murder. This might be the
pate of a politician which this ass now o'er-offices, one
75 that would circumvent God, might it not?

Horatio

It might, my lord.

Hamlet

Or of a courtier, which could say, 'Good morrow, sweet
lord. How dost thou, sweet lord?' This might be my
Lord Such-a-one, that praised my Lord Such-a-one's
80 horse when 'a meant to beg it, might it not?

Horatio

Ay, my lord.

Hamlet

82 *chopless*: lacking a jaw.
83 *mazard*: headpiece.
84 *revolution*: turn-around.
   trick: knack.
85 *cost no more*: only worth.
   loggets: tossing pieces of wood at a
   target.

88 *For and*: and in addition.
92 *quiddities*: quibbling arguments about
   meanings (*quidditas* = essential
   nature of a thing; 'quillities' is
   Hamlet's own coinage).
93 *tenures*: land rights.
94 *sconce*: head.
95–6 *action of battery*: charge of assault.
97 *buyer of land*: property dealer; lawyers
   were often accused of using legal
   expertise for personal advantage in
   such deals.
97–8 *statutes . . . recoveries*: legal terms
   relating to property-dealing and debt-
   recovery: 'statutes' = securities for
   debt; 'recognizances' =
   acknowledgements of debt; 'fines'
   = actions leading to agreement;
   'recoveries' = suits for obtaining
   possession; 'double vouchers' = third-
   party securities.
98 *fine*: a) end; b) handsome; c) small,
   finely ground.
99 *recovery*: whole gain.
100 *vouch*: assure.

Why, e'en so, and now my Lady Worm's, chopless, and
knocked about the mazard with a sexton's spade. Here's
fine revolution and we had the trick to see't. Did these
85 bones cost no more the breeding but to play at loggets
with 'em? Mine ache to think on't.

Gravedigger

[*Sings*] *A pickaxe and a spade, a spade,*
          For and a shrouding-sheet,
          O a pit of clay for to be made
90   *For such a guest is meet.*

[*Throws up another skull*]

Hamlet

There's another. Why, may not that be the skull of a
lawyer? Where be his quiddities now, his quillities, his
cases, his tenures, and his tricks? Why does he suffer this
mad knave now to knock him about the sconce with a
95 dirty shovel, and will not tell him of his action of
battery? Hum, this fellow might be in's time a great
buyer of land, with his statutes, his recognizances, his
fines, his double vouchers, his recoveries. Is this the fine
of his fines and the recovery of his recoveries, to have
100 his fine pate full of fine dirt? Will his vouchers vouch
him no more of his purchases, and double ones too,

102 *indentures*: documents used in
  conveyancing; the details were
  duplicated (hence 'pair') on a single
  sheet of paper which was divided by a
  jagged cut.

103 *conveyances*: documents relating to
  ownership of land.
103–4 *this box*: probably the grave.
104 *th'inheritor*: the man who acquires the
  'box'.
108 *sheep and calves*: i.e. fools.
  assurance: certainty of possession—
  and the deed securing this.
110 *sirrah*: sir (a form used only to address
  inferiors).
113 *thine*: Hamlet speaks to the
  Gravedigger using the familiar second
  person singular, while the Gravedigger
  replies with the polite (second person
  plural) form.
114 *You lie*: The pun is expected.
117 *quick*: living.

122 *none*: no woman.

125 *absolute*: strict in his use of language,
  pedantic.
  card: book—literally, a shipman's
  navigation chart.
126 *equivocation*: ambiguity.
  undo: ruin.

than the length and breadth of a pair of indentures? The very conveyances of his lands will scarcely lie in this box, and must th'inheritor himself have no more, ha?

Horatio
105 Not a jot more, my lord.
Hamlet
Is not parchment made of sheepskins?
Horatio
Ay, my lord, and of calveskins too.
Hamlet
They are sheep and calves which seek out assurance in that. I will speak to this fellow.—Whose grave's this,
110 sirrah?
Gravedigger
Mine, sir.
[*Sings*] *O a pit of clay for to be made—*
Hamlet
I think it be thine indeed, for thou liest in't.
Gravedigger
You lie out on't, sir, and therefore 'tis not yours. For my
115 part, I do not lie in't, yet it is mine.
Hamlet
Thou dost lie in't, to be in't and say 'tis thine. 'Tis for the dead, not for the quick: therefore thou liest.
Gravedigger
'Tis a quick lie, sir, 'twill away again from me to you.
Hamlet
What man dost thou dig it for?
Gravedigger
120 For no man, sir.
Hamlet
What woman then?
Gravedigger
For none neither.
Hamlet
Who is to be buried in't?
Gravedigger
One that was a woman, sir; but rest her soul, she's dead.
Hamlet
125 How absolute the knave is. We must speak by the card or equivocation will undo us. By the Lord, Horatio, this

126–7 *this . . . note of it*: I have watched it happening over the past few years.
127 *the age*: people nowadays.
127–8 *grown so picked*: become so refined.
128–9 *the toe . . . kibe*: there's not much difference between poor and rich—one comes so close to the other that he rubs ('galls') his chilblain ('kibe').

135 *young Hamlet was born*: From the evidence presented in this scene, various critics have attempted to calculate Hamlet's age; but precise chronology seems unimportant.

41–2 *as mad as he*: The madness of the English became a national joke.

152 *pocky*: diseased.
hold: survive.
152–3 *laying in*: i.e. burying.

three years I have took note of it, the age is grown so picked that the toe of the peasant comes so near the heel of the courtier he galls his kibe.—How long hast thou
130 been grave-maker?

Gravedigger
Of all the days i'th' year I came to't that day that our last King Hamlet o'ercame Fortinbras.

Hamlet
How long is that since?

Gravedigger
Cannot you tell that? Every fool can tell that. It was that
135 very day that young Hamlet was born—he that is mad and sent into England.

Hamlet
Ay, marry. Why was he sent into England?

Gravedigger
Why, because 'a was mad. 'A shall recover his wits there. Or if 'a do not, 'tis no great matter there.

Hamlet
140 Why?

Gravedigger
'Twill not be seen in him there. There the men are as mad as he.

Hamlet
How came he mad?

Gravedigger
Very strangely, they say.

Hamlet
145 How 'strangely'?

Gravedigger
Faith, e'en with losing his wits.

Hamlet
Upon what ground?

Gravedigger
Why, here in Denmark. I have been sexton here, man and boy, thirty years.

Hamlet
150 How long will a man lie i'th' earth ere he rot?

Gravedigger
Faith, if 'a be not rotten before 'a die—as we have many pocky corses nowadays that will scarce hold the laying

in—'a will last you some eight year or nine year. A
tanner will last you nine year.

Hamlet

155 Why he more than another?

Gravedigger

Why, sir, his hide is so tanned with his trade that 'a will
keep out water a great while, and your water is a sore
decayer of your whoreson dead body. Here's a skull now
hath lien you i'th' earth three and twenty years.

Hamlet

160 Whose was it?

Gravedigger

A whoreson mad fellow's it was. Whose do you think it
was?

Hamlet

Nay, I know not.

Gravedigger

A pestilence on him for a mad rogue! 'A poured a flagon
165 of Rhenish on my head once. This same skull, sir, was
Yorick's skull, the king's jester.

Hamlet

This?

Takes the skull

Gravedigger

E'en that.

Hamlet

Alas, poor Yorick. I knew him, Horatio, a fellow of
170 infinite jest, of most excellent fancy. He hath bore me on
his back a thousand times, and now—how abhorred in
my imagination it is. My gorge rises at it. Here hung
those lips that I have kissed I know not how oft. Where
be your gibes now, your gambols, your songs, your
175 flashes of merriment, that were wont to set the table on
a roar? Not one now to mock your own grinning? Quite
chop-fallen? Now get you to my lady's chamber and tell
her, let her paint an inch thick, to this favour she must
come. Make her laugh at that.—Prithee, Horatio, tell
180 me one thing.

158 *whoreson*: An expression of
contemptuous familiarity.
159 *lien*: been lying. The 'you' is merely
for emphasis.

165 *Rhenish*: Rhine wine.

170 *fancy*: imagination.

172 *my gorge rises*: I feel sick at the sight.

177 *chop-fallen*: down in the mouth.
178–9 *to . . . come*: she will end up
looking like this.

'Alas, poor Yorick. I knew him, Horatio, a fellow of infinite jest' (*5*, 1, 169–70), Alan David as Gravedigger, Samuel West as Hamlet, and Conor Moloney as Other Gravedigger, Royal Shakespeare Company, 2001.

Horatio
What's that, my lord?
Hamlet
Dost thou think Alexander looked o' this fashion in 'th'
earth?
Horatio
E'en so.
Hamlet
185 And smelt so? Pah!

Puts down the skull

Horatio
E'en so, my lord.
Hamlet
To what base uses we may return, Horatio! Why, may
not imagination trace the noble dust of Alexander till 'a
find it stopping a bung-hole?
Horatio
190 'Twere to consider too curiously to consider so.
Hamlet
No, faith, not a jot, but to follow him thither with
modesty enough, and likelihood to lead it. Alexander
died, Alexander was buried, Alexander returneth to
dust, the dust is earth, of earth we make loam, and why
195 of that loam whereto he was converted might they not
stop a beer-barrel?
Imperious Caesar, dead and turn'd to clay,
Might stop a hole to keep the wind away.
O that that earth which kept the world in awe
200 Should patch a wall t'expel the winter's flaw.
But soft, but soft awhile. Here comes the king,
The queen, the courtiers.

Enter Bearers *with a Coffin, a* Priest, King, Queen,
Laertes, Lords *Attendant*

Who is this they follow?
And with such maimed rites? This doth betoken
The corse they follow did with desp'rate hand

182 *Alexander*: Alexander the Great
(356–323 BC) was the greatest
conqueror known to the classical
world, and often cited in meditations
on Death the Leveller; he was also
noted for the beauty of his body.

190 *curiously*: ingeniously.

192 *modesty*: moderation.
likelihood to lead it: consideration of
what is likely.
194 *loam*: plaster (made with clay and
water).

197 *Imperious Caesar*: The emperor Julius
Caesar was often cited together with
Alexander; the rhyme seems to be
Hamlet's own.
200 *flaw*: storm.

203 *maimed rites*: maimèd; i.e. the
minimum of ceremony.

205 *Fordo*: destroy.
　it: its.
　estate: worldly position.
206 *Couch we*: let's hide ourselves.

210 *enlarg'd*: extended.
211 *have warranty*: As the Priest explains, some additional sanction (other than the findings of the coroner) was necessary when there was any doubt of the cause of death.
212 *o'ersways . . . order*: overrules normal practice.
214 *last trumpet*: This should signal the end of the world.
　for: instead of; as a rejection of social and religious values, suicide was punished by deprivation of the usual rites.
215 *Shards*: broken stones.
216 *virgin crants*: wreath of virginity.
217 *maiden strewments*: flowers strewing the grave in token of chastity.
217–18 *bringing . . . burial*: carrying to the grave with tolling bell and burial rites.
221 *sage requiem*: solemn mass.

224 *violets*: symbolic of love and chastity (see *4, 5, 181*).

226 *howling*: i.e. in hell.
229 *deck'd*: decorated.

231 *cursed*: cursèd.

205 Fordo it own life. 'Twas of some estate.
　Couch we awhile and mark.
　　　Laertes
　What ceremony else?
　　　Hamlet
　That is Laertes, a very noble youth. Mark.
　　　Laertes
　What ceremony else?
　　　Priest
210 Her obsequies have been as far enlarg'd
　As we have warranty. Her death was doubtful;
　And but that great command o'ersways the order,
　She should in ground unsanctified been lodg'd
　Till the last trumpet: for charitable prayers
215 Shards, flints, and pebbles should be thrown on her.
　Yet here she is allow'd her virgin crants,
　Her maiden strewments, and the bringing home
　Of bell and burial.
　　　Laertes
　Must there no more be done?
　　　Priest
　　　　　　　　　　　　No more be done.
220 We should profane the service of the dead
　To sing sage requiem and such rest to her
　As to peace-parted souls.
　　　Laertes
　　　　　　　　　　Lay her in'th' earth,
　And from her fair and unpolluted flesh
　May violets spring. I tell thee, churlish priest,
225 A minist'ring angel shall my sister be
　When thou liest howling.
　　　Hamlet
　　　　　　　　　　What, the fair Ophelia!
　　　Queen
　[*Scattering flowers*] Sweets to the sweet. Farewell.
　I hop'd thou shouldst have been my Hamlet's wife:
　I thought thy bride-bed to have deck'd, sweet maid,
230 And not have strew'd thy grave.
　　　Laertes
　　　　　　　　　　　　O, treble woe
　Fall ten times treble on that cursed head

232 *ingenious*: alert, lively.

234 *caught her*: The coffin would be open.

Whose wicked deed thy most ingenious sense
Depriv'd thee of.—Hold off the earth awhile,
Till I have caught her once more in mine arms.

Leaps into the grave

235 *quick*: living.
236 *flat*: level ground.
236–8 *a mountain . . . Olympus*: The
giants of classical mythology heaped
Mt. Pelion on top of Mt. Ossa in their
attempt to storm Mt. Olympus, the
home of the gods.

235 Now pile your dust upon the quick and dead,
Till of this flat a mountain you have made
T'o'ertop old Pelion or the skyish head
Of blue Olympus.
Hamlet
              What is he whose grief
Bears such an emphasis, whose phrase of sorrow

239 *Bears . . . emphasis*: is so vehemently
expressed.
240 *Conjures . . . stars*: casts a spell on
the planets (called 'wandering stars'
to distinguish them from the 'fixed
stars' of the firmament).

240 Conjures the wand'ring stars and makes them stand
Like wonder-wounded hearers? This is I,
Hamlet the Dane.
Laertes
[*Grappling with him*] The devil take thy soul!

243s.d. The comments of the bystanders
suggest that this fight takes place on
the stage, not in the grave (which
would be represented by a trap-door in
the stage).

Hamlet
                    Thou pray'st not well.
I prithee take thy fingers from my throat,

245 *splenative*: hot-tempered (caused by
excess of spleen).

245 For though I am not splenative and rash,
Yet have I in me something dangerous,
Which let thy wiseness fear. Hold off thy hand.
King
Pluck them asunder.

Queen

Hamlet! Hamlet!

All

250 Gentlemen!

Horatio

Good my lord, be quiet.

Hamlet

Why, I will fight with him upon this theme

Until my eyelids will no longer wag.

Queen

O my son, what theme?

Hamlet

255 I lov'd Ophelia. Forty thousand brothers

Could not with all their quantity of love

Make up my sum. What wilt thou do for her?

King

O, he is mad, Laertes.

Queen

For love of God forbear him.

Hamlet

260 'Swounds, show me what thou't do.

Woo't weep, woo't fight, woo't fast, woo't tear thyself,

Woo't drink up eisel, eat a crocodile?

I'll do't. Dost come here to whine,

To outface me with leaping in her grave?

265 Be buried quick with her, and so will I.

And if thou prate of mountains, let them throw

Millions of acres on us, till our ground,

Singeing his pate against the burning zone,

Make Ossa like a wart. Nay, and thou'lt mouth,

270 I'll rant as well as thou.

Queen

This is mere madness,

And thus awhile the fit will work on him.

Anon, as patient as the female dove

When that her golden couplets are disclos'd,

His silence will sit drooping.

Hamlet

Hear you, sir,

275 What is the reason that you use me thus?

I lov'd you ever. But it is no matter.

---

253 *wag*: flutter (show the least sign of life).

259 *forbear him*: leave him alone.

260 *thou't*: thou wilt. Hamlet uses the 'thou' of insult.
261 *Woo't*: wilt thou.
262 *eisel*: vinegar.
crocodile: Perhaps because these were said to shed false tears?

265 *quick*: alive.

267 *our ground*: i.e. where we are buried, the 'flat' of line 236.
268 *his*: its.
burning zone: the sphere of the sun.
269 *Ossa*: See line 237; Hamlet will outdo Laertes—even in the vehemence of his rhetoric.

273 *golden couplets*: twin chicks.
disclos'd: hatched.

276 *ever*: always.

277 *Hercules*: the superman of Greek mythology, who was dramatically presented with roaring speeches.
278 'A cat cannot be silenced for ever, and even a dog cannot always be kept down.'
279 *wait upon him*: look after him.
280 *in our last night's speech*: by thinking of what we talked about last night.
281 *to the present push*: into action immediately.

283 *living*: everlasting.

Act 5 Scene 2
A challenge is issued and accepted: the duel is arranged, the king prepares the chalices, and Hamlet fights Laertes.

1 *see the other*: i.e. as promised in 4, 6, 22–3.

6 *mutines in the bilboes*: mutineers in shackles (which were attached to a fixed bar on board ship).
7 *let us know*: let us remember. Hamlet never fails to meditate on his experience.
9 *pall*: falter.
   learn us: teach us.
10 *divinity*: divine power.
10–11 *shapes . . . will*: Hamlet's metaphor is from building, where the workmen cut ('rough-hew') the stone or timber which is then shaped by the master-craftsman.
13 *sea-gown*: short-sleeved garment of coarse fabric.
   scarf'd: wrapped (not properly put on).
14 *them*: Rosencrantz and Guildenstern.
15 *Finger'd*: got my hands on.
   in fine: finally.

Let Hercules himself do what he may,
The cat will mew, and dog will have his day.   [*Exit*
    King
I pray thee, good Horatio, wait upon him.
                                              [*Exit* Horatio
280 [*To* Laertes] Strengthen your patience in our last
        night's speech:
We'll put the matter to the present push.—
Good Gertrude, set some watch over your son.
This grave shall have a living monument.
An hour of quiet shortly shall we see;
285 Till then in patience our proceeding be.   [*Exeunt*

SCENE 2

Enter Hamlet *and* Horatio

Hamlet
So much for this, sir. Now shall you see the other.
You do remember all the circumstance?
    Horatio
Remember it, my lord!
    Hamlet
Sir, in my heart there was a kind of fighting
5 That would not let me sleep. Methought I lay
Worse than the mutines in the bilboes. Rashly—
And prais'd be rashness for it: let us know
Our indiscretion sometime serves us well
When our deep plots do pall; and that should learn us
10 There's a divinity that shapes our ends,
Rough-hew them how we will—
    Horatio
                                    That is most certain.
    Hamlet
Up from my cabin,
My sea-gown scarf'd about me, in the dark
Grop'd I to find out them, had my desire,
15 Finger'd their packet, and in fine withdrew
To mine own room again, making so bold,
My fears forgetting manners, to unseal

20 *Larded*: garnished.

21 *Importing*: concerning.
health: well-being, security.

22 *bugs and goblins*: i.e. imaginary dangers.
in my life: if I remain alive.

23 *on the supervise*: as soon as the letter is read.
no leisure bated: without wasting time.

24 *stay*: wait for.
grinding: sharpening.

29 *benetted*: entangled.

30–1 *Or . . . play*: before I even started thinking about it, my mind had begun the action.

32 *fair*: properly.

33–4 *I . . . fair*: I used to think, as statesmen ('statists') do, that it was beneath me to have good handwriting.

36 *did . . . service*: served me well (as the untrained English yeomen served their feudal lords).

37 *Th'effect*: the contents.

38 *conjuration*: injunction.

39 *As England*: since England.

40 *As love*: so that friendship.
the palm: 'The righteous shall flourish like the palm-tree' (Psalm 92:12); Hamlet imitates Claudius's flowery style.

41 *wheaten*: made of wheat stalks (emblematic of rural prosperity).

42 *stand a comma*: join them as a comma links parts of a sentence.

43 *charge*: significance.

44 *view and knowing*: reading and understanding.

45 *debatement*: argument.

46 *sudden*: immediate.

47 *shriving-time*: time for spiritual confession.

Their grand commission; where I found, Horatio—
Ah, royal knavery!—an exact command,
20 Larded with many several sorts of reasons
Importing Denmark's health, and England's too,
With ho! such bugs and goblins in my life,
That on the supervise, no leisure bated,
No, not to stay the grinding of the axe,
25 My head should be struck off.

Horatio
                                    Is't possible?

Hamlet
Here's the commission, read it at more leisure.
But wilt thou hear now how I did proceed?

Horatio
I beseech you.

Hamlet
Being thus benetted round with villainies—
30 Or I could make a prologue to my brains,
They had begun the play—I sat me down,
Devis'd a new commission, wrote it fair—
I once did hold it, as our statists do,
A baseness to write fair, and labour'd much
35 How to forget that learning, but, sir, now
It did me yeoman's service. Wilt thou know
Th'effect of what I wrote?

Horatio
                                    Ay, good my lord.

Hamlet
An earnest conjuration from the king,
As England was his faithful tributary,
40 As love between them like the palm might flourish,
As peace should still her wheaten garland wear
And stand a comma 'tween their amities,
And many such-like 'as'es of great charge,
That on the view and knowing of these contents,
45 Without debatement further more or less,
He should those bearers put to sudden death,
Not shriving-time allow'd.

Horatio
                                    How was this seal'd?

Hamlet
Why, even in that was heaven ordinant.
I had my father's signet in my purse,
50 Which was the model of that Danish seal,
Folded the writ up in the form of th'other,
Subscrib'd it, gave't th'impression, plac'd it safely,
The changeling never known. Now the next day
Was our sea-fight, and what to this was sequent
55 Thou knowest already.
Horatio
So Guildenstern and Rosencrantz go to't.
Hamlet
Why, man, they did make love to this employment.
They are not near my conscience, their defeat
Does by their own insinuation grow.
60 'Tis dangerous when the baser nature comes
Between the pass and fell incensed points
Of mighty opposites.
Horatio
                              Why, what a king is this!
Hamlet
Does it not, think thee, stand me now upon—
He that hath kill'd my king and whor'd my mother,
65 Popp'd in between th'election and my hopes,
Thrown out his angle for my proper life
And with such coz'nage—is't not perfect conscience
To quit him with this arm? And is't not to be damn'd
To let this canker of our nature come
70 In further evil?
Horatio
It must be shortly known to him from England
What is the issue of the business there.
Hamlet
It will be short. The interim is mine.
And a man's life's no more than to say 'one'.
75 But I am very sorry, good Horatio,
That to Laertes I forgot myself;
For by the image of my cause I see
The portraiture of his. I'll court his favours.
But sure the bravery of his grief did put me
80 Into a tow'ring passion.

48 *ordinant*: ordination; Hamlet sees the shaping hand of 'divinity' (line 10) everywhere.
49 *signet*: signet-ring.

51 *writ*: writing.
52 *Subscrib'd*: signed underneath.
53 *changeling*: substitute for the one stolen (literally, a replacement for a child stolen by fairies).
54 *what . . . sequent*: what followed this.
56 *go to't*: will die; Horatio is shocked.
57 *they . . . employment*: they were willing participants.
59 *insinuation*: intruding into the matter.
60 *the baser nature*: a lowly person.
61–2 *the pass . . . opposites*: the cruel and angry sword-fighting of powerful opponents.
61 *incensed*: incensèd.
63 *stand . . . upon*: give me your opinion.
65 *Popp'd . . . hopes*: defrauded me of my hopes of election (to succeed his father).
66 *angle*: fishing-rod.
   proper: own.
67 *coz'nage*: cheating.
68 *quit him*: repay him.
69 *canker*: malignant sore.

72 *issue*: outcome.

73 *interim*: interval.

74 *say*: count.

77 *image*: representation.
78 *court his favours*: make friends with him .
79 *bravery*: passionate expression.

Horatio

Peace, who comes here?

Enter Osric, *a Courtier*

Osric

Your Lordship is right welcome back to Denmark.

Hamlet

I humbly thank you, sir.—Dost know this water-fly?

Horatio

No, my good lord.

Hamlet

Thy state is the more gracious, for 'tis a vice to know
85 him. He hath much land and fertile. Let a beast be lord
of beasts and his crib shall stand at the king's mess. 'Tis
a chuff, but, as I say, spacious in the possession of dirt.

Osric

Sweet lord, if your lordship were at leisure, I should
impart a thing to you from his Majesty.

Hamlet

90 I will receive it, sir, with all diligence of spirit. Your
bonnet to his right use: 'tis for the head.

Osric

I thank your lordship, it is very hot.

Hamlet

No, believe me, 'tis very cold, the wind is northerly.

Osric

It is indifferent cold, my lord, indeed.

82 *water-fly*: mosquito; the return to
prose lightens the atmosphere.

86 *crib*: manger, beast's feeding-rack.
mess: dining-table.
87 *chuff*: peasant.
spacious . . . dirt: a great land-owner.

90 *diligence*: attentiveness.
90–1 *Your . . . use*: put on your hat;
Elizabethans wore their hats indoors,
but removed them in the presence of
a superior.

92 *I . . . hot*: Osric, reluctant to offend
etiquette, excuses himself from
obeying Hamlet's courtesy.

94 *indifferent*: fairly, rather.

96 *complexion*: temperament.

104 *absolute*: perfect.
105 *differences*: distinctions.
106 *soft society*: pleasing manners.

107 *feelingly*: knowledgeably.
     card or calendar: model or epitome.
     gentry: gentlemanly behaviour.
108 *continent*: container.

110–17 *his . . . more*: Hamlet parodies
     Osric's speech mannerisms.
110 *his . . . you*: he loses nothing in your
     description.
111 *divide . . . inventorially*: list his
     different attributes.
     dozy: stupefy.
112–13 *yaw . . . sail*: waver from the
     course in trying to keep up with him.
113 *in . . . extolment*: to praise him truly.
114 *article*: theme.
114–15 *his . . . rareness*: his quality so
     rare and precious.
115 *make . . . diction*: speak truly.
116–17 *his . . . umbrage*: his only likeness
     is in his mirror and in those who
     follow in his line.
119 *The concernancy*: what is all this
     about.
119–20 *wrap . . . breath*: describe him in
     our rough speech.

122 *Is't . . . tongue*: can't you speak in
     another way.
122–3 *You will to't*: you provoke him.

124 *What . . . nomination*: what is the
     name.

Hamlet

95 But yet methinks it is very sultry and hot for my
complexion.

Osric

Exceedingly, my lord, it is very sultry—as 'twere—I
cannot tell how. My lord, his Majesty bade me signify to
you that 'a has laid a great wager on your head. Sir, this

100 is the matter—

Hamlet

[*Signing to him to put on his hat*] I beseech you
remember—

Osric

Nay, good my lord, for my ease, in good faith. Sir, here is
newly come to court Laertes—believe me, an absolute

105 gentleman, full of most excellent differences, of very
soft society and great showing. Indeed, to speak
feelingly of him, he is the card or calendar of gentry; for
you shall find in him the continent of what part a
gentleman would see.

Hamlet

110 Sir, his definement suffers no perdition in you, though I
know to divide him inventorially would dozy
th'arithmetic of memory, and yet but yaw neither, in
respect of his quick sail. But, in the verity of extolment,
I take him to be a soul of great article and his infusion

115 of such dearth and rareness as, to make true diction of
him, his semblable is his mirror and who else would
trace him his umbrage, nothing more.

Osric

Your lordship speaks most infallibly of him.

Hamlet

The concernancy, sir? Why do we wrap the gentleman

120 in our more rawer breath?

Osric

Sir?

Horatio

Is't not possible to understand in another tongue? You
will to't, sir, really.

Hamlet

What imports the nomination of this gentleman?

Osric

125 Of Laertes?

Horatio

His purse is empty already, all's golden words are spent.

Hamlet

Of him, sir.

Osric

I know you are not ignorant—

Hamlet

I would you did, sir. Yet in faith if you did, it would not
130 much approve me. Well, sir?

Osric

You are not ignorant of what excellence Laertes is—

Hamlet

I dare not confess that, lest I should compare with him
in excellence; but to know a man well were to know
himself.

Osric

135 I mean, sir, for his weapon; but in the imputation laid
on him, by them in his meed, he's unfellowed.

Hamlet

What's his weapon?

Osric

Rapier and dagger.

Hamlet

That's two of his weapons. But well.

Osric

140 The king, sir, hath wagered with him six Barbary horses,
against the which he has impawned, as I take it, six
French rapiers and poniards, with their assigns, as
girdle, hanger, and so. Three of the carriages, in faith,
are very dear to fancy, very responsive to the hilts, most
145 delicate carriages, and of very liberal conceit.

Hamlet

What call you the carriages?

Horatio

I knew you must be edified by the margin ere you had
done.

Osric

The carriages, sir, are the hangers.

---

130 *approve*: compliment.
132–4 *I . . . himself*: Hamlet's riddling
  sense perhaps means that to
  appreciate excellence one must know
  it in oneself.
135 *imputation*: estimation.
136 *by . . . meed*: those who can judge
  such matters.
138 *Rapier and dagger*: The fashionable
  weapons of the time; the dagger was
  held in the left hand to ward off the
  opponent's rapier.

140 *Barbary*: Arab.
141 *impawned*: staked.
142 *poniards*: daggers.
  assigns: accessories.
143 *hanger*: the straps and pad attaching
  the sword to the girdle.
144 *dear to fancy*: well-designed.
  responsive to: appropriate for.
145 *delicate*: finely-wrought.
  liberal conceit: richly decorated.
146 *call you*: do you mean by.
147 *you . . . margin*: would need the
  explanation of a marginal note.

150 *german*: appropriate; a 'carriage' was used to transport a cannon.

156 *laid*: wagered.
passes: bouts.
157-8 *exceed . . . hits*: hit you three times more than you hit him.
158 *twelve for nine*: Perhaps these are the given odds for the duel.
159-60 *vouchsafe the answer*: accept the challenge.
164 *breathing . . . me*: my exercise period.
165-6 *hold his purpose*: keep his word.
166 *and*: if.
167 *the odd hits*: i.e. the extra three hits of the wager.
168 *deliver you so*: return this answer.
169 *flourish*: ceremony.
170 *commend*: a) present; b) praise.
171 *Yours*: Hamlet is curtly dismissive.
173 *for's turn*: to do it for him.
174 *lapwing*: silly young bird (who leaves the nest as soon as it is hatched); perhaps Osric's hat suggested the image to Horatio.

175 *did . . . dug*: paid formal compliments to the nipple.
176 *bevy*: batch, flock.
177 *the drossy age*: the degenerate time.
got the tune: learned the fashionable speech.
178 *out . . . encounter*: through meeting with it regularly.
yeasty collection: bubbly conversation.
179 *carries them through*: enables them to confront.
179-80 *the most . . . opinions*: men of the most carefully sifted (tested) ideas.

Hamlet

150 The phrase would be more german to the matter if we could carry a cannon by our sides—I would it might be hangers till then. But on. Six Barbary horses against six French swords, their assigns, and three liberal-conceited carriages—that's the French bet against the Danish.

155 Why is this—impawned, as you call it?

Osric

The king, sir, hath laid, sir, that in a dozen passes between yourself and him he shall not exceed you three hits; he hath laid on twelve for nine. And it would come to immediate trial if your lordship would vouchsafe the

160 answer.

Hamlet

How if I answer no?

Osric

I mean, my lord, the opposition of your person in trial.

Hamlet

Sir, I will walk here in the hall. If it please his Majesty, it is the breathing time of day with me. Let the foils be

165 brought, the gentleman willing, and the king hold his purpose, I will win for him and I can; if not, I will gain nothing but my shame and the odd hits.

Osric

Shall I deliver you so?

Hamlet

To this effect, sir, after what flourish your nature will.

Osric

170 I commend my duty to your lordship.

Hamlet

Yours.   [*Exit* Osric
'A does well to commend it himself, there are no tongues else for's turn.

Horatio

This lapwing runs away with the shell on his head.

Hamlet

175 'A did comply with his dug before 'a sucked it. Thus has he—and many more of the same bevy that I know the drossy age dotes on—only got the tune of the time and, out of an habit of encounter, a kind of yeasty collection, which carries them through and through the most

180 fanned and winnowed opinions; and do but blow them
to their trial, the bubbles are out.

Enter a Lord

Lord
My lord, his Majesty commended him to you by young
Osric, who brings back to him that you attend him in
the hall. He sends to know if your pleasure hold to play
185 with Laertes or that you will take longer time.
Hamlet
I am constant to my purposes, they follow the king's
pleasure. If his fitness speaks, mine is ready. Now or
whensoever, provided I be so able as now.
Lord
The king and queen and all are coming down.
Hamlet

190 *In happy time*: most fortunately.

191–2 *use . . . entertainment*: show some courtesy.

190 In happy time.
Lord
The   queen   desires   you   to   use   some   gentle
entertainment to Laertes before you fall to play.
Hamlet
She well instructs me.   [*Exit* Lord
Horatio
You will lose, my lord.
Hamlet

196 *at the odds*: the 'three hits' of line 157–8.
197 *how . . . heart*: how worried I am about everything.

195 I do not think so. Since he went into France, I have been
in continual practice. I shall win at the odds. Thou
wouldst not think how ill all's here about my heart; but
it is no matter.
Horatio
Nay, good my lord.
Hamlet

200 *gaingiving*: misgiving.

200 It is but foolery, but it is such a kind of gaingiving as
would perhaps trouble a woman.
Horatio
If your mind dislike anything, obey it. I will forestall
their repair hither and say you are not fit.

204 *We*: Hamlet assumes the royal plural.
204–5 *There . . . sparrow*: 'Are not two sparrows sold for a farthing? And one of them shall not fall to the ground without your Father' (Matthew 10:29).
205 *it*: death.

Hamlet
Not a whit. We defy augury. There is special providence
205 in the fall of a sparrow. If it be now, 'tis not to come; if it

be not to come, it will be now; if it be not now, yet it will come. The readiness is all. Since no man, of aught he leaves, knows aught, what is't to leave betimes? Let be.

A table prepared. Trumpets, Drums, *and* Officers *with cushions. Enter* King, Queen, Laertes, Osric, *and all the* State, *and* Attendants *with foils and daggers*

King
Come, Hamlet, come, and take this hand from me.

Puts Laertes's *hand into* Hamlet's

Hamlet
210 Give me your pardon, sir. I have done you wrong;
But pardon't as you are a gentleman.
This presence knows, and you must needs have heard,
How I am punish'd with a sore distraction.
What I have done
215 That might your nature, honour, and exception
Roughly awake, I here proclaim was madness.
Was't Hamlet wrong'd Laertes? Never Hamlet.
If Hamlet from himself be ta'en away,
And when he's not himself does wrong Laertes,
220 Then Hamlet does it not, Hamlet denies it.
Who does it then? His madness. If't be so,
Hamlet is of the faction that is wrong'd;
His madness is poor Hamlet's enemy.
Sir, in this audience,
225 Let my disclaiming from a purpos'd evil
Free me so far in your most generous thoughts
That I have shot my arrow o'er the house
And hurt my brother.
Laertes
                              I am satisfied in nature,
Whose motive in this case should stir me most
230 To my revenge; but in my terms of honour
I stand aloof, and will no reconcilement
Till by some elder masters of known honour
I have a voice and precedent of peace

207 *readiness*: 'Be ye also ready' (Matthew 24:44).
207–8 *no man . . . betimes*: no man knows what he leaves behind when he dies, what does it matter if he dies early.
208s.d. *State*: court.

212 *presence*: royal assembly.
213 *I am . . . distraction*: I am suffering from severe mental affliction.
215 *nature*: natural (filial) feelings. *exception*: disapproval.

224 *in this audience*: before these listeners.
225 *purpos'd*: intended.
228 *my brother*: Their shared love for Ophelia (and the similarity of their revenge causes) perhaps links Hamlet and Laertes as brothers. *in nature*: in my human feelings.
229 *Whose . . . most*: which should be my strongest motive.
230 *terms*: sense.
231 *stand aloof*: hold back.
233 *a voice and precedent*: an authoritative pronouncement quoting precedents.

234 *name ungor'd*: reputation unscarred.

To keep my name ungor'd. But till that time
235 I do receive your offer'd love like love
And will not wrong it.
> **Hamlet**
>   I embrace it freely,

236 *freely*: without reservation.
237 *frankly*: honestly.

And will this brothers' wager frankly play.—
Give us the foils.
> **Laertes**
> Come, one for me.
> **Hamlet**

240 *foil*: background to show off a jewel.

240 I'll be your foil, Laertes. In mine ignorance
Your skill shall like a star i'th' darkest night

242 *Stick fiery off*: shine out brilliantly.

Stick fiery off indeed.
> **Laertes**
>   You mock me, sir.
> **Hamlet**
> No, by this hand.
> **King**
> Give them the foils, young Osric. Cousin Hamlet,
245 You know the wager?
> **Hamlet**
>   Very well, my lord.
> Your Grace has laid the odds o'th' weaker side.

246 *laid the odds*: placed your bet.

> **King**
> I do not fear it. I have seen you both,

248 *better'd*: said to be better.

But since he is better'd, we have therefore odds.
> **Laertes**
> This is too heavy. Let me see another.

249 *too heavy*: While the duellists are
selecting their weapons, Laertes must
find the 'unbated' rapier and poison
its point.
250 *likes me well*: suits me.
have . . . length: are all the same
length.

> **Hamlet**
250 This likes me well. These foils have all a length?
> **Osric**
> Ay, my good lord.

They prepare to play

Enter Servants *with flagons of wine*

> **King**
> Set me the stoups of wine upon that table.

252 *stoups*: goblets.
254 *quit . . . exchange*: surrender after the
third bout; the king's meaning is not
clear.

If Hamlet give the first or second hit,
Or quit in answer of the third exchange,

255 *ordnance*: cannon; compare *1, 2, 126*
and *1, 4, 8–12*.
256 *better breath*: renewed energy.
257 *union*: uniquely precious pearl (which
would dissolve in the wine); the
extravagant gesture would conceal the
king's real intention.
260 *kettle*: kettledrum.

255 Let all the battlements their ordnance fire:
The king shall drink to Hamlet's better breath,
And in the cup an union shall he throw
Richer than that which four successive kings
In Denmark's crown have worn—give me the cups—
260 And let the kettle to the trumpet speak,
The trumpet to the cannoneer without,
The cannons to the heavens, the heaven to earth,
'Now the king drinks to Hamlet.' Come, begin.
And you, the judges, bear a wary eye.
Hamlet
265 Come on, sir.
Laertes
Come, my lord.

They play

Hamlet
One.
Laertes
No.
Hamlet
Judgement.
Osric
270 A hit, a very palpable hit.
Laertes
Well, again.
King
Stay, give me drink. Hamlet this pearl is thine.
Here's to thy health.

Drums; trumpets; and shot goes off

Give him the cup.
Hamlet
I'll play this bout first. Set it by awhile.
275 Come.

They play again

Another hit. What say you?

'A hit, a very palpable hit' (5, 2, 270). Michael Pennington as Hamlet and John Bowe as Laertes, Royal Shakespeare Company, 1980.

277 *confess't*: admit it.

Laertes
I do confess't.
   King
Our son shall win.
   Queen
                              He's fat and scant of breath.

278 *fat*: sweating.
    scant of breath: breathless.
279 *napkin*: handkerchief.

Here, Hamlet, take my napkin, rub thy brows.
280 The queen carouses to thy fortune, Hamlet.
   Hamlet
Good madam.

281 *Good madam*: Hamlet acknowledges
    the queen's salutation.

   King
Gertrude, do not drink.
   Queen
I will, my lord, I pray you pardon me.

She drinks and offers the cup to Hamlet

   King
[*Aside*] It is the poison'd cup. It is too late.
   Hamlet
285 I dare not drink yet, madam—by and by.
   Queen
Come, let me wipe thy face.
   Laertes
My lord, I'll hit him now.
   King
                              I do not think't.
   Laertes
[*Aside*] And yet it is almost against my conscience.
   Hamlet
Come for the third, Laertes. You do but dally.

290 *pass*: thrust.

291 *make a wanton of me*: are just fooling
    around with me. Hamlet's taunt
    dispels Laertes' momentary wavering.

290 I pray you pass with your best violence.
I am afeard you make a wanton of me.
   Laertes
Say you so? Come on.

They play

   Osric
Nothing neither way.

Laertes

Have at you now.

Laertes wounds Hamlet; then, in scuffling, they change rapiers

King

295 Part them; they are incensed.

Hamlet

Nay, come again.

He wounds Laertes. The Queen falls

Osric

Look to the queen there, ho!

Horatio

They bleed on both sides. How is it, my lord?

Osric

How is't, Laertes?

Laertes

300 Why, as a woodcock to mine own springe, Osric.

I am justly kill'd with mine own treachery.

Hamlet

How does the queen?

King

She swoons to see them bleed.

Queen

No, no, the drink, the drink! O my dear Hamlet!

The drink, the drink! I am poison'd.   [*Dies*

Hamlet

305 O villainy! Ho! Let the door be lock'd.

Treachery! Seek it out.   [*Exit* Osric

Laertes

It is here, Hamlet. Hamlet, thou art slain.

No medicine in the world can do thee good;

In thee there is not half an hour's life.

310 The treacherous instrument is in thy hand,

Unbated and envenom'd. The foul practice

Hath turn'd itself on me. Lo, here I lie,

Never to rise again. Thy mother's poison'd.

I can no more. The king—the king's to blame.

300 *woodcock*: a proverbially foolish bird. *to mine own springe*: caught in my own trap (see *1*, 3, 115).

311 *Unbated and envenom'd*: see *4*, 7, 138–48. *practice*: trickery.

315 *to thy work*: Hamlet finally achieves revenge—although the king must be doubly punished, to pay for his second crime in causing Gertrude's death.

318 *damned*: damnèd.

319 *thy union*: your pearl; Hamlet also puns on 'union' (= marriage) as he forces the king to drink from his poisoned chalice.

321 *temper'd*: concocted.

322 *Exchange forgiveness*: As he asks for Hamlet's forgiveness, also forgiving Hamlet for killing Polonius, Laertes acquires some of the prince's nobility.

323 *come not upon thee*: i.e. you are not responsible for.

325 *make thee free*: absolve you.

327 *chance*: happening.

328 *mutes*: actors without speaking parts.

329–30 *this . . . arrest*: The personification of Death as an officer of the law—a sergeant-at-arms—is not uncommon in Elizabethan drama.

329 *fell*: stern, cruel.

330 *strict*: just, inescapable.
I could tell you: Elizabethans believed that those near death had the gift of prophecy.

333 *unsatisfied*: those who are ignorant.

334 *antique*: ancient. The pre-Christian Romans preferred to commit suicide rather than live an ignoble life.

339 *hold me in thy heart*: love me.

340 *Absent . . . awhile*: i.e. do not die yet. For Hamlet now, death is seen as the end of a painful life and the beginning of eternal bliss.

Hamlet

315 The point envenom'd too! Then, venom, to thy work.

Wounds the King

All
Treason! treason!
   King
O yet defend me, friends. I am but hurt.
   Hamlet
Here, thou incestuous, murd'rous, damned Dane,
Drink off this potion. Is thy union here?

320 Follow my mother.   [King *dies*
   Laertes
                              He is justly serv'd.
It is a poison temper'd by himself.
Exchange forgiveness with me, noble Hamlet.
Mine and my father's death come not upon thee,
Nor thine on me.   [*Dies*
   Hamlet

325 Heaven make thee free of it. I follow thee.
I am dead, Horatio. Wretched queen, adieu.
You that look pale and tremble at this chance,
That are but mutes or audience to this act,
Had I but time—as this fell sergeant, Death,

330 Is strict in his arrest—O, I could tell you—
But let it be. Horatio, I am dead,
Thou livest. Report me and my cause aright
To the unsatisfied.
   Horatio
                              Never believe it.
I am more an antique Roman than a Dane.

335 Here's yet some liquor left.
   Hamlet
                              As th'art a man
Give me the cup. Let go, by Heaven I'll ha't.
O God, Horatio, what a wounded name,
Things standing thus unknown, shall I leave behind
   me.
If thou didst ever hold me in thy heart,

340 Absent thee from felicity awhile,

And in this harsh world draw thy breath in pain
To tell my story.

A march afar off and shot within

What warlike noise is this?

Enter Osric

Osric
Young Fortinbras, with conquest come from Poland,
To the ambassadors of England gives
345 This warlike volley.
    Hamlet
                    O, I die, Horatio.
The potent poison quite o'ercrows my spirit.
I cannot live to hear the news from England,
But I do prophesy th'election lights
On Fortinbras. He has my dying voice.
350 So tell him, with th'occurrents more and less
Which have solicited—the rest is silence.   [*Dies*
    Horatio
Now cracks a noble heart. Good night, sweet prince,
And flights of angels sing thee to thy rest.

March within

Why does the drum come hither?

Enter Fortinbras, *and the English* Ambassadors, *and*
Soldiers *with drum and colours*

    Fortinbras
355 Where is this sight?
    Horatio
                    What is it you would see?
If aught of woe or wonder, cease your search.
    Fortinbras
This quarry cries on havoc. O proud Death,
What feast is toward in thine eternal cell,
That thou so many princes at a shot

346 *o'ercrows*: triumphs over (like a victorious fighting-cock).

348 *election*: i.e. for the new king of Denmark.
    lights: favours, chooses.
349 *my dying voice*: my deathbed vote. Hamlet was himself promised the 'voice' of Claudius (*3, 2*, 326–7).
350 *occurrents more and less*: everything that has happened.
351 *solicited*: persuaded me to speak for him.

354 *the drum*: i.e. the marching soldiers following the drum.

354s.d. *colours*: standards, banners.

356 *woe or wonder*: sorrow or disaster.

357 *quarry*: heap of dead bodies (usually animals killed in hunting).
    cries on havoc: proclaims wholesale slaughter.
358 *toward*: being prepared.

360 *dismal*: full of terror.

362 *The ears*: i.e. the king's ears.

366 *Had . . . life*: even if he were alive.

368 *so jump upon*: so precisely at the right
moment.
question: business.

371 *stage*: platform. Horatio is asking for a
public inquiry, open 'to the view' of
all.
placed: placèd.
374 *carnal*: i.e. the marriage of Gertrude
and Claudius.
375 *accidental judgements*: divine justice
in what looked like accidents.
casual: happening (apparently) by
chance.
376 *put on*: contrived.
forc'd: faked.
377 *this upshot*: i.e. the final outcome.

382 *of memory*: unforgotten.
383 'This seems a good time to claim
them.'

385 *draw on more*: persuade other voices.
386 *this same*: i.e. the inquiry.
presently: immediately.
387 *wild*: agitated.
388 *On*: on top of, in addition to.

389 *stage*: platform (see line 371).

390 *put on*: put to the test.
391 *for his passage*: to mark his passing.

360   So bloodily hast struck?
First Ambassador
                                    The sight is dismal;
And our affairs from England come too late.
The ears are senseless that should give us hearing
To tell him his commandment is fulfill'd,
That Rosencrantz and Guildenstern are dead.
365 Where should we have our thanks?
Horatio
                                    Not from his mouth,
Had it th'ability of life to thank you.
He never gave commandment for their death.
But since, so jump upon this bloody question,
You from the Polack wars and you from England
370 Are here arriv'd, give order that these bodies
High on a stage be placed to the view,
And let me speak to th'yet unknowing world
How these things came about. So shall you hear
Of carnal, bloody, and unnatural acts,
375 Of accidental judgements, casual slaughters,
Of deaths put on by cunning and forc'd cause,
And, in this upshot, purposes mistook
Fall'n on th'inventors' heads. All this can I
Truly deliver.
Fortinbras
                        Let us haste to hear it,
380 And call the noblest to the audience.
For me, with sorrow I embrace my fortune.
I have some rights of memory in this kingdom,
Which now to claim my vantage doth invite me.
Horatio
Of that I shall have also cause to speak,
385 And from his mouth whose voice will draw on more.
But let this same be presently perform'd
Even while men's minds are wild, lest more mischance
On plots and errors happen.
Fortinbras
                                    Let four captains
Bear Hamlet like a soldier to the stage,
390 For he was likely, had he been put on,
To have prov'd most royal; and for his passage,

The soldier's music and the rite of war
Speak loudly for him.
Take up the bodies. Such a sight as this

395   Becomes the field, but here shows much amiss.
Go, bid the soldiers shoot.

[*Exeunt marching, bearing off the bodies,*
after which a peal of ordnance is shot off

395   *Becomes the field*: is suitable for the
battlefield.

The songs in *Hamlet*

The songs in Shakespeare's plays have attracted much attention in recent years. Sometimes they are versions of the 'pop songs' of the day, whose original tunes can be found in contemporary music-books. Detailed studies have been made by Dr F. W. Sternfeld, and published in his *Music in Shakespearian Tragedy* (1963) and *Songs from Shakespeare's Tragedies* (1964).

How should I your true love know
Hamlet, *Act 4*

Shakespeare's text

Ballad tune: *Walsingham*
harmonized by Francis Cutting

*[*Singing interrupted:*] (QUEEN) Alas, look here, my lord.

Tomorrow is Saint Valentine's day
Hamlet, *Act 4*

Shakespeare's text   Linley: *Shakespeare's Dramatic Songs*

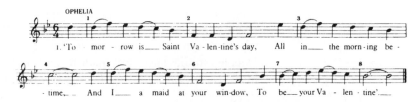

2. Then up he rose and donn'd his clothes
    And dupp'd the chamber door,
    Let in the maid, that out a maid
    Never departed more.

3. By Gis and by Saint Charity,
    Alack, and fie for shame!
    Young men will do't if they come to't,
    By Cock, they are to blame.

4. Quoth she, 'Before you tumbled me,
    You promis'd me to wed.'
[*He answers:*]   'So would I ha' done, by yonder sun,
    And thou hadst not come to my bed.'

They bore him bare-faced
Hamlet, *Act 4*

Shakespeare's text   Ballad tunes: *Walsingham*
                                            and *Bandalashot* (adapted)

For bonny sweet Robin
Hamlet, *Act 4*

Shakespeare's text   Ballet Lute Book

For bon - ny sweet__ Ro - bin is all____ my joy.

And will he not come again?
Hamlet, *Act 4*

Shakespeare's text   Linley: *Shakespeare's Dramatic Songs*

1st stanza: And will he not come a - gain?____ And will he not come__ a -
2nd stanza: His beard__ as white as snow,____ All fla - xen was__ his
They bore__ him bare - faced on the bier, Hey non non-ny, non - ny, hey

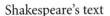

- gain?____ No, no, -gain?____ No, no, no, he is dead, Go
poll,____ He is poll,____ no - ny, And in his grave rained
non - ny, And non - ny, And

to thy death - bed, [and] He ne - ver will come a - gain.____
cast a - way moan, Gra - mer - cy on his soul!____
ma - ny a tear . . .

In youth when I did love
Hamlet, *Act 5*

Shakespeare's text   Nott: *Songs and Sonnets*

FIRST CLOWN (GRAVEDIGGER)

1. In youth when__ I did love, did love, Me -
2. But age with his steal - ing steps, Hath
3. A pick - axe__ and a spade, a spade, For

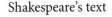

- thought it was ve - ry sweet: To__ con - tract O! the time for a
claw'd me__ in his clutch: And__ hath____ shipp'd me in -
and a__ shroud - ing sheet; O! a pit____ of clay for

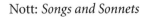

my be - hove, O! me - thought there a was no - thing - a meet.
- til the land, As____ if there had ne - ver been__ such.
to be made, For____ such____ a guest is meet.

What the Critics have said

Shakespeare has been well served by critics of *Hamlet* and interpreters of the character of the Prince. This is a selection of their comments.

The play is 'almost one continued *Moral*; a series of deep Reflections, drawn from *one* Mouth'.

Earl of Shaftesbury, 1710

'Who can read the Speech with which young *Hamlet* accosts him [the Ghost] without trembling?'

Joseph Addison, 1711

'The pretended madness of *Hamlet* causes much mirth, the mournful distraction of *Ophelia* fills the heart with tenderness.'

Samuel Johnson, 1765

'We do not like to see our Author's plays acted, and least of all *Hamlet*. There is no play that suffers so much in being transferred to the stage.'

William Hazlitt, 1817

'A Maxim is a conclusion upon observation of matters of fact, and is merely retrospective: an Idea, or, if you like, a Principle, carries knowledge within itself, and is prospective. Polonius is a man of maxims. While he is descanting on matters of past experience, as in that excellent speech to Laertes before he sets out on his travels, he is admirable; but when he comes to advise or project, he is a mere dotard. You see, Hamlet, as the man of ideas, despises him.'

S. T. Coleridge, 1827

'*Hamlet* . . . is the most popular play in our language. It *amuses* thousands annually, and it stimulates the minds of millions . . . The lowest and most ignorant audiences delight in it. The source of the delight is twofold: First its reach of thought on topics the most profound; for the dullest soul can *feel* a grandeur which it cannot *understand*, and will listen with hushed awe to the outpourings of a great meditative mind obstinately questioning fate; Secondly, its wondrous dramatic variety.'

G. H. Lewes, 1855

Classwork and Examinations

The works of Shakespeare are studied all over the world, and this classroom edition is being used in many different countries. Teaching methods vary from school to school—even *within* the United Kingdom—and there are many different ways of examining a student's work. Some teachers and examiners expect detailed knowledge of Shakespeare's text; others ask for imaginative involvement with his characters and their situations, and there are some teachers who want their students, by means of 'workshop' activities, to share in the theatrical experience of directing and performing a play. Most people use a variety of methods. This section of the book offers a few suggestions for approaches to *Hamlet* which could be used in schools and colleges to help with students' understanding and *enjoyment* of the play.

A   Discussion of Themes and Topics
B   Character Study
C   Activities
D   Context Questions
E   Critical Appreciation
F   Essays
G   Projects

A   Discussion of Themes and Topics

It is most sensible to discuss each scene as it is read, sharing impressions (and perhaps correcting misapprehensions): no two people experience any character in quite the same way, and we all have different expectations. It can be useful to compare aspects of this play with other fictions—plays, novels, films—or with modern life. A large class can divide into small groups, each with a leader, who can discuss different aspects of a single topic and then report back to the main assembly.

Suggestions

A1   How does Shakespeare create the 'atmosphere' for his ghost story in *Act 1*, Scene 1? Would modern theatre or film techniques be able to help him at all?

A2   In *Act 1*, Scene 4 we see a father (Polonius) giving advice to his children. How do you rate Polonius as a father? How would you react to the kind of advice that he gives to Laertes and Ophelia?

A3 How would you, as a director, stage the Ghost in its *Act 1* appearances? Consider *both* the resources of the Elizabethan theatre *and* those of modern stage/film technology, and compare this Ghost with other fictional apparitions.

A4 Do you blame Hamlet for stabbing the spy behind the arras? Would you feel the same if the listener had been Claudius and not Polonius?

A5 Suppose Hamlet had killed Claudius when he found him at the end of *Act 3*, Scene 3. Would you have more, or less, respect for the Prince?

A6 Why should a king—or other head of state—take more care of him/her self, and be better protected, than any other citizen (see 3, 3, 5–23)?

A7 How would you, as a director, stage the episode in the closet when the Ghost appears to Hamlet?

A8 Can you share Hamlet's admiration for Fortinbras and his 'divine ambition' (4, 4, 49)?

A9 At the burial of Ophelia, Laertes asks 'What ceremony else?' (5, 1, 209). Discuss the importance which this play attaches to the rites and ceremonies of death.

A10 At the beginning of the play, Hamlet said that 'The time is out of joint' and that he 'was born to set it right' (1, 5, 196–7). In your opinion, has he done this?

A11 Hamlet believes that 'There is special providence in the fall of a sparrow' (5, 2, 204–5). Does Providence have any part in this play?

A12 Hamlet is a very long play, and most directors find it necessary to make cuts. Where would you choose to cut?

B Character Study Shakespeare's characters can be studied in many different ways, either from the *outside*, where the detached, critical student (or group of students) can see the function of every character within the whole scheme and pattern of the play; or from the *inside*, where the sympathetic student (like an actor) can identify with a single character and can look at the action and the other characters from his/her point of view.

Suggestions   a) from 'outside' the character

B1   What do we learn of the character and function of Horatio in the first act of the play?

B2   In Shakespeare's plays, the style of a person's speech often tells us a lot about his character. Show how true this is of Polonius.

B3   Consider the characters of Laertes and/or Fortinbras, and suggest how they compare and contrast with Hamlet.

B4   Describe the character of Ophelia, remembering the scenes at the beginning of the play where she was present with her brother and her father, the middle scenes with Prince Hamlet, and her final appearance before her death. Did her madness surprise you?

B5   'Despite all that he tells us about himself, Hamlet still remains a mystery—we can never feel that we fully understand him.' How well do you understand Hamlet? Write an account of his character, and compare your account with those of other students.

b) from 'inside' the character

B6   Assuming the character of Horatio, write an account of your attitude to ghosts and describe how this was changed by your experience in *Act 1*. You could perhaps be writing a diary entry, or a letter to a friend at university, or a paper for publication in a learned journal.

B7   Imagine yourself to have been present—perhaps as a courtier or lady-in-waiting—when the new king addressed his court at Elsinore; describe the scene in a letter to your wife/husband. What impression did Claudius's first speech make on you? Did you think his nephew was rather odd?

B8   'O woe is me T'have seen what I have seen, see what I see' (3, 1, 160–1). In the character of Ophelia, write a confidential diary describing Hamlet as he used to be, and as he now appears. Try to describe your own feelings.

B9   As one of the Players, now returned to London, give an account of your reception and performance at Elsinore.

B10   Imagine you are Gertrude. What are your thoughts as you wait for Hamlet to come to your closet?

B11 As Gertrude, confide your thoughts to your diary after Hamlet has left your room.

B12 Tell 'Ophelia's story' in letters to her girl-friend.

B13 At the end of the play, Fortinbras says that Hamlet—had he lived—'was likely . . . to have prov'd most royal'. In the character of Fortinbras, describe your real feelings about the Prince of Denmark.

B14 What version of the whole affair—or of any part of it—would Gertrude have given to a confidante (in letters discovered after her death)?

B15 If Claudius had been writing his autobiography, how might he have described the events that followed his marriage to Queen Gertrude?

C **Activities**   These can involve two or more students, preferably working *away from* the desk or study-table and using gesture and position ('body-language') as well as speech. They can help students to develop a sense of drama and the dramatic aspects of Shakespeare's play—which was written to be *performed*, not studied in a classroom.

C1 Speak the lines—act the scenes! To familiarize yourselves with Shakespeare's verse, try different reading techniques—reading by punctuation marks (where each person hands over to the next at every punctuation mark); reading by sentences; and reading by speeches. Begin acting with small units—about ten lines—where two or three characters are speaking to each other; rehearse these in groups of students, and perform them before the whole class. Read the lines from a script—then act them out in your own words.

C2 Devise a scene in which Marcellus tries to persuade the reluctant Horatio (who does not believe in ghosts) to accompany the Guards on their midnight watch.

C3 'Never make known what you have seen tonight' (1, 5, 149). Hamlet swears his companions to secrecy—but suppose that Marcellus cannot keep a secret. How would he tell Barnardo (who witnessed the Ghost's first appearance) about this latest manifestation? Improvise such a scene.

C4 *Hamlet* is famous for the Prince's soliloquies. Speak any one of these aloud, using *your own words*.

C5 Arrange the seating of the royal party at *The Murder of Gonzago*—so that the audience for *Hamlet* can see and hear everything that is happening.

C6 Imagine you are a television reporter covering the fencing match between Hamlet and Laertes. Give a running commentary on the fight, and its unexpected outcome.

D Context Questions

Questions like these, which are sometimes used in written examinations, can also be helpful as a class revision quiz, testing knowledge of the play and some understanding of its words.

D1 Moreover that we much did long to see you,
The need we have to use you did provoke
Our hasty sending. Something have you heard
Of Hamlet's transformation . . .

(i) Who is speaking, and who is addressed?
(ii) Why does the speaker say 'we'?
(iii) What is 'Hamlet's transformation'?

D2 And I, of ladies most deject and wretched,
That suck'd the honey of his music vows,
Now see that noble and most sovereign reason
Like sweet bells jangled out of tune and harsh,
That unmatch'd form and feature of blown youth
Blasted with ecstasy.

(i) Who is the speaker, and to whom does she refer?
(ii) What has she just seen?
(iii) Who else witnessed the scene?

D3 See what a grace was seated on this brow,
Hyperion's curls, the front of Jove himself,
An eye like Mars to threaten and command,
A station like the herald Mercury
New-lighted on a heaven-kissing hill,
A combination and a form indeed
Where every god did seem to set his seal
To give the world assurance of a man.

(i) Who speaks these lines, and who hears them? What is their relationship?
(ii) Who is being described, and how is he related to the speaker?

(iii)   What has the speaker just done?

D4   And then it started like a guilty thing
Upon a fearful summons. I have heard
The cock, that is the trumpet to the morn,
Doth with his lofty and shrill-sounding throat
Awake the god of day, and at his warning,
Whether in sea or fire, in earth or air,
Th'extravagant and erring spirit hies
To his confine; and of the truth herein
This present object made probation.

(i)   Who is speaking, and to whom does he speak?
(ii)   What has just happened?
(iii)   What does the speaker decide to do next?

D5   My liege and madam, to expostulate
What majesty should be, what duty is,
Why day is day, night night, and time is time,
Were nothing but to waste night, day, and time.
Therefore, since brevity is the soul of wit,
And tediousness the limbs and outward flourishes,
I will be brief.

(i)   Who is the speaker?
(ii)   Who does he call 'My liege and madam'?
(iii)   What has he really come to say?

E   Critical Appreciation   These present passages from the play and ask questions about them. Some examination boards allow candidates to take their copies of the play into the examination room, asking them to re-read specified sections of the play and answer questions on them.

E1   Read again the opening of *Act 1*, Scene 1 as far as line 42 (**Marcellus** ' . . . Look where it comes again'), and comment on Shakespeare's skill in compelling the audience's attention and creating suspense.

E2   Having re-read *Act 4*, Scene 5, lines 1–72 (**Queen** 'I will not speak with her' to **Ophelia** 'good night, good night'), discuss Shakespeare's ability to focus the interest on more than one character in a single moment.

E3   Hamlet and Fortinbras are contrasted throughout the play in various ways. Read again *Act 4*, Scene 4, lines 9–66 (**Hamlet** 'Good sir, whose powers are these' to **Hamlet** 'My thoughts be bloody or be nothing worth'), and give your own opinions on the value of this contrast.

F   Essays   These will usually give you a specific topic to discuss, or perhaps a question that must be answered, in writing, *with a reasoned argument*. They *never* want you to tell the story of the play—so don't! Your examiner—or teacher—has read the play, and does not need to be reminded of it. Relevant quotations will always help you to make your points more strongly.

F1   'Horatio has no personality of his own; he is merely a device for imparting information.' Do you agree?

F2   Show how the two kings—Hamlet's dead father and Claudius, his brother—are contrasted with each other throughout the play.

F3   Hamlet accuses himself for failing to act (see 2, 2, 535–67). What do *you* think is the main cause of his delay?

F4   Compare Laertes and Hamlet as revengers.

F5   Hamlet calls Denmark 'an unweeded garden' (1, 2, 135). Where do *you* see signs of rottenness?

F6   Polonius thinks it is necessary that someone should 'o'erhear' Hamlet's conversation with his mother (3, 3, 32). Describe other scenes in the play where characters spy—or plan to spy—on other characters.

F7   Describe the character of Polonius, remembering that we see him both as a father and a politician.

F8   Can you distinguish between Hamlet's madness and that of Ophelia?

F9   'Behind the mask of madness, both Hamlet and Ophelia can speak freely.' To what extent is this true?

F10   At the graveside Hamlet declares, 'I lov'd Ophelia' (5, 1, 255). Considering the way he has behaved to her, do you believe him now?

F11   How would you describe the character of Gertrude? Do you detect any change in her as the truth of the situation is gradually revealed to her?

F12 Hamlet is sure that 'There's a divinity that shapes our ends' (5, 2, 10). What events in the play have given him this impression?

F13 Will Horatio's description of events ('so shall you hear . . . inventors' heads' 5, 2, 373–8) be a satisfactory account of what has happened in Denmark?

G Projects In some schools, students are asked to do more 'free-ranging' work, which takes them outside the text—but which should always be relevant to the play. Such projects may demand skills other than reading and writing: design and artwork, for instance, may be involved. Sometimes a 'portfolio' of work is assembled over a considerable period of time; and this can be presented to the examiners as part of the student's work for assessment.

The availability of resources will, obviously, do much to determine the nature of the projects; but this is something that only the local teachers will understand. However, there is always help to be found in libraries, museums, and art galleries.

G1 'Hamlet through the ages': make a study of famous actors who have played the part of Hamlet.

G2 Prepare one scene of the play for performance, and produce a director's script with details of staging, lighting, costume and movement, etc.

G3 Explore Shakespeare's sources.

G4 Shakespeare's Theatre.

G5 Actors on Tour.

G6 Revenge in Life and Art.

G7 *Hamlet* as inspiration.

Background

England c. *1602*

When Shakespeare was writing *Hamlet*, most people still believed that the sun went round the earth. They were taught that this was a divinely ordered scheme of things, and that—in England—God had instituted a Church and ordained a Monarchy for the right government of the land and the populace.

'The past is a foreign country; they do things differently there.'

L. P. Hartley

Government For most of Shakespeare's life, the reigning monarch was Elizabeth I. With her counsellors and ministers she governed the nation (population five million) from London, although fewer than half a million people inhabited the capital city. In the rest of the country, law and order was maintained by the land-owners and enforced by their deputies. The average man had no vote—and his wife had no rights at all.

Religion At this time, England was a Christian country. All children were baptized, soon after they were born, into the Church of England; they were taught the essentials of the Christian faith, and instructed in their duty to God and to humankind. Marriages were performed, and funerals conducted, only by the licensed clergy and in accordance with the Church's rites and ceremonies. Attendance at divine service was compulsory; absences (without good—medical—reason) could be punished by fines.

By such means, the authorities were able to keep some check on the populace—recording births, marriages, and deaths; being alert to any religious nonconformity, which could be politically dangerous; and ensuring a minimum of orthodox instruction through the official 'Homilies' which were regularly preached from the pulpits of all parish churches throughout the realm.

Following Henry VIII's break away from the Church of Rome, all people in England were able to hear the church services *in their own language*. The Book of Common Prayer was used in every church, and an English translation of the Bible was read aloud in public. The Christian religion had never been so well taught before!

Education

School education reinforced the Church's teaching. From the age of four, boys might attend the 'petty school' (French '*petite école*') to learn the rudiments of reading and writing along with a few prayers; some schools also included work with numbers.

At the age of seven, the boy was ready for the grammar school (if his father was willing and able to pay the fees). A thorough grounding in Latin grammar was followed by translation work and the study of Roman authors, paying attention as much to style as to matter. The arts of fine writing were thus instilled from early youth.

A very few students proceeded to university; these were either clever scholarship boys, or else the sons of noblemen. Girls stayed at home, and acquired domestic and social skills—cooking, sewing, perhaps even music. The lucky ones might learn to read and write.

Language

At the start of the sixteenth century the English had a very poor opinion of their language: there was little serious writing in English, and hardly any literature. Latin was the language of international scholarship, and Englishmen admired the eloquence of the Romans. They made many translations, and in this way they extended the resources of their own language, increasing its vocabulary and stretching its grammatical structures. French, Italian, and Spanish works were also translated and, for the first time, there were English versions of the Bible.

By the end of the century, English was a language to be proud of: it was rich in synonyms, capable of infinite variety and subtlety, and ready for all kinds of word-play—especially the *puns*, for which Elizabethan English is renowned.

Drama

The great art-form of the Elizabethans was their drama. They inherited a tradition of play-acting from the Middle Ages, and this was reinforced in the sixteenth century by the reading and translating of the Roman playwrights. At the beginning of the century, plays were performed by groups of actors, all-male companies (boys acted the female roles) who travelled from town to town, setting up their stages in open places (such as inn-yards) or, with the permission of the owner, in the hall of some noble house.

The touring companies continued, in the provinces, into the seventeenth century; but in London, in 1576, a new building was erected for the performance of plays. This was the Theatre, the first purpose-built playhouse in England. Other playhouses followed, (including Shakespeare's own theatre, the Globe); and the English drama reached new heights of eloquence.

There were those who disapproved, of course. The theatres, which brought large crowds together, could encourage the spread of disease—and dangerous ideas. During the summer, when the plague was at its worst, the playhouses were closed. A constant censorship was imposed, more or less severe at different times. The Puritan faction tried to close down the theatres, but—partly because there was royal favour for the drama, and partly because the buildings were outside the city limits—they did not succeed until 1642.

Theatre From contemporary comments and sketches—most particularly a drawing by a Dutch visitor, Johannes de Witt—it is possible to form some idea of the typical Elizabethan playhouse for which most of Shakespeare's plays were written. Hexagonal in shape, it had three roofed galleries encircling an open courtyard. The plain, high stage projected into the yard, where it was surrounded by the audience of standing 'groundlings'. At the back were two doors for the actors' entrances and exits, and between these doors was a curtained 'discovery space' (sometimes called an 'inner stage'). Above this was a balcony, used as a musicians' gallery or for the performance of scenes 'above'; and projecting over part of the stage was a roof, supported on two pillars, which was painted with the sun, moon, and stars for the 'heavens'. Underneath was space (concealed by curtaining) which could be used by characters ascending and descending through a trap-door in the stage. Costumes and properties were kept backstage in the 'tiring house'. The actors dressed lavishly, often wearing the secondhand clothes bestowed by rich patrons. Stage properties were important for defining a location, but the dramatist's own words were needed to explain the time of day, since all performances took place in the early afternoon.

A replica of Shakespeare's own theatre, the Globe, has been built in London, and stands in Southwark, almost exactly on the Bankside site of the original.

Shakespeare's Globe, Southwark, London, England. Photograph by Richard Kalina.

Selected Further Reading

Sources: Muir, Kenneth, *The Sources of Shakespeare's Plays* (London, 1977).

Date and Text: Honigmann, E. A. J., 'The Date of *Hamlet*', *Shakespeare Survey* 9, (Cambridge, 1956).
Jenkinson, Harold, Introduction to the Arden edition of *Hamlet*, (Methuen, 1982).
Walker, Alice, 'The Textual Problem of *Hamlet*: A Reconsideration' (*Review of English Studies*, 1951).

Criticism: a) *Books*
Alexander, Nigel, *Poison, Play, and Duel*, (London, 1971).
Alexander, Peter, *Hamlet, Father and Son*, (London, 1955).
Granville-Barker, Harley, *Preface to 'Hamlet'*, (London, 1937).
Knights, L. C., *An Approach to 'Hamlet'*, (London, 1960).
Prosser, Eleanor, *Hamlet and Revenge*, (Stanford, Calif., 1967).
Wilson, J. Dover, *What Happens in 'Hamlet'?*, (Cambridge, 1935).

b) *Essays*: Valuable essays on *Hamlet* are included in:
Barton, Anne, Introduction to the Penguin edition of *Hamlet*, (Penguin Books, 1980).
Bayley, John, *Shakespeare and Tragedy*, (Routledge, 1981).
Eliot, T. S., *Selected Essays*, (London, 1932).
Gardner, Helen, *The Business of Criticism*, (Oxford, 1959).
Honigmann, E. A. J., *Shakespeare: Seven Tragedies*, (London, 1976).
Knight, G. Wilson, *The Wheel of Fire*, (Methuen, 1930).

c) *Essay Collections*
Jump, J. D. (ed.), *'Hamlet': A Casebook*, (London, 1968).
Muir, Kenneth, and Wells, Stanley (eds.), *Aspects of 'Hamlet'*, (Cambridge, 1979).
Parker, Patricia, and Hartman, Geoffrey (eds.), *Shakespeare and the Question of Theory*, (Routledge, Chapman & Hall, 1985).
Patterson, Annabel (ed.), *Shakespeare and the Popular Voice*, (Basil Blackwell, 1989).

Background reading: Bate, Jonathan, *The Genius of Shakespeare* (Picador [Macmillan], 1997).

Blake, N. F., *Shakespeare's Language: an Introduction* (London, 1983).

Gibson, Rex, *Shakespeare's Language* (Cambridge, 1997).

Honan, Park, *Shakespeare: A Life* (Oxford, 1998).

Langley, Andrew, *Shakespeare's Theatre* (Oxford, 1999).

Muir, K., and Schoenbaum, S., *A New Companion to Shakespeare Studies* (Cambridge, 1971).

Thomson, Peter, *Shakespeare's Theatre* (London, 1983).

William Shakespeare, 1564–1616

Elizabeth I was Queen of England when Shakespeare was born in 1564. He was the son of a tradesman who made and sold gloves in the small town of Stratford-upon-Avon, and he was educated at the grammar school in that town. Shakespeare did not go to university when he left school, but worked, perhaps, in his father's business. When he was eighteen he married Anne Hathaway, who became the mother of his daughter, Susanna, in 1583, and of twins in 1585.

There is nothing exciting, or even unusual, in this story; and from 1585 until 1592 there are no documents that can tell us anything at all about Shakespeare. But we have learned that in 1592 he was known in London, and that he had become both an actor and a playwright.

We do not know when Shakespeare wrote his first play, and indeed we are not sure of the order in which he wrote his works. If you look on page 179 at the list of his writings and their approximate dates, you will see how he started by writing plays on subjects taken from the history of England. No doubt this was partly because he was always an intensely patriotic man—but he was also a very shrewd businessman. He could see that the theatre audiences enjoyed being shown their own history, and it was certain that he would make a profit from this kind of drama.

The plays in the next group are mainly comedies, with romantic love-stories of young people who fall in love with one another, and at the end of the play marry and live happily ever after.

At the end of the sixteenth century the happiness disappears, and Shakespeare's plays become melancholy, bitter, and tragic. This change may have been caused by some sadness in the writer's life (one of his twins died in 1596). Shakespeare, however, was not the only writer whose works at this time were very serious. The whole of England was facing a crisis. Queen Elizabeth I was growing old. She was greatly loved, and the people were sad to think she must soon die; they were also afraid, for the queen had never married, and so there was no child to succeed her.

When James I came to the throne in 1603, Shakespeare continued to write serious drama—the great tragedies and the plays based on Roman history (such as *Julius Caesar*) for which he is most famous. Finally, before he retired from the theatre, he wrote another set of comedies. These all have the same theme: they tell of happiness which is lost, and then found again.

Shakespeare returned from London to Stratford, his home town. He was rich and successful, and he owned one of the biggest houses in the town. He died in 1616. Although several of his plays were published separately, most of them were not printed until 1623, in a collection known as 'the First Folio'.

Shakespeare also wrote two long poems, and a collection of sonnets. The sonnets describe two love-affairs, but we do not know who the lovers were. Although there are many public documents concerned with his career as a writer and a business-man, Shakespeare has hidden his personal life from us. A nineteenth-century poet, Matthew Arnold, addressed Shakespeare in a poem, and wrote 'We ask and ask—Thou smilest, and art still'.

There is not even a trustworthy portrait of the world's greatest dramatist.

Approximate order of composition of Shakespeare's works

Period	Comedies	History plays	Tragedies	Poems
I	Comedy of Errors Taming of the Shrew	Henry VI, part 1 Henry VI, part 2	Titus Andronicus	
1594	Two Gentlemen of Verona Love's Labour's Lost	Henry VI, part 3 Richard III King John		Venus and Adonis Rape of Lucrece
II	Midsummer Night's Dream Merchant of Venice	Richard II Henry IV, part 1	Romeo and Juliet	Sonnets
1599	Merry Wives of Windsor Much Ado About Nothing As You Like It	Henry IV, part 2 Henry V		
III	Twelfth Night Troilus and Cressida		Julius Caesar Hamlet	
1608	Measure for Measure All's Well That Ends Well		Othello Timon of Athens King Lear Macbeth Antony and Cleopatra Coriolanus	
IV	Pericles Cymbeline			
1613	The Winter's Tale The Tempest	Henry VIII		